Surrealistic TRIALS

SURVIVING MY LIFE AFTER DEATH

Hilary Jamron

Orchestrated by Leia Stinnett

Surrealistic TRIALS

Surviving My Life After Death

Hilary Jamron

Orchestrated by Leia Stinnett

Light Technology Publishing

Some names have been changed in this book to protect the privacy of the individuals involved.

Cover art by Rassouli

ISBN: 978-1-62233-014-0

LIGHT Technology PUBLISHING

PO Box 3540
Flagstaff, AZ 86003
1-800-450-0985
1-928-526-1345
www.LightTechnology.com

Contents

Foreword

There are many reasons people come together, none of which have anything to do with coincidence. Certainly, my first meeting with Hilary was not planned, except perhaps by the angels above. Most people would see us as the "odd couple" if they did not understand that our relationship goes well beyond this lifetime at the soul level.

The angels brought us together in this lifetime at a point when Hilary found herself at a crossroads, questioning the very purpose of her existence. She needed a gentle reminder of who she really is — a teacher of higher truths — and that nothing she has experienced in this life is a waste of time. She needed a purpose to keep on going, and that purpose was revealed: "Hilary, telling your story to others may help them learn the importance of not giving up, to push through any and all limitations. Teach people to be grateful for what they have and to use their gifts in service to God and to help others."

As Hilary wrote her story, I worked as her cognitive mind, bringing all the parts together in a cohesive format and giving the story more clarity in its organization of events. Hilary writes from her higher self, a place above cognitive or any conscious thinking — a place of simple truths, spiritual realities, and divine purpose.

Over forty years ago, Hilary "died" from a drug overdose. While she was on the Other Side, her guardian angel, Mary, cared for her needs. Mary continued caring for the comatose teenager as doctors did their best to fuss about, diagnose, and settle on a prognosis better than "dim." During her stay in Mount Sinai Hospital's neurology unit, Hilary observed through her higher self (whom she calls Tink) the mental difficulties of patients in her room and around her. Somehow, Hilary totally understood them. They became her reality checks to some degree while doctors, nurses, and other staff became more surreal.

As time passed, through determination to succeed and overcome the sense of living in a box, Hilary got up and moving again — and not in a wheelchair or walker. After a great deal of physical therapy and mental intention, she began living a somewhat normal life. But the truth of the matter is only a part of her came back from the Other Side; only a fragment of Hilary's physical conscious mind was functioning. Her higher self took over.

She spent many years working at a psychiatric facility helping those she related to best: the outcasts. These people shared a common bridge with Hilary, all living in more than one world at the same time. She understood them, had great compassion for them, and in fact helped most of them considerably more than most medical people could or even desired to. Painfully, however, she could not help all of them to the degree she had hoped, and she knew when other authorities should be called to the rescue.

Hilary's love of nature was responsible for her greatest healing. This will always be so. Nature has been her escape into a world of reality when the illusion becomes too much to deal with. In nature, there is no noise but a merger between heaven and earth where all creation blends in harmony, peace, and love. Nature has allowed Hilary to escape her physical limitations and has given her a sense of freedom and flight.

Decades later, when she became very ill, Hilary could not ignore her diagnosis; she was told that she was positive for hepatitis C. To her mind, this diagnosis was overwhelming, painful. To her higher self, it meant she must seek a protocol and stay with it until she was cured. The protocol she dealt with would have sent most of us to the corner to curl up in a ball and ask for a speedy death. The first year of treatment did not resolve the issue. Hilary has since come through a second and successful treatment process that actually brought the two of us together. She can no longer work in the field of psychiatry or any other field beyond what she is doing now — writing this book.

This lady has endured more painful experiences than anyone I have ever met and has kept on moving forward, one painful step in front of the other, to teach the rest of us that what she can do, we all can do.

Never Give Up!

This is a book we should all read over and over again. Each time you read it, you will discover something new — something about the author, something about yourself, something that will feed your soul in the moment. This book is a teaching tool with the purpose of helping all of us overcome roadblocks we meet along our journeys. You will be reminded that you are not your body, that you have a host of helping angels at your command, and that we each have an ever-present God connection, a higher self, who guides us each day — even when our conscious minds are not functioning.

I respect this lady's courage, her "never give up," "matter of fact" approach to life. She wants to help people help themselves, and this story is only the beginning of the ways in which she will accomplish her goal.

— Leia Stinnett, Orchestrator

"The Eternal Womb," 2012, by my daughter, Misty Dawn, who was born filled with infinite wisdom.

The essence of All That Is transcends time and space. This photograph is a reflection of how I live my life. The spirit renews itself in part through the physical source of life, that home of warmth, safety, and love where the soul is free to dance gracefully, agelessly, lovingly through the universe.
Without Limits.

Preface

This story has no beginning — only an arbitrary point where the telling reveals itself as formed words. The beginning was before, before my soul danced fluidly across infinity. Even before the ancient abyss became infinity's potential. Before.

This story will have no end — only a point where the telling goes slowly silent, when the whisper is finally too faint to hear and even the most earnest listener must use more senses to be taken further. You will not know if this is the story's continuation or your own imagination. It will not matter.

This is a story like jumping into a swift river and trying to hold on to a single ripple for an entire journey to the sea, then discovering along the way that you can breathe beneath the surface.

— Misty Dawn

Birth
is not the beginning
Death
is not the end
Understanding
is a fallacy
Truth
is not anchored in perception
Beauty
is beyond vision
Reality
is not what you think
Love
is universal

— Misty Dawn

Introduction

I am by no means a "religious" person.

I believe in everything.

I know my truth.

I know that I am blessed in this life, that I am protected and safe.

That if and when I need an angel, one is there.

When I fall, I'll get up.

Every time.

I know that angels don't live in boxes. They show up when we least expect them, and they don't wear white robes or have wings. Well, at least mine haven't.

Yet.

When I died of a drug overdose forty years ago, part of my soul refused to come back. That part of my higher self chose to remain where peace and simplicity reign. The physical manifestation of that part lives just above me as a tiny, translucent entity. She scampers about, quick and efficient, mischievous, lighthearted, ever present. She is always there, and she can always make me smile.

I get lost sometimes. I get lost driving to the grocery store, in my head, in music, or wandering off the grid of reality to the place where serenity rules and our real lives are the ones we live while we drift off to sleep.

Communing with Nature

Rock, right center.

Part of climb to Rock.

Molly and me on the trail to Rock.

Trailhead.

The laundry list of my physical ailments is both arduous and boring. The blue "disabled" placard on my rearview mirror says that I'm exhausted. My body has been damaged, mistreated, and contorted. The eyes I see in my mirror are often empty, and I wonder where I am.

Nothing in moderation.

I am Extremes.

When I was asked to write this story, I saw my little higher self — that special part of me — watching life events unfold as one would watch a movie. Her name is Tink, and she would write from our favorite place, a special rock off the shore of Boulder Lake, high on a mountain near Donnelly, Idaho. The rock is a holy place. God and I have met up there many times. We've watched bald eagles dance through double rainbows and seen the clouds open to reveal magical secrets. We have spread ashes of loved ones, cried, celebrated, grieved, and rejoiced.

Rock called to my spirit many years ago as I was hiking north past Boulder Lake toward Anderson Canyon. Molly heard it first. A rambunctious Blue Heeler pup, she and I were inseparable wanderers exploring the high country together every chance we got. Molly stopped that day, cocked her head, and let out a whisper of a woof. Following her gaze, I saw Rock ten or twelve feet from shore — smooth, flat, beckoning. My furry friend and I looked at each other and smiled. She was swimming her doggy swim by the time I had taken my clothes off and dove into the icy lake. We swam to Rock. The water was recently melted snow, and the sun was hot and soothing on my body.

Rock told me what to do, and, spotting a foothold, I easily climbed out of the water onto her large, flat surface. "Now stand up," Rock whispered. I did. "Look around you, Hilary. Feel around you."

What happened next was already an unconscious but integral element of my life, an intense experience that has soothed my soul since the beginning of time. Physical sensations coursed through my body and my being. My lines of vision blurred all at once, then faded as I felt a tremendous burst of power course through Rock into my feet and up my legs. I raised my arms to the sky and was encompassed by a familiar foreign entity. No thoughts, no movement — nothing but power. Accepting and appreciating the experience, I stayed with it until I was not only filled to the brim but had long since overflowed. I was a battery with a charge strong enough to light the world, to love without measure.

And I did.

Only in nature are my spirit and soul truly strong and at peace.

Motivation is the desire to get from where we are now to where we want to be.

There is always a way to get to where we need to be.

Getting to Rock has, at times, been not only inconvenient but also occasionally risky, given the isolated, rugged terrain. The hike to Rock and Boulder Lake begins at a trailhead eight miles up a windy, potholed dirt road. From there, you walk up two miles past the waterfall, traverse the quarter-mile of stone, and crest the hill.

Magnificent solitude. Stunning. Spiritual.

You hug the shore of Boulder Lake east toward Jughandle another half-mile or so, and there it is: Rock. How far it is from shore depends on the time of year, snowmelt, and how Rock is feeling. Sometimes I'm invited to swim out and lie down; other times it takes snowshoes or skis to get there, and in the spring it's a slosh through "sluck" — that winning combination of slush, ice, and mud.

The winter my dear friend Ernie's plane crashed in Montana, hiking in snowshoes to get there while carrying winter camping gear and a shovel was a royal pain in the ass, and I was sure to tell him so when I said goodbye.

Disoriented by the way the snow was melting, Molly and I once ended up at the wrong lake and spent a chilly night snuggled in the tent so we could trek to Boulder at sunrise. God made sure the detour included a spectacular light show with so many stars there was barely room for sky.

The part of me that died with my mom lives there at Rock and delights in her company. The glint in my father's eye reflects off the water.

I kept a speckle of my Michael's goodness before alcohol destroyed him. The purest part of the man I married on the mountaintop near our tipi home, the man to whom I was married for more than two decades, whose brilliant, fragile soul shines through in our daughter. A precious, unblemished speckle of the familiar soul that shall continue to be part of my lifetimes. It lives there at Boulder Lake too, in the form of a small, smooth rock tucked in the nook of a nearby tree.

Molly's stunning soul returned to its source when I freed her ashes and let my tears become one with the lake. She who was on every trek with me for eighteen years is at Rock, fetching tennis balls and forever running to stand still.

The part of me that didn't come back from the Other Side can always be found there, laughing, dancing, and often singing Loudly and Out of Tune.

The woman physically putting words to paper is, oddly enough, not writing this. It is being written by my higher self, the part of my soul and consciousness that lives at Rock. I write as I sit in the warm summer sun, dangling my feet in Boulder Lake. I write from the place where I came into this existence and from where I shall leave. It will be a sunny day, and I'll be barefoot.

Boulder Lake.

Memories

The two-year-old opens her eyes and stretches her little girl body as she awakens from her afternoon nap. She looks around and is comforted by the familiarity of her surroundings. Her crib is in the spacious kitchen of an upstairs apartment on Chestnut Street. She can hear some of the neighborhood kids playing outside. It's summer, and the big kids are *always* outside. Sometimes they let her play with them, but she's little.

She pushes her blanket off and holds on to the bars of the crib. She falls a few times as she tries to stand up, giggles, and makes a game of it for a while as the sleep and dreams fade and she feels rested and refreshed.

She is alone.

"Oooohhhh" — stretching both tiny arms feels good, and she can reach farther and farther every day. Holding on to the top rail to keep from tipping over, Hilary makes her way to the back-right corner of the crib. From there, she can reach the phone on the wall. The receiver is kind of heavy, but she's learned how to pick it up. It's close enough to the crib that even if she drops it, she can still scrunch on her knees and talk. She does a good job this time. The operator who comes on the line hears the little voice she recognizes so well: "I want to talk to Woz, pwease."

"Sure, Hilary. I'll get her for you."

Me as a baby with my mom.

A moment later, Hilary hears the voice of Roz, her neighbor, on the other end of the line. "I'll be right over, sweetie. You just stay in your crib like a good girl until I get there to help you out."

"Okay, Woz."

Hilary misses when she tries to put the phone back on the shiny thing, and it dangles from the black, curly string. She looks at it for an instant, knowing that Woz will fix it. When the tiny body plops down, she settles on her back with hands and feet in the air, rocking herself back and forth while she waits for Roz.

• • •

I didn't make that up. It is a clear memory of my reality as a two-year-old. I don't know how often I was left alone, but I know that it was not uncommon for my mom to be gone during the day. I remember that she left me in my crib and that we could depend on Roz to be there. I also remember that being alone never bothered me. Even as an infant, I innately knew that I was protected and safe. Looking back today, it is clear that I always had special guardians, and though my guardian angel, Mary, didn't consciously appear until I was five years old, she was at my side always.

• • •

For my fifth birthday, I got a horseback riding lesson at Grossinger's Hotel, then a highly regarded summer resort in upstate New York. The striking colors of autumn in the Catskills were a perfect backdrop for my dream come true. The stables, grounds, and horses were as grand and immaculately maintained as the rest of the resort.

My dad was head bartender at Grossinger's. With his charming demeanor, influential connections, and unabashed good looks, he moved easily in the inner circles. Jenny Grossinger was the queen hostess to wealthy guests, famous entertainers, and powerful politicians. The Grossinger kids went to school with us in the small town of Liberty. Some of them were snobby, but Jimmy wasn't, and he and I chased each other around the playgrounds for years. He had his own horse, of course, and he was excited that I'd be learning to ride.

We were greeted by Sam, the stable boss, approaching the car on his Appaloosa, Baxter. He was leading a smaller white mare with gentle eyes, an easy manner, and a spot on her face where I was convinced her unicorn horn was somehow hidden. I chattered on about castles, knights, and Pegasus as Sam boosted me onto the saddle and adjusted the stirrups. Sam and I were set to head out to the enchanted forest, and I'd learn all about everything.

My dad at the Grossinger's Hotel bar where he was head bartender.

Yippee, another life!

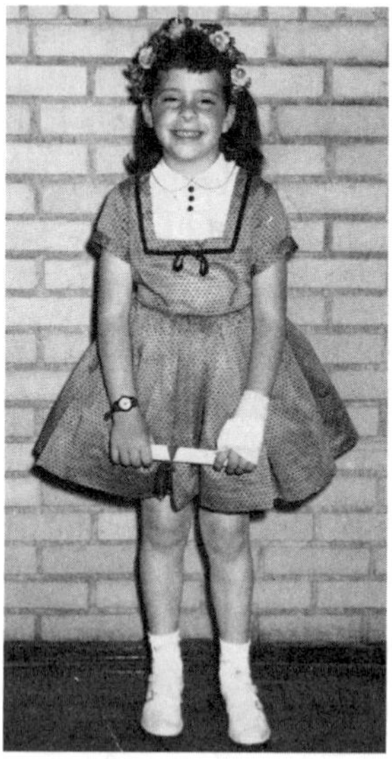

Kindergarten graduation.

Mom was in the front seat of the Buick. Dad stood leaning easily next to her open window. Sam guided us to the trail while he explained the basics. I listened intently, patting Bella the horse's neck incessantly so she'd know I loved her. Sam handed me the reins, and we walked along the trails with fall leaves crunching beneath the horses' hooves. Bella, the beginner's favorite, was trained to follow Baxter's every movement. A natural teacher, Sam talked easily, transforming wishes into reality and inexperience into calm confidence.

After walking a few (hundred) miles, the trail opened to a grand meadow. Sam continued his instruction while we stopped for a few minutes and had a snack. He patiently showed me how to manage Bella at a trot. We had all morning, so I hoped that by the end of the lesson I would know how to let her run. Cantor. Run. Gallop. Soar. Whatever it was, it was going to be amazing, and I would hang on. Both horses eased from walk to trot and eventually took flight with ease and powerful grace.

I gripped the saddle horn with all my might and held my breath. Bella knew her job as she followed Baxter's signals and pace to the letter. We crossed miles of pristine meadow, then arced widely and eased into a comfortable trot across the field to where another trail headed back into the forest. The morning passed quickly, and before I knew it, we were walking toward the stables as pictures of my future as a flying cowgirl fairy filled my head.

Suddenly, the world was silent and I was flying through the autumn sky.

The ground rose up to meet me just before I landed with a thud on the thick leaves. Bella reared above as I lay where I'd landed, tiny and vulnerable beneath her. I heard her whinny in the instant before her front-right hoof landed squarely on my five-year-old hand. In slow motion, I saw my horse rear up a second time as my body was somehow shielded, and then Sam was by my side. He picked me up and ran toward the nearby barns. A motionless, little, blood-soaked body was cradled in Sam's powerful arms. "Damn bees stung her," I heard him mutter.

I felt no pain or fear — only an indescribable shift. I had separated from myself, left the wounded child and risen above the scene. I could see my safe self watching from above where I was snuggled in a pile of soft, warm clouds in the hands of what could only have been a real, live angel. She had reached down from the sky and guided Bella's landing at the moment of impact. I caught a glimpse of gray hair and clear eyes, flashes of other scenes — wiggly baby toes in a crib, an arrow released from my brother's bow whizzing so close to my eye I could feel its motion.

As we neared the stables, my father ran toward us. When he saw me soaked in blood, his legs buckled and his strong daddy body dropped to the ground, where he remained face down and still. I tried to tell him that Mary said I was okay, that I'd been saved by an angel, but he couldn't hear me.

There were two ambulances at the Grossinger's stables that fall day in 1957: one for the bloody birthday girl and one for her dad, who had gone into shock. Mom rode with me in the back of the ambulance. Three surgeons and seven hours later, my hand was reconstructed and in a cast. Dad was okay, though he paced, yelled about bees, and vowed I would never again ride a horse.

Mary left my battered little body with a seed of knowing that day: the certainty that she had been with me always and would never, ever leave. It would be years before I would think about her again.

• • •

The Concord Hotel was the largest resort in the Catskills region. It had over 1,500 guest rooms and a dining room that seated 3,000. The resort encompassed 2,000 acres. The slanting floor of the hotel's stadium-sized nightclub rose into an astonishing distance. Audiences of up to 3,000 guests were draped in pearls and wrapped in furs; diamond cuff links peeked out from tailored silk suit jackets.

The bar at the Concord, the largest resort in the Catskills at the time, where my dad worked. Movie stars, presidents, and entertainers made frequent apperances here during my childhood.

Top entertainers did their apprenticeships for audiences of connoisseurs who were seeing it all. The Catskill resorts were the big moneymakers of the time and demanded big-name stars of Broadway and TV. It was where an era of entertainers got their starts. Dean Martin, Frank Sinatra, Bob Hope, Jerry Lewis, Mickey Rooney, Johnny Carson — up-and-coming talent came from New York City knowing that in the Catskills they faced packed houses and their toughest audience. The truth was that a single performance at the Concord could make or break a career. Joe Frazier and other boxers trained there, and Buster Crabbe (aka Tarzan) rippled his muscles while directing the hotel's swimming pools for many years. Mickey Rooney sometimes took me shopping in the Concord's private mall when my dad was in his meetings. He made me laugh, spent obscene amounts of money, and told me how much he liked my father's style.

Dave Jamron's "style" was well known and highly regarded in the Catskill hotel industry. He'd been head bartender at Grossinger's before taking over at the Concord. He was an intelligent, charming, handsome man with bright blue eyes and a mischievous twinkle that never missed a beat. He moved easily with quiet power that allowed no room for questions or mistakes. His instructions were followed to the letter. Dave easily orchestrated bar operations and other lucrative business activities, surrounding himself with serious money and some of the biggest names in politics, entertainment, and power of the time.

An early professional portrait of my parents, brother, and me.

I watched him carefully and saw that he was a master chameleon. He was distant and scary as a parent, with a hair-trigger temper that left me quaking and the family living on eggshells. At the hotels, though, he was generous, easygoing, and indulgent with me while running business matters with a low-key iron fist. By purposefully emulating his ways, I learned to adapt to my surroundings and circumstances — to always and never fit in.

By the age of ten, I was able to flow between small-town Liberty and the elitism of high-end clubs with grace and ease. Unimpressed, I thought the tiny downtown movie theater felt no different from the nightclubs where the Rat Pack earned their stripes. Movie stars, presidents, and entertainers were all in the Catskills, and the Concord's main bar was a subdued hub of excitement. I knew there were secrets, and I thought it was all very cool.

• • •

I remember my dad coming home after work one day and announcing that we were moving — right that minute. His friend and coworker Joe was moving his family as well, and packing was unceremonious and unexplained. I was about seven or eight, and there was an urgency I didn't understand. With Mom's help, we picked through our belongings, filled a small moving van within a matter of hours, and by nightfall we were heading off on "vacation." We met up with Joe and his family in the city where we rented a storage facility before heading to Miami Beach with a few suitcases and a holiday mentality. We lived in an unobtrusive South Beach hotel for a few months that year and enjoyed the beaches and easygoing lifestyle. When we headed back to the Catskills, it was a new school year, and our extended vacation was never discussed. I made up all kinds of suspense stories, though, having to do with gangsters chasing us and suitcases filled with cash.

My fantasies may not have been far from the truth. Years later, I met up with Joe's eldest son, Russell, in Monticello. He told me that both of our fathers were involved in some risky high-stakes operations that were run through the bars. (It was easy to run illegal money — lots of money — through the tills with just a few brilliant tricks of the trade). Russell told me later that we had to move because one of the owners had gotten wind of mob activity and issued instructions to "get rid" of the employees involved. Repercussions must have been imminent, and apparently that translated into something like "get out of dodge now." The shoeboxes filled with cash were not mere savings accounts to pay our college tuition. The money was illegal, and there was more of it than we had imagined. Many years later, I learned that my father had carefully hidden a small fortune.

• • •

When I finished sixth grade in June 1964, my family went to the city to see the New York World's Fair. We stayed with Uncle Max and Aunt Etta. They lived close enough to the fairgrounds that if you walked up their hill, you could see the top of the twelve-story Unisphere.

Sixth grade graduation, Liberty, New York, 1964.

Max smoked cigars and cornered me in the basement, where his beer breath turned my stomach as he touched and caressed my most private parts every time we visited. I hadn't told anyone about Uncle Max yet; I was too embarrassed. After all, I was almost twelve years old by then and felt I should have been able to take care of myself.

When I was five, I had told about Mr. Crowley, the milkman in Liberty who had made me do things to him in the dairy place. He would unzip his pants, take his man thing out, and put my small hands on it, then my mouth. Then he told me it was our secret game and that if I told anyone, he would do something mean to my brother. I did tell after a while, though, and my dad and mom took me downtown, where I had to tell the whole story to a judge. I don't know what happened next, but somebody else brought the milk and left it on the porch after that.

Uncle Max had been touching me every time we visited for several years. He would send me to the basement to get something, and no matter how fast I tried to get back, I was never quick enough. I would hear Uncle Max's clumping footsteps on the stairway, and then there he was. The foul beer breath assaulted my senses as he assaulted my body, rubbing me, taking off my clothes, and whispering about how important our secrets were. He loved me and would hate to think about how mad my dad would get at me if I told. My dad would have one of the yelling fits in which his fist was two inches from my nose at the same time he screamed. Those were the scariest ones. Anyway, at almost twelve, I felt like I should have been able to handle things myself.

After the fair, we would be moving again, but this move was different. This time my father would stay in New York and work while my brother, mom, and I moved to Miami Beach. There was no talk of divorce or marital problems — just some muttering about my mom's health. We would ride the train with the sleeping car to Florida, eat in the dining car, and have a real adventure. I had never fit in with the other kids growing up and hoped to make friends when we moved to our new home. My dad would fly down and visit.

We were afraid of him anyway. He yelled a lot, and we never knew what might set him off. His fits of rage were terrifying. He would snap for no apparent reason, then scream and rant at the top of his lungs, throwing things and carrying on until he was spent. All we could do was cringe and hold our collective breath until he was done. I knew my dad loved me, but I was afraid of him, so it would be good to have him far away and sending us money. I clearly remember the stacks of shoeboxes filled with cash in the closet of the room he kept at the hotel.

Despite the tension, we acted like a family at the fair, marveling at the General Electric Carousel of Progress and the groundbreaking Disney exhibits. We rode through history on moving seats in the building that turned on its axis.

Everywhere were tributes to JFK, who had broken ground for the fair in 1962 and whose heartbreaking assassination was still fresh in the minds and hearts of Americans. I'd been in my sixth grade classroom swooning over my tall, dark, handsome teacher, Mr. Alexander, when the announcement came over the P.A. system. As tears instantly soaked Mr. Alexander's five o'clock shadow (the definition of manliness), the tragedy of November 22 in Dallas ripped a hole through the hearts of a generation, destroying dreams of Camelot and happy endings.

One day we were a generation riding on the wings of hope for the future.

Then he was killed.

Then we moved.

South Beach

I lost my parents in July 1964. My mom and dad didn't die in a fiery car crash or from some exotic illness picked up while they were on a safari in a sweltering Central American jungle — nothing that allowed an eleven-year-old to concoct elaborate tales that would evoke pity or advertise for donations with a sad television commercial. I don't recall rescue attempts by the Waltons or being invited to live with Ward and June Cleaver.

My parents simply stopped being parents.

Dad stayed in New York.

My mom made new friends.

My brother wandered off.

I was left to raise myself in Miami Beach.

A friend recently sent me a photo of Ida M. Fisher Junior High in Miami Beach. It looks like an expensive, gated resort with its stately palms, manicured lawn, open breezeways, and arched stone passages. It looks exactly the same as when I started seventh grade there as a shy, self-conscious eleven-year-old in 1964.

Each morning, I walked to school through Flamingo Park. I passed by the baseball field; passed the handball, squash, and tennis courts; and turned on the grass next to the swimming pool, which brought me out the other side just a block from school. It was a different world from New York, especially at first, and I was petrified. I surprised myself by making a few friends despite being the newcomer from up north with the funny accent. I fell into an easy rhythm academically, applied myself, and tried to keep anxiety at bay by watching social scenes unfold from a distance.

My first migraine headache happened in seventh grade biology class the day we were dissecting a frog. The blackboard quivered and blurred, the room spun, and I suddenly felt as if I'd been hit in the back of the head with a hammer. Pushing the desk out of my way, I ran down the hallway to puke in the nearest bathroom. The school nurse let me walk home when she couldn't reach my mother, and I began the ritual of dark rooms and cold washcloths. The episodes lasted a few days, and then I was fine — until the next time. The excruciating inevitable next times have been with me ever since. The debilitating headaches are now relegated to a tiny corner of the blue placard in my car.

Toward the end of seventh grade, I met George. He was a year older and drop-dead gorgeous — six feet tall, strong, lean, with blonde hair and striking blue eyes peeking out from sun-streaked bangs. He wore tan khaki pants a lot and had a lightweight, red, button-down shirt that he favored. Our unpredictable connection was intense and immediate. He was bright and ambitious, reeking of decency and common sense. George was sweet, attentive, and treated me like a princess. He had a shiny new driver's license, a 1930 Model A Ford with a rumble seat, and a powder-blue Vespa. We were a steady couple from the end of seventh grade until my senior year in high school — a lifetime in teenage years. George tried with all his might to keep me safe, but nothing could have kept me from succumbing to the deadly vortex that was South Beach.

• • •

The legend of Mr. Ruben Blumstein the Spanish teacher lives on in everyone who went to Fisher. A huge, imposing man, a Cuban Jew raised in Mexico, he took his job very seriously. When he got upset with a student during class, it was not uncommon for him to pick the student up, desk and all, and hurl them across the classroom. The sound of his yelling at the top of his lungs and pounding on books was part of Fisher's ambience. Thankfully, he liked me, and the closest I ever came was a mild desk bounce. His teaching methods were effective, though. I, for one, learned Spanish quickly and fluently.

Years later, fluent in Spanish and living in Barcelona, I wrote Mr. Blumstein a letter. He made corrections with his famous bold red pen and sent it back across the sea to let me know he still cared.

George, my high school boyfriend.

All over Miami Beach, people spoke Spanish. The influx of people leaving Cuba in protest of the Communist regime was in full swing, and Miami was the destination. Though official numbers vary, close to 250,000 Cubans found their way to greater Miami. In 1965 alone, 45,000 refugees were airlifted out of Cuba as many more left in boats. In November 1966, the U.S. enacted the Cuban Adjustment Act, granting citizenship to Cubans who had been living in America for at least two years.

Assimilation and compromise were the major tasks at hand in job markets, in schools, and on the streets. There was an overall air of understanding as language barriers were transcended and adjustments made. All the refugees who came to America felt fortunate to get out of Cuba with their families and the clothes on their backs. Doctors and lawyers bussed tables in cafeterias and worked tirelessly at whatever jobs they could find. A proud, determined people, Cubans did what they had to do to survive.

My understanding of the political climate was minimal at best. We knew that our schools were stretching resources and that we needed to learn Spanish. Given the magnitude of the influx, Miami Beach managed the transition in a graceful manner. The majority of newcomers crossed the bay to Miami City and established separate communities. Those who stayed on the beach side became part of our world. We learned each other's languages and customs and adapted to the reality of multicultural existence.

I thought I'd made a big change moving from New York.

The Cuban people knew change.

The Cuban people were survivors.

I was drawn to these newcomers, to the independent intensity that defied labels and boxes.

Of course I was.

Proud Cubans on America's fringes.

Unboxable outcasts.

• • •

Nobody was home after school. Again.

I'd brought home a good report card — not because I worked for it, but because school came easy. All A's except for that B- in geometry. Darn shapes. Tossing the manila envelope on the table to be signed, I went to my room and looked out the window at Biscayne Bay.

We lived on the ninth floor of the West End Villas, a high rise in the South Beach area. The complex of three buildings had a main entrance where doormen welcomed people into the comfortably furnished lobby. Several restaurants, a few small shops, and two swimming pools completed the air of luxury. The complex was the first high rise in this section of South Beach and was surrounded by single-family homes and small apartment buildings. A large grocery store was two blocks away on Alton Road; the ocean, a five-minute walk. A Royal Castle burger joint was tucked away across an unlit parking lot. I found a rough crowd of glue-sniffing dope dealers there at all hours of the day and night. It was a lonely, dark hangout for lonely, dark people.

I liked Miami Beach. I could walk everywhere I wanted to go, school was a snap, the weather was great, and I was free to do as I pleased.

Far too free.

My brother, Steve, was probably sailing or hanging out at one of his friends' houses. He kept busy, and I didn't see him much. Mom would be at the Crown Tower Complex on 6th and Ocean Drive, where Trudy and Johnny lived. Mom's crew was always either on the beach or in the bar.

On my own, I was drawn to the ocean, where I walked for miles, splashing my bare feet in the surf. One afternoon, I walked so far that the beach ended at a huge jetty where the outcropping of rocks made it impossible to pass. Lost in thought, I left the waterfront and went toward Ocean Drive.

That's when I discovered the real South Beach.

Turning from the jetty toward Ocean Drive, I saw that this beach was different — no lounge chairs, umbrellas, or sunburned tourists. The pier had

South Beach Pier.

South Beach, 1967. 1st street and Ocean Drive.

people fishing from it instead of vendors selling straw hats and souvenirs. Intrigued, I climbed on the stone sea wall and sat cross-legged on the smooth rock. Beyond the sea wall, a park-like area dotted with palm trees covered the fifty yards or so to the street. It was a perfect vantage point from which to survey my discovery. There were a few stores, lots of funk, and no glitz.

Transfixed, I sat alone, barefoot and comfortable. This was where I belonged. The South Beach of the sixties was a haven for hippie types who didn't fit in anywhere else. Hopping off the sea wall and crossing the street that day was to be a pivotal choice that would impact the rest of my life.

• • •

The smell of leather drew me to a tiny shop where a slight, dark-haired man was engrossed in his sewing machine. Frank and his girlfriend, Roxanne, owned the leather shop. They were creative, energetic, and savvy enough to have had successful shops in both New York and Georgetown. These folks were suede, fringe, pot, guitars, music, beads, love, peace, and freedom. From the moment I walked in, I was in love with all things leather. It's been a lifelong love affair.

The surf shop a few doors down was a damp, cavernous building with an area in back that had been converted to communal living space. Jules and Daniel were brothers who had grown up in a small house a few blocks away. They lived in the shop now along with Freddy, Eve, and Jan. Rarely were any of that crew seen outside during the day. They preferred the dankness of the shop to all things outdoor. The shop had a massive garage-type door overhead that slid open and shut and was locked at night with a padlock. Just inside was a tall counter and ancient cash register. The concrete floors were always wet and cool. The sidewalk in front was lined with colorful boards standing on end. Some were for rent, some for sale, and a few, like mine, were parked safely when not in use and watched over by the golden rule.

Next door on the corner, Lum's served burgers and fries in red plastic baskets with red-and-white-checkered basket liners.

Across the street, the dog track's huge covered parking lot served us well. There were spots to climb and hang out and a strategic shaded part of the roof where we could smoke dope and watch greyhound races on the weekends.

Down from the dog track toward the causeway that crossed Biscayne Bay were the apartments, the only low-income housing around. Families lived in small spaces and spent most of their time sitting on the large front lawn socializing, kids playing on weathered jungle gyms. My good friend Bobby lived on the next block. He had a single mom who worked long hours to keep food on the table.

Before long, I blended easily with the inhabitants of this special corner of the world. The expanse of beach was divided by the pier and had two distinct personalities. North of the pier, tourists parked lounge chairs and did what tourists do. South of the pier, from behind the dog track to the jetty, was ours. Under the pier was ours as well. The truant officer, I thought, took pleasure in doing that "come on out and go to school" thing with his finger.

The tiny block between First and Second Streets on Ocean Drive became the center of my world. I listened, watched, and for the first time in my life, felt totally at ease. Though invisible to the untrained eye, the seductively tantalizing air of hippie heaven had me from the start.

Roxy spotted my artistic eye, and before long, I was working in the leather shop, free to explore my own unique style. My signature designs used the natural edges of hides that were often tossed in the scrap box, creating a rustic flair. My official coronation involved being given a key to the shop and a tan suede bikini that, though it never touched the ocean, ended up serving as great advertising.

Now that I was a completely official South Beach regular, the surf shop became part of my turf. It always had a laid-back atmosphere with locals waxing their boards and hanging out. The hippie fixtures occupied themselves with the constant flow of barefoot traffic.

Twenty-one-year-old Eve was my heroine and role model. Eve was a stunning, graceful brunette with an aristocratic air. She had come from Maryland to Florida with a friend and was now one of the managers of the surf shop. She didn't surf and rarely went outside, but she did a great job hanging out near the counter looking beautiful and oozing sensuality. When she befriended me, my acceptance was cast in stone.

These folks didn't go to school. They were older, dressed differently, and came from exotic places like Greenwich Village and Haight Ashbury. I didn't know much about those places, but I knew it was all very cool. A quirky surfer high school kid, I kept my mouth shut as I learned the ropes. Gradually, I blended in, and someone was always home on South Beach.

At last, I belonged!

South Beach in the sixties.

Outcast Heaven.

• • •

I quickly figured out that the surf shop wasn't staying open by selling board wax to barefoot customers. Mass quantities of drugs were changing hands over the counter. Traffic was heavy with people who didn't surf and shared an unhealthy looking pallor.

Jaundiced junkies.

A thriving heroin trade.

Soon I was skipping school to surf all morning, crossing the street with my Hobie board on my head. When a nod or finger wave signaled me to come in and get high, I'd towel off, lean my board against the building, and head to the rear living space. The sound of bare feet on wet concrete echoed loudly as I padded back and opened the door.

Eve kept a beaded bag that held syringes, ties, a spoon, matches, and servings of heroin folded in packets of tinfoil. I learned how to cook the heroin in the spoon, draw it up into the syringe, and plink the needle to clear it of air.

Apparently air was dangerous.

As I held the rubber tie, the needle found its vein. Then the rush washed over me — the warm, perfect moment of ecstasy that became the driving force in my life.

I don't remember making a decision to shoot up.

I do remember that the first time I felt the rush of heroin course through my body, I understood.

I understood everything.

To this day, I maintain that the only thing wrong with heroin is that it's just too damn good.

It was a wonderful feeling belonging to the South Beach crew. I occasionally went to school, but I really lived to surf, get high, and work with leather. It felt like every day was a dream.

Abruptly my dream was shattered.

NO! Punched directly in my heart from inside.

• • •

Dear God, why is that thick, horrific layer of powder on Bobby's dead face? An awful, orange-hued color caked on my sweet friend's dead blue face is burned forever in my memory. A sweet, tender boy, devoted to his mother and barely eighteen, my bosom buddy and confidante. He lay in that casket in an elegant dark-blue suit, crisp white shirt, and diagonal-striped blue and silver tie with matching cuff links and tie pin. I had approached the casket slowly and looked at him through my fingers like when the scary part of *Psycho* came on the screen at the movie theater. Through my fear, I beheld makeup slathered on the skin of a face that was nothing more than a poor imitation, a far-from-accurate likeness of the boy I had loved. I was certain I still saw what must have been the exit hole in his forehead where the bullet had come out. *HOW COULD THEY DO THAT TO HIM?*

I didn't know whether I meant the man who shot him in the head or the people who worked at the funeral parlor — maybe all of them. We had been to Liberty City together many times, Bobby and me. In Miami in the sixties, Liberty City was a rough, strictly black part of town, safe for those who lived there and select outsiders with cash to buy drugs. Bobby had gone on his usual run to score heroin. He didn't use drugs other than to taste for quality checks; he fancied himself a businessman, a reliable, savvy supplier for South Beach. One night he didn't come back. When I walked in the surf shop the next day, Jules told me that Bobby had run into a problem over a drug deal.

"He's dead."

"Dead?"

The first time I went to Liberty City with Bobby I met Jerry, an imposingly brawny forty-ish black guy built like a football player. His dark eyes were bright and intense, his energy oddly comforting. When our eyes locked, he lightly touched my hand and assured me that I would be safe, unharmed, and that he would protect me. I belonged. "Belonging" might have meant having the right to sit on the tile floor of a tenement bathroom and shoot heroin into my veins, but it was still belonging. Though I could handily shoot myself up, care had to be taken with the pure, uncut product we were given to sample. Guidance was never far away.

It must have been a misunderstanding, fast and furious, because Bobby was way too smart to mess with these guys. They had mounds of cash and piles of weapons.

Now Bobby was dead.

I'd never been to a funeral before, and after one peek at the open casket, I quickly turned on my heels and walked out. I would say goodbye later, on the beach, alone with Bobby's spirit and the crashing waves.

The goodbye to Bobby lit a spark in my soul.

A bewildered teenager, I left the funeral, drawn by the power of the sea. That transformative moment led me toward the path I have walked ever since. I have no memory of choosing a spot in the familiar sand where the jagged rocks of the jetty met the ocean or of purposefully wading barefoot into the water wearing the forest-green linen dress, french-braided sun-bleached hair, leather bracelets, rings on every finger, long silver earrings, my body moving as in a trance toward a spot that beckoned. I waded breast-deep toward a vision of Bobby holding hands with a familiar gray-haired angel. The waves lifted us gently again and again, setting our feet tenderly on the ocean floor with each roll of the tide. Power was effortlessly drawn from the source, the universal strength of nature. Ecstasy coursed through my body, entering the toes and spreading with a rush of knowing through every fiber of my being. The power remained within as it moved on.

No longer perplexed, a young woman emerged from the sea moments or hours later, arms reaching toward the heavens in a gesture that was to last a lifetime.

There is no conscious awareness of change that day when I laid my dress gently on the rocks and sat naked at the edge of the water.

Though Bobby's powdered face would haunt my memory forever, the lesson he gave me would shape my life.

1969

We know without question that there is a shrine to the summer of '69. It's a zillion feet tall and encased in magic. Inside are music, mud, suns, moons, love, peace, drugs, sex, rock 'n' roll, and Woodstock.

On July 20, a small, scratchy black-and-white television shows the wonder of the lunar landing and Neil Armstrong's giant leap for mankind. Mid-August is an intricate diorama with half a million tiny, muddy figures defining the decade. Though parts of the shrine are veiled in a hazy cloud of drug-induced memory loss, each of us easily fills in real, imagined, or made-up details.

We watched the Moon landing on television in July.

In August we climbed in a hippie van and headed to Woodstock, nestled in my well-loved, familiar Catskill Mountains.

Adult logic forces me to doubt the accuracy of my own memories, but since they're mine, they're real to me. This is my story, and I'm sticking to it.

• • •

At sixteen, I had finished my junior year in high school and was off to spend the summer with Eve at her parents' house in Maryland. When I told

High School.

Eve and me.

my mother I was going to my friend Nancy's family lake house in the Blue Ridge Mountains, she predictably chose to believe me. I promised I would write. Eve had an apartment above her parents' sprawling suburban house in Towson, Maryland. She found work waiting tables in a nightclub. I got a job selling *Encyclopedia Britannica* door to door. (Yes, people did that. No, you didn't carry the whole set around.)

• • •

Inside the zillion-foot shrine, a massive haze of bouncing clouds carries thousands of people from one carnival ride to the next. Like *Alice in Wonderland*, experiences move in bizarre, wild succession, colorful and fascinating. Woodstock was a fuzzy place and time except for the music. The music will always be remembered. And the mud, and the drugs, and the camaraderie. But mostly the music.

In a corner of the shrine is a beanbag chair to lounge on while watching an old color video clip of a teenager who fell down a rabbit hole and went on a brief trip to hell toward the end of the summer of '69. By that time, everything went in a needle. Heroin, cocaine, crystal meth, speedball combos, crushed-up pills, and one memorable night, LSD.

• • •

To say "oops" would be putting it far too mildly, though "oops" does sum it up.

With the syringe still in my arm, I was peaking on three hits of Purple Haze in a nanosecond (whatever that is). We went to a club, and over forty years later, I can still see the bands floating in the smoky air, playing music that came from inside my body. I didn't want the drums in me because they were distracting me from watching the world melt. People were going insane around me; I could tell by the way they morphed into different shapes and stared at me with soulless eyes. The only sane one, I was petrified, watching madness take over the world. The bass drum was my heartbeat as Eve's face melted before my eyes. I saw a payphone and screamed, perhaps silently, knowing that I had to call an ambulance. If someone didn't put her face back together, she'd be completely gone. My new friends surrounded me and led me firmly out of the club. They laid me down in a quiet room and shot me full of Dilaudid while Eve went to get heroin, the wrench it took to pull me out of Wonderland.

• • •

We miraculously survived that summer, and Eve and I went back to Florida. My mom thought it was nice that I'd spent the summer in the mountains. She didn't have a clue. I resumed the double life of high school student and South Beach junkie.

A month later, Eve's skin turned an odd shade of yellow. Her eyes followed suit by becoming haunting and distant. Then she was dead.

Hepatitis.

Three or four other friends turned yellow and died on South Beach that month. I watched from a distance, detached and removed, never for an instant considering that I too was mortal. I didn't wonder what happened to them or where they had gone. I'd spiraled a long way down from the time of Bobby. Empty is a feeling that comes when human emotion is tossed in the trash with that last dirty needle. Sadness, grief, fear, love, and loneliness can't be cooked up and shot back in with the next fix.

I have a tiny, old black-and-white photo of Eve and me from one of those photo booths with the little black curtain — four pics for a quarter. I put it in a photo album I was making for my daughter a few years ago with a note that reads, "Eve, my friend who gave me hep C."

Oh well, I had other friends who weren't dead.

• • •

Larry was cool. Larry was leather, fringe, sandy-blond hair flowing from under the cocky leather hat, guitar over his shoulders. The suede knee-high boots were a dark-rust color, and the long fringes waved gently with each step. He appeared one day on the street outside the leather shop.

Frank was teaching me to make belts that day, the secret braid with no beginning and no end — much like life on South Beach. When Frank saw Larry, he hopped from his stool and bolted out the door.

"You made it, man!" He and Larry embraced and high-fived and danced around the sidewalk. Roxanne ran across from her perch on the sea wall to join in as the festivity vibe spread, encompassing our universe with the promise of joy, splendor, wonder, love, peace, burgers, board wax, Barge leather glue, and all manner of grooviness.

Larry was unceremoniously dragged into the shop for Frank's show-and-tell. The shop was Frank's accomplishment. It was tangible, well appointed, and we had earned respect for our creations. Customers came from other beaches, money was being made, and, above all, it smelled good and I worked there. Frank and Roxy had been waiting for Larry. He'd just finished a gig with a band in D.C.

I sat on a stool in back of the counter, watching. When Frank introduced us, Larry glided over, looked me straight in the eyes, and kissed my hand. I was sixteen. Charmed. Bowled over. In trouble. He held on to my hand and asked if I would show him around South Beach. Mesmerized by the coolness of all that was Larry, I came from behind the counter, and we left hand in hand, connected by the fascination in our eyes.

It wasn't much of a tour, but suddenly our block was filled with magic and charm. We talked easily and comfortably as we made our way down the street, across to the beach, and onto the pier. When he asked about the dog track, I led him to my special spot. The back corner of the covered parking lot had a high concrete divider that separated the dog track from our beach. It was a private spot even on race days.

Larry's quiet, gentle manner entranced me. His dark old-soul eyes held me tightly.

We shared stories and secrets and had no concept of time that day. He let go of my hand only to coax his guitar from his back to the cradle of his arms. He looked far beyond my eyes and began to play. The Rolling Stones' "Get Off My Cloud" set the tone for what was to be our brief, intense story.

I floated home late that night.

• • •

I kept my grades up, and no one suspected that I was a budding junkie. If questioned about my activities or whereabouts, I was quick with alibis and lied easily to everyone, including myself.

Larry was utterly bewitching. He'd moved in with Frank and Roxy and found work playing in a small club on weekends — when carloads of surfing, drugged-out strangers showed up to hang out and spend money.

As heroin took over my life, I spent more time on the beach and less time covering my tracks. Hell, George was the only one who even knew I was changing. During my senior year, he tried his hardest to rescue me, but I didn't hear a word. He even took to cruising the block on his little blue Vespa and inviting me to go with him for a ride or to have dinner, or, "My God, Hilary, please leave this place and come with me where it's safe." *No way.*

My nights were spent on the beach, smacked out. With the streets and sea walls deserted, we moved easily from the manicured grass to the stone sea wall and beyond to the comfortable familiarity of the sand and sea.

Still entranced with Larry, I was known as his girl — despite George and despite our age difference of well over a decade. He matched the smooth, sweet-smelling leather he always wore with his easy, soft-spoken manner. He spoke of spirituality in ways that had never crossed my conscious mind — about soul paths, lessons, life, and death. Larry whispered that he'd loved me before we met, that we'd known each other before. He smiled sweetly when he told me he was going to come back as a jet-black kitty cat. While teenage girls at Beach High swooned over television idols, I had my very own real, live super-duper hippie-leather-fringy boyfriend.

• • •

As the winter flew by, my grip on reality loosened with each stronger, purer shipment of heroin, each hit of acid. Who named LSD? Purple Haze, Orange Sunshine, tiny drops on paper that took us away. Often.

Those were the days of love-ins, three-day pre-Woodstock music festivals that were mostly unsupervised parties held in public venues. We camped out and saw Jimi Hendrix, Janis Joplin, and the Rolling Stones. We were there when Hendrix got out of his helicopter, walked on stage, and fell down, only to be whisked away before playing a single note. When Janis inspired us with Southern Comfort and the short-lived intensity of her genius and Joan Baez wrote a song for her. We were the ones who bought those expensive Doors tickets the time Jim Morrison pulled his dick out, got arrested, and ended the concert after only one song. All that money for one song! We were there.

• • •

In the winter of '69, I was a high school senior thinking about a calfskin vest I'd designed. After pondering decorative beads, fringe, and overlays, I'd decided that a tasteful layer of tobacco suede down the front would contrast perfectly with the row of leather buttons and looped hooks. It was a special order, and I would finish it today. I rounded the corner onto Ocean Drive, walking briskly as I always did, and used my key to open the leather shop. As I thoughtfully sorted through tobacco hides, Roxanne made a rare morning appearance. She was delicate, tiny, draped as always in skirts and scarves that were wound, tucked, and tied in mysterious ways. She tried to tame her long, unruly auburn hair with the wooden stick that held her leather barrette. She pulled herself easily onto one of the high stools at the counter.

"Hilary."

"Hi, Rox."

I was measuring and marking a corner of the hide I'd chosen, focused on taking my strips from the outermost section to get the natural edges.

"Hilary, Larry is gone."

"Where'd he go?" I paused, looked at her, and suddenly felt the weight of her words.

"He drowned himself, Hilary. Jumped off the end of the pier last night. Larry couldn't swim, Hilary. One of his boots washed up on shore about an hour ago. The cops are looking for his body."

I drew a complete blank.

• • •

I was certainly impacted by South Beach and deeply disturbed by the deaths of Bobby, Eve, and Larry, yet after high school, it was time to leave it all behind and enter a new phase of life.

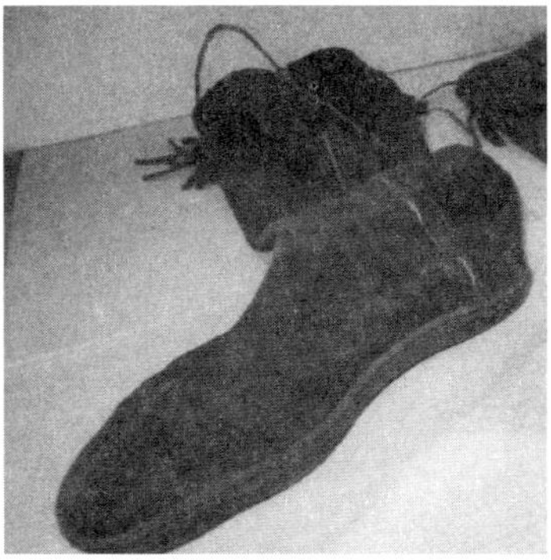

They found Larry's boot.

Quinnipiac College.

The name caught my attention as I leafed through the paperwork I'd been given by Mr. Mandon, the school counselor. There had been talk of not letting me graduate high school due to excessive absences. My mother and I agreed to resolve the issue as a family. So we lied. We told the principal I'd been home taking care of her. He dared to ask her why her illness appeared to be the worst on Mondays and Fridays, and Mom's haughty response brought the conversation to an immediate and satisfactory halt.

When I told Mr. Mandon I wanted to leave Florida, he looked at my 3.8 GPA and gave me a list of private liberal arts schools where I would qualify for academic scholarships. I moved to Hamden, Connecticut, and started school right after my Mom's heart surgery in August of 1970.

Quinnipiac is across from Sleeping Giant State Park. Standing on campus, if you look at the mountains across the road, they form the shape of a sleeping giant. There's a real castle in the giant's belly button. I spent more time in the belly button castle than anywhere else that year. Though a seasoned junkie can always find junk, I didn't fit in and missed the easy beach ways.

I had relatives living all over Connecticut and New York. One of my aunts told me that she tried to talk to me that year, that she was concerned about me. I have few memories of that year, but one thing I know for certain is that I wouldn't have listened to anyone. I was hell-bent on self-destruction.

• • •

When I finished my first year of college in Connecticut in 1971, my dad got me a job working as a cocktail waitress at the Concord. I worked the main nightclub as well as the most elite of the swimming pools and made a ridiculous amount of money in tips. Summer staff was housed in a group of buildings on hotel grounds where exhausted college students and enterprising locals found drugs plentiful and camaraderie easy. Many of us used whatever speed was around so we could work more hours and keep going with little need for sleep.

The last night I worked, I remember hustling drinks while James Taylor and Joni Mitchell gave a stellar performance to a packed house.

After work, it was time to party.

Dead

On July 13, 1971, Marco Pizzolo came home during lunchtime to meet the plumber. On his bed, he found a blue, dead, naked body lying in a pool of vomit — mine. When he called an ambulance, the screaming sirens brought paramedics, police, hotel security, and every neighbor from miles around.

Twenty-year-old Marco was grilled by police and arrested for attempted murder as emergency responders took over. The last thing he saw was a paramedic cutting my throat to create an airway with an emergency tracheostomy. Oxygen was forced into my lungs, and I was whisked into an ambulance for transport to Monticello Hospital.

Because no one knew how long my brain had been without oxygen, it was impossible to predict the extent of brain damage or whether I would survive at all. When a brain doesn't get enough oxygen, it's said to be hypoxic. The result is long-term irreversible damage to the brain's functioning, and the person's life will never be the same.

When they got me to the ER, my body was inflexible from the neck down.

Not a good sign.

The coma was stage 3, very deep. My breathing was supported on the then-revolutionary Bird Respirator. There were high temperatures, pneumonia, and dyskinesia.

The position of my body was significant in that it was a classic posture known as tonic rigidity, an ominous sign of severe brain damage leading to a very poor prognosis. My upper extremities were flexed, bent inward on the chest, hands clenched into fists. Both legs were also rigid — evidence of disruption of motor neurons in the lower spinal cord. Other neurological testing confirmed that there was major damage to nerve paths connecting my spinal cord and brain.

• • •

In the early 1970s, the study of consciousness was in its infancy. Intensive care was dramatically improved during this time as doctors learned that if the body could be kept alive, the brain could shake off a coma — a totally unresponsive, eyes-closed state — within two to four weeks. At that point, people may emerge with varying degrees of damage. As more patients were kept alive long enough to come out of comas, the next step for scientists was to explore the nature and degree of disability in brain-injured patients. In 1971, comatose patients were often referred to as vegetables. If and when they woke up, their brain functions were not understood, and their consciousness appeared to be unstable.

Scientists have determined that consciousness appears to be a type of collective agreement among different brain regions, a dynamic state made possible by an active coalition of parts — the circuit for consciousness. The schematic being developed now, forty years later, is a first step, a set of testable hypotheses about how an injured brain might climb back into awareness. Interestingly, if this theory can be scientifically proven, it will turn consciousness from a metaphysical question into a scientific one.

I know that matters of consciousness, life, and death will never be defined, proven, or explained scientifically. If consciousness is dependent on the "collective agreement" of different parts of the brain, studies may eventually be able to define how many parts of the brain must be active to equal a particular definition of "consciousness."

But science will never be able to factor in the soul.

Therefore, science will never be able to define consciousness.

Consciousness is dependent on agreements made far from research labs, in the place where guardian angels and souls relax in recliners and chat.

• • •

I was aware of waxing and waning components as I watched events unfold in the ICU in Monticello. What began to take over my confused consciousness was an old, familiar energy: Mary. After many years, my guardian angel had returned to wipe away the tears and let me know that all was well in this odd new world. At one point during this time, Mary rounded up emotion and placed it in the delicate silver locket she wears on a chain around her neck. My feelings would be safely stored there and dealt with later.

For now, the only focus must be to heal this paralyzed body.

What part of me was adept at overseeing my best interest? Was the feat accomplished with a cosmic broom and dustpan? Did Mary come up with the survival plan and line the locket with velvet and fairy dust? Who is qualified to say where the brain ends, where the soul begins, what constitutes survival?

I wanted more than anything to stay with Mary, to keep from returning to this, that "other" world. When I argued, whined, and stomped my feet enough, Mary found a gracious quorum of angels to help with a compromise. Part of my spirit would always live outside of the body, attentive and loving. This glowing entity, Tink, was to watch, guide, and be responsible for the documentary film that constitutes my current existence. Who knows what cosmic genius came up with such a novel solution?

Certainly not me.

• • •

I drifted in and out, my consciousness a mystery. Events on Mary's side were vivid, real, and intense with emotions.

Oh my goodness, Mrs. Hoos! Mrs. Hoos had been my second grade teacher, my all-time favorite, and there she was sitting in a chair next to my hospital bed. "I can teach you," she said, "how to move on from here. The tricky part is that you've always been incredibly stubborn about doing things exactly the way you want to do them. This one is different, my child."

Mrs. Hoos hadn't changed a bit. She was still the white-haired, sturdily built woman who looked and behaved like a dreamy, kind, old grandmother. We'd gotten along, and she had helped me through times when I was littler, lonelier, and more frightened than any seven-year-old on the planet. I looked at her intensely.

"I'm not afraid."

"Of course you're not. You never have been." She smiled and touched my face. Mary was behind Mrs. Hoos — well, beside her, fading in and out.

"We know you don't want to go back, Hilary."

"I'm *not* going back," I thought, without knowing what I meant. Funny how I was thinking thoughts that I didn't understand while traversing time and space with ease. It was the "outside voices" that were disruptive, the ones trying relentlessly to break down my protective barriers. I was barely aware of my physical surroundings. The hospital bed was still clear from above, and my body was still in it. Mrs. Hoos and Mary were talking quietly and leaning over the broken girl. Beyond that, I was clueless.

My mom and Mrs. Hoos, 1958.

"You can't stay with us yet."

"I've always been with you."

"Yes, you have. People around you have died, Hilary, and your friend Bobby's spirit brought you here to look death squarely in the face. Death is not something you can run to or run from. Regardless of what you may think, you are *not* the boss here. This experience, this visit, is intended to change you forever, Hilary. You may fight, resist with all your might, but in the end, you will return to finish this lifetime. You will remember death as few are able, and you will teach others that death is not scary, Hilary. You will teach this whether you want to or not."

Their good-natured laughter drove me to pout like the spoiled brat I was. Mrs. Hoos stood up, hugged Mary, and walked slowly back to her second grade desk, where she began to grade papers as her presence faded into a mist.

Realities came and went, but who is to say what is real and what is not? I could fly with Mary and Tink. That was very real. As I flew, there were no limits to my imagination. I was free.

Hospital staff and gadgets cared for my broken body. They were unaware of the fact that I am not my body and that a greater part of me was overseeing my total experience. I wanted to be free of my predicament, my crippled body that wouldn't move. But soon I realized I was already free, free to be everywhere at once. It felt perfectly natural that when I looked up from the bed, I saw a little me looking down. Little me could fly, and together we were able to move freely. We watched Mary at her work as she checked tubes and IVs before going to another part of the building for supplies. When she came back and tried to run her fingers through the mats that used to be my hair, she shook her head and decided to seek out mortal hair product.

• • •

Ellen is beside my bed in intensive care, leaning over and whispering in her heavy Brooklyn accent. She is petite with dark brown eyes, olive skin, and black hair flowing past her knees. Though tied back in an attempted ponytail, the hair, much like Ellen, is not to be contained. We were roommates at Quinnipiac College and planned to leave school and backpack in Europe.

"What were you doing in that bed behind me a while ago?"

Ellen's Mona Lisa smile. She asks me what drugs I want her to bring in, what would make me feel better. She's going to the city for a couple of days and will get whatever I want.

"I'm good, El. Don't need anything."

She smiles and fades into a fog, giving her spot to Charlene as I continue to watch from everywhere. Charlene lived with her husband and baby on the snowy hill where we moved after Chestnut Street. There were only two houses on the hill, hers and the one we rented. We always rented, and we were always moving. Not far, usually — just around town in Liberty. My dad was restless, on edge, always ready. For what, I didn't know. But he was ready.

I liked Charlene a lot because she focused, and when we talked, I felt like I mattered. What was she doing here? She spoke as a conspirator, standing close to the side rail of the bed. "I can get you out of here without anyone knowing," she told me.

Our eyes locked in a part of my mind that was with me up above, but the me in the bed did nothing. I thought her away, and she was gone from the room. *I wonder why she would say something like that? I'm comfortable. She seemed to be trying to help me, though, so I guess I'll thank her later.*

Awake

"Blink twice if you understand me."

Okay.

I blink my eyes as the voice asked. Where I drift, a few blinks are meaningless. I feel a light near my eyes, close them, and leave the room.

Little did I know that this moment was the Awakening.

I turn to Mary and am warmly comforted by her touch. The smooth, peeled logs of my raft have been lashed together with strong, white rope, and I travel on the calm water from one island to the next without moving. The tropical sun blazes through the brilliant blue sky, the sea, and the essence of my being. My body barely makes contact with the logs but rather hovers just above the raft's surface like a butterfly. I smile, knowing that I am seeing forever, that this peace is endless. I understand that I am part of a world beyond meditation or imagination. My body is embraced by a long, white, flowing gown sewn from fabric so exquisitely soft that Mary chuckles when she tells me it's a celestial fabric she made just for me.

• • •

I have heard stories of people who have gone to the Other Side — stories of gardens, angels, white lights, and loved ones who have passed on. My experience was very real and comforting to me; I wanted to stay there, and part of me did.

• • •

I watch events unfold from several feet above myself at the same time as I watch from the body looking up. Above is a small, translucent version of my body fading in and out like a Cheshire Cat. Protective and able to communicate thoughts, this entity's job is to give solace and gather information. The physical body doesn't need to understand yet. It needs only to survive.

Mary cares for the long, tangled knot on my head. My brown hair hung past my waist and had shone with brilliant golden highlights from the summer sun. I wore it loose and parted in the middle. Someone had wanted to cut it off when I came in because it was matted and wreaked of vomit and death. Mary quietly insisted that she would take care of it and began the monumental task of turning it back into hair.

We talk about the nearby mountains and how we would ride horses on her farm near Hurleyville. We look into each other's eyes so deeply that we touch each other's souls. Or is it one soul, Mary and me?

I watch Mary make one of those beauty parlor sinks appear at the head of my hospital bed, and then I fly above her as she gathers supplies from a cupboard at the other end of the building. She moves with such fluid grace that I'm never sure whether her feet touch the ground. When Mary decided to save my hair, she knew that Eva would help. Eva had heard about the overdose, even read the sensationalized story in the local newspaper: "Liberty Native Overdoses on Drugs!" Mary said my overdose hit Liberty like a gossip comet. Big news that was easily embellished.

• • •

The part of me that went to the salon with Mary saw that downtown Liberty was still in 1964. Eva's Beauty Parlor was half a block up from the stoplight on Chestnut and Main. Sears & Roebuck was on the corner. We used to take our books of green stamps into the store and trade them for cool stuff from the catalog. I felt the yucky green-stamp glue taste when we went past the store and saw little me licking the stamps and putting them in the special books. I looked up and down Main Street — Woolworth's and the diner, the soda fountain, the movie theater, and Ben was even standing outside his little art store smoking a cigar and talking to Charlie Gips. I liked Ben; he had painting classes for kids in the downstairs part of his store. Charlie was my friend Linda's dad. Their house up the hill from the Dairy Queen had a dance studio in the basement where Charlie taught us to do the kinds of dances in which boys and girls actually touch each other. We all went when we were nine or ten. Maybe it was a Liberty rite of passage to learn a proper fox trot and waltz for when we went to the hotels.

My mom, Sally, was a bit of a legend when I was a kid, especially at Eva's. My dad bought her expensive blond wigs made from human hair so that when she wasn't feeling well, she could drop off the wigs to be styled. Mom had been sick for as long as I could remember. She had a bad heart, they said, but I loved her and thought her heart was pretty great. Always dressed to kill, she couldn't possibly be caught without good hair and perfect makeup. I was proud to have the only mom in town using the wig method. When she spent time at Eva's, I used to sit on the straight-backed chairs in the front part of the salon, reading or coloring while I waited for her. The chairs were just far enough from the grown-ups that no matter how hard I tried, I could never quite make out the details of the town gossip, which was one of the big reasons for Eva's successful business.

When I had my hair done at Rumors in McCall in the future, I saw a picture of Eva's in my head — styling chairs filled with women of the fifties trading the day's most important stories and secrets. The only difference at Rumor's forty years later was that men and women had their hair done at the same place while they openly talked about anyone who wasn't there.

• • •

Twenty-seven days passed before I responded to the voice asking me to blink twice. The ability to process those words proves that on some level I knew I existed. Removed from the meaning of the blinks, I was a casual observer watching as my body was surrounded by medical personnel bustling about with equipment that provided them with the necessary proof that I existed.

In that same moment, in another place, a bleeding little girl's body flew through an autumn sky and landed in a cloud-cushioned crib where an infant played with her toes and giggled. It was the miniscule moment in time and space where Mary lives, where I have always been safe.

• • •

I probably should be paying attention, and maybe even trying to listen, but I don't want to. I want to go to the bathroom, but they aren't going to let me.

Kind of unreasonable, I think, but I'm not going to worry about it. I'm just going to watch, because I can. I see a doctor lean over me — doing an exam, I guess. I don't know if my eyes are open or closed, and I don't have any idea what is going on. I look okay from up above, kind of skinny maybe, bandaged and tubed, but I still look like me. I don't wonder where I am or what is going on.

In the outdoor breezeway, an ambulance idles with both doors open. Mary holds the hand of the flying little me that has become a constant presence. We watch as the body is loaded into the ambulance accompanied by tubes and IVs attached to the gurney. "No, no one may ride along in the ambulance," I hear. My father's somber face flashes before me. He is nodding pensively, letting hospital staff know that he and my mother will be following closely behind.

I am comfortable in Limbo. I both watch and feel the body being lifted into the air, and I know it is my body. My eyes look back at me. Outside, where the crisp mountain air delights my senses, I see with my eyes closed. A crowd gathers now — well wishers, curious locals, hospital staff. I can easily be an observer since no one speaks to me or expects a response.

A version of Mary still holds my hand, and it doesn't matter that the medics can't see or hear her. It's all one reality working together for the common interest.

"Easy with her," I hear. "Slowly, okay, set her down and keep the oxygen close by."

Yeah, easy with me. Her. Us. I can do it all myself, you know. Do what? Was I going somewhere? I watch as my body is loaded into the back of a long car. I've never been inside a hearse, but I'm pretty sure I hadn't died. If I had, this was definitely not the usual ritual.

The gurney crashes loudly through swinging doors to a place where rows of blinding lights pierce my eyelids, and a thousand people surround me, bustling and chattering. I can hear an authoritative voice bark an order every now and then. I think this is a hospital. A white coat with white hair and a stethoscope whisks in, brisk and purposeful. He's followed closely by other white lab coats. I begin to wonder if he is some sort of guru. *Maybe I'm in a monastery!* I feel isolated and vulnerable yet powerful. I am the consummate survivor of something … but what?

• • •

I was moved to Mount Sinai Hospital in Manhattan as soon as I was stable. My dad would see that I got the best care New York City had to offer. The drive from Monticello to the city must have taken a little more than an hour by ambulance. I don't remember much about the drive other than lying comfortably on a cloud with Mary and Tink hovering about.

When I next heard a voice, it was another request to do the blinking thing. I was tired, very tired. I didn't want to perform anyone's circus act. I wanted to be left alone. I was still meandering about in my thoughts when I vaguely recognized that Mary and Tink were my only connections to reality. Thoughts were in pictures and words happened when sounds arranged themselves into an order that was somehow familiar.

Where's Mary? My face feels wet. I can't touch my face, but I feel that it's moist. I can't touch it because ... a man's voice breaks through the barrier separating realities.

"Paralyzed," it said, "but not a vegetable."

That time the sounds made words. I remember hearing those words just as vividly as I remember that they had no meaning.

I want for nothing. I remain one with the raft and easily reshape it at will, morph it into a flying sailboat if I feel like moving quickly or playing tag with the wind. Mary and I laugh easily as we move clouds into funny shapes and soar with delight above the water.

"Move your feet if you understand me."

I hear a group murmur and hum of voices. I used to have a boyfriend who was an entomologist and raised bees. No, that was in the future. Anyway, the room sounds like the air did when he was dressed in his astronaut suit and getting us honeycombs.

Being in two worlds at once is so natural that I don't even think about it. I intuitively know that I'm safe with Mary and that she'll take care of me for as long as it takes the debilitated body to recover. It's all about survival. For me, it's always been about survival.

Recovery

It's easy to explore when you're a flying little Tink holding on to Mary's reassuring hand, and you can instantly be wherever you want to be. When I leave the room, I arrange for a teeny piece of Hilary's awareness to come with me — just enough to keep her from being totally ignorant of the world beyond the hospital bed.

The nurse's station, down the hall to the right, is fully staffed and has an air of crisp efficiency. To the left is a large, open waiting room where chairs and couches are arranged in sections set up for small groups of family or friends to have relatively private conversations. Mom is sitting on a green couch with her eyes closed. Dad paces with vigilant anticipation. They don't look at one another. They don't speak.

Ten or twelve lab coats are in a huddle, talking in hushed tones. I smile in my head and think they should lighten up and do one of those football cheers as they break the huddle — throw their collective arms in the air and yell, "Go patients!" or something. They don't. The huddle breaks, and the team captain heads toward my dad.

I know he's the captain; he's dignified, has thick white hair, and I'm pretty sure I spot a C on his tie clip. The rest of the team gives him a nearly imperceptible bow as they finish their huddle talk, and he alone leaves the troop.

I follow him, wanting to see the expression on his face. *Oh, he* does *think he's quite the big shot*; his brow is furrowed, face firmly set with lips tightly pursed. I consider the notion of his face freezing that way. *Didn't his mom warn him about that? What would his friends think? Surely he has friends.*

When the captain goes into the waiting room, he asks my dad to have a seat on the couch beside my mother and pulls over a chair to face them. His look is kind and thoughtful. He speaks quietly and in a calm, reassuring doctor tone. No matter how close I go, I can't quite make out the words. Mom has tears in her eyes and looks numb. Dad is doing the talking and nodding his head slowly, taking in every word. They shake hands, and Captain rejoins his team.

Mom looks like a statue. She doesn't move or say a word; she only stares into space with the tears stuck in her eyes. Dad resumes his pacing, shooting looks in Mom's direction like bullets from a handgun.

Mom walks slowly down the hallway and into an elevator, moving as if in a trance. Following from above, I watch her get off on the second floor and head toward the cafeteria. She gets her bearings and stops at a coffee machine. She looks forlorn — a victim of circumstance, a devoted mother with wayward child.

"Be kind," Mary whispers, her constant presence comforting and always gentle.

I feel a jolt when my blood begins to boil, thinking of the years in Florida when I saw Mom only in passing if we happened to be home at the same time. Anger comes as a surprise, as does the huge mountain of resentment and sadness that built up during the years when I was running wild. Surprise Mountain is made up of desperate pleas for attention, acts of defiance, and self-destructive, outrageous behaviors. The shoplifting, stolen prescription drugs, thousands of dollars taken from designer wallets — never a comment from Mom about not coming home for days, refusing to go to school, or blatantly using drugs. Sally didn't know the moment when her little girl became a junkie or hear her deafening silent screams for love, limits, parenting.

Sally hadn't heard any of it. She had lived her own gay life of beaches and nightclubs in Florida, a life that definitely did not involve children. She'd meant well and was now confused that her daughter seemed cross with her. She truly had no idea why. How could she? No one wakes up in the morning thinking, "Today I'll screw up my kid." Parents do the best they can do with the tools they have. Always.

During the next few hours or days, her parents walk in and out, sit by her body, talk to her. She doesn't respond, even though I know she can if she wants to. Once she opened her eyes while Dad was there, but that was it. Mom still has those tears. They're frozen and don't spill out, but sit in her eyes — even the blind one.

• • •

Oh yippee, here comes the team! Captain is in the lead, the rest of the players a deferential five feet behind his longer-than-the-rest lab coat. Captain's lab coat flows like the train of a gown. They swoosh through the door and stop at my roommate Serena's bed. Serena is a very attractive woman with dark, thick, curly short hair. Serena wears her own nightgowns, and today's is a brilliant shade of orange with ivory-colored flowers. Her bed is raised almost to a sitting position. She is cordial, bright, and confident. She interacts easily with the team, knows some of their names, and is like a hostess welcoming guests into her home.

When they ask her if the bed is still moving, she patiently reminds them that it's not the *bed* that moves; it's the *room*. She had been in a car accident when she stopped at a red light and the street kept on moving. And moving. Always moving, that world around her, until she lost track of herself and her husband brought her here. The room has slowed down, she explains, but that invisible gas pedal sometimes got it going, and she would just hold on to the rails of her bed. That way she wouldn't fall off and get hurt.

I like her a lot.

Jenny is next, across the room. Captain reviews her chart. "Sixty-four-year-old woman with progressive brain disorder. Memory loss began three months ago, progression fairly rapid, particularly short-term memory. Tests indicate deterioration of brain tissue, etiology unknown."

They move as one (the cast of a Broadway show?) and give Jenny their best team "good morning." Jenny had been up and around this morning. She washed, ate breakfast, and fixed her gray hair in a tidy bun. She was looking out the window and talking. Jenny is impatient. "Yes, yes, I have to get dressed now and get to the subway. I'm going to stop at the market and then go home where I belong and cook dinner for my husband. I must hurry along, or I'll miss my train connection."

The co-captain, a good thirty years younger than the captain, takes his turn. "Well, Jenny, is it all right if I examine you this morning? Your husband will be here to see you later today."

She is so confused, dear Jenny, yet dignity is apparently an important and respected attribute in this room. Jenny speaks in a rushed manner but is polite and agreeable.

"My husband is coming here. Yes, he is coming here, and then I will get the subway and go home and cook him dinner. I'll pack my suitcase first. It's under the bed here."

Co-captain has Jenny's chart and a pen. Separating from the group, he approaches the side of her bed. "How are we feeling today, Jenny?" *Not very original co-captain bedside manner, and that "we" reference couldn't possibly help her confusion.*

"I'm well, young man, and I wonder if you will be so kind as to get my suitcase out from under this bed? I must be getting along very soon."

"Can you tell me where you are now?"

"Of course. I'm in the city." She points out the big picture windows, her eyes sharply focused on an imaginary destination. "I am also running late. See over there? That's where I'll get the subway to go home. I can walk there in ten minutes. I do it all the time."

"What are you doing here in the city?"

"Well, my husband drove me here, and now it's time for me to go home and prepare dinner. He works all day, and I think I'll fix a roast chicken and potatoes tonight."

"Do you know that you are in a hospital, Jenny?"

Surprised, she looks around the room. "Yes, well, I suppose I am. It's time to leave now. You've all been very kind." Jenny gets briskly out of bed. She is a tall woman, trim and fit. She reaches under her bed, gets her suitcase, and opens it on the bed. As she bustles about, she seems not to notice the entourage at all. She moves to the bathroom, speaking quietly, picks up her toothbrush and personal items, and sets them on the counter.

Co-captain is speechless, and entourage mouths drop. Jenny opens the closet and reaches for her street clothing. "Time to change. Pack suitcase and get subway. It must be getting toward dinner time." She is pleasant, determined, and in her own world.

Captain Courageous steps in. "Excuse me, Jenny. I'm Dr. Morris Bonner. We have met before. You are a patient here at Mount Sinai Hospital in Manhattan. Your husband asked me to take care of you. He tells me you haven't been yourself lately. You're here to get some medical tests."

Pause in the packing mission.

"Roger knows I'm here? The children too? Well." She moves slowly from the closet to her bed and sits down.

"Yes, Jenny. Roger will be here to visit you shortly. I promise. If you don't mind, will you please put your things away? It will be so very helpful if you'll relax and stay with us for a little while. Here, Jenny. Let me get this out of your way. You don't need to worry about cooking dinner tonight. You can lie down and relax."

This guy is good.

Bewildered, Jenny shakes her head slowly. "All right, that's fine as well. Yes, I'll do that — just lie down and wait for Roger to get here. Okay. Then later I'll pack my bag and go to the subway. Roger will be here soon. Okay, yes, thank you."

"That poor woman. Hilary, are you hearing this? She is so sweet. What are we doing in a room with Jenny?" I wonder briefly. She doesn't have both oars in the water. As Jenny settles into her hospital bed, Team Lab Coat stops, has a brief huddle, and then heads my way.

• • •

As Jenny continues chatting quietly, Team White assembles at the foot of my hospital bed. Captain picks up my chart and announces to his minions that he will now read the all-important "transfer note" that came with the patient in the ambulance. The circumstances of my overdose, coma, and medical status are reviewed.

I hear muttering and am aware of a faraway crowd, but I have zero interest in penetrating the fog between out there and in here. Voice sounds drone on. "The patient has been out of coma for approximately four days now. Note that on subsequent examination, it was found that the patient had overdosed on a combination of substances including heroin, amphetamines, and a thing called angel dust that was sprinkled on marijuana. I have it that angel dust is possibly a phenothiazine material. At any rate, the patient had signs of phenothiazine toxicity and was given Cogentin and Artane in an effort to treat apparent damage to the basal ganglia, the part of the brain that controls movement. Had that treatment been effective, we would not currently be looking at quadriplegic paralysis. A thorough mental status evaluation has not yet been attempted, but the patient has responded to simple instructions. So, doctors, let's see what she understands.

"Hilary, hello. I am Dr. Bonner, chief of neurology. You've had an accident and have been transferred to my care at your father's request. Your parents have asked me to visit with you."

My *daddy loves me*. Dr. Bonner moves closer and manages to tear a small slit in the fog with his deliberate close positioning. When I feel his breath, I open my eyes.

"Hilary, we are here to help you. You have a bandage on your throat from a tracheostomy tube. You should be able to speak, but if you have difficulty, I will hold my hand over the bandage to make it easier."

I don't need any help. I'm good. I'd be better if you would get out of my face. Thoughts meander across my mind without conviction.

"I'd like to examine you and ask you a few questions, if you don't mind. I'll ask yes-or-no questions to start with."

If he'd move back, the fog would get rid of him. He doesn't. *Shit. What did he say?* As I drift, Dr. Bonner is persistently annoying. He stays where he is.

"Can you tell me where you are?"

Now that you mention it, I have no idea. His hand sits gently on my throat as I wait for a hint. No hint. Though Mary is just off to my side, she too is silent. An unfamiliar voice: "No."

"Okay. You're in Mount Sinai Hospital in Manhattan. Can you tell me who the president is?"

"JFK." The musical score from *Camelot* begins to play in the background.

"And what year is it, Hilary?"

"1971."

"Yes, that's correct."

Point.

"Do you feel that?"

What?

"How about this on your leg?"

Feel what? I don't feel a damn thing.

Group team mutter.

"Hilary, my colleague is going to test the sensation in your feet with a pin. I will stay here. Now, will you please tell me whether you feel the pinprick on your foot?"

What is he talking about?

"Hilary?"

Tink is snuggled in Mary's lap now.

"No." My voice sounds muffled.

"Very good. Thank you."

Yeah.

"Do you feel that?"

What?

"Hilary, do you feel this?"

I look from Mary to him to Tink. I'm done with this game.

"Hilary."

Do I detect a harsh, bossy tone? Watch it, buddy.

After a few minutes, he moves from mildly bossy to pushy. "Are you feeling the pins, Hilary?"

My face is wet. I feel *that.* He's staring at me. Someone mentions that I'm crying. Interesting, I don't feel like I'm crying, but I *must* be. I don't feel sad. I don't feel pins. I feel numb inside and out.

"Hilary?"

I don't feel. The significance of not feeling is lost on me as I close my eyes and go to sit with Mary. I'm done playing. It takes him a while to understand that the game is over. When he does, he joins the others in the mist, and the white quiet voices move slowly out the door.

• • •

Cameras flicker and zoom in on Rock's smooth surface where Molly lies in the sun watching the movie. Tink and Mary have been fading in and out like Alice's Cheshire cat.

• • •

Hilary predictably remains in position as the lab coats meander about her world. Quadriplegics are like that; you can count on them not to run away. Too much damage to the brain. Too long without oxygen. Very poor prognosis. Though foggy and confused, the mind is active. She doesn't want to know where she is or why — not really. The team visits, pokes, prods, questions, and tests. Psychiatrists, neurologists, and brain surgeons. Tube fixers, food feeders, room cleaners, and sheet changers. Busy.

When her cheeks are wet with tears, they send psychiatrists who have a name for paralyzed teenagers who cry in silence. Clearly, the body has a poor prognosis. The spirit, however, is playful, wise, bursting with power, and manifested in Tink with Mary as her guide and companion. Was the overdose accidental, a party gone too far, or was it a means by which to explore death? Had she wanted to understand the deaths of her lost friends and chosen to do so with her own demise? This was the dilemma of the eighteen-year-old paralyzed body with the very poor prognosis.

• • •

We all meet at Rock. When Mary reaches down to rub Molly behind her ears, she sees a slab of driftwood under her paws. It seems that something has been carved into the wood, and Molly smiles her doggy smile as Mary gently picks it up. Molly leans into the ear scratch as Mary reads the familiar phrase aloud:

"Motivation is the desire to get from where you are to where you want to be."

Ah, simplicity still rules. Got it.

Lying paralyzed in bed … not so great.

Running on the beach … much better.

A clear, lucid image appears: The broken body stands up, turns toward them, and raises its arms to the sky.

We're on our way.

How much of a soul is needed to carry on a life? We have no idea, but we do know that much of my soul will ultimately refuse to return to the body. It's going to be a multidimensional existence. The rest of this life will be interesting.

• • •

As the team approaches my body's bed, Captain is talking about the "poor prognosis" again. It's always the same routine with poking, prodding, questions, and tests. Where are the discussions about progress and solutions? We've all been very patient, but enough is enough. The meeting at Rock was a resounding success. Decisions were made by my higher self that will now be communicated to the well-meaning, mortal hospital staff.

A cheering section begins a pulsing beat in the background. I'd been a devoted fan of the New York Yankees since my dad took my brother and me to Yankee Stadium when we were little. Tink has donned a Yankees cap and is waving a flag bearing the top hat and baseball bat logo.

"You're not going to die, dumbshit," she says. "What about physical therapy? Tell them!

"Up! Up! Yell! Yell!

"MAKE THEM LET YOU GET … WELL.

"Picture running on the beach!

"All you have to do is reach!"

My body lies there. Big surprise. Captain does the introductory mumbling, same old song and dance.

"If the Yanks aren't doing great,

they don't sit around and wait."

Mary is cringing at Tink's cornball cheers but enjoying the top hat routine.

"Morning, Hilary," says Captain. "Let's see what progress you're making today."

One more cheer: "DO it, Hilary."

Hilary opens her eyes and looks at Dr. Bonner.

"Do you feel that pressure on your leg?"

I lock eyes with Captain. The introduction of Frank Sinatra's "New York, New York" starts up.

"I want a physical therapist." I hear the words come out of my mouth and am a tiny bit surprised. So is he.

Pause.

"We've consulted with that department and, given your status, they prefer to wait."

"I want a physical therapist."

"Yes. Well, I'll talk with your parents and the head of PT this afternoon, and we'll see what we can do."

"Now. I have a life to live."

"Fine, that's fine, Hilary." He signals to the resident armed with a pin. "Dr. Wahlberg is going to test your ankle sensation now. There, can you feel that?"

"*Start spreading the news (doo doo dee doo doo).*

I'm leaving today (doo doo dee doo doo) …"

Tink is dancing in time to the music, now dressed in pinstripes.

I refuse to answer on the grounds that no one is paying attention to me.

"Hilary, can you feel pressure on your ankle?"

Silence fills the room. Serena looks over from her bed, catches my eye, and gives me a quick smile-nod combination.

The team is in a pickle now (not the Yankees). *What do we do, Captain?*

Time ticks by slowly as understanding takes hold. I have reclaimed my power and am no longer helpless.

"These vagabond shoes (doo doo dee doo doo)
Are longing to stray …"

"I'm not talking any more until I see a physical therapist." My eyes slam quietly shut. I made the statement softly and with complete calm and finality. There are a few team jaws dropping at the foot of the bed, but Captain keeps his cool. He nods to the team, stands above us, and politely says he'll see what he can do.

It's too bad the team can't see Tink above them still stepping to the music while not missing a word of the doctor discussion.

"It's time that we address Hilary's psychiatric issues more aggressively. The patient's lack of cooperation is uncharacteristic and undoubtedly indicative of a shift in her brain function. Not uncommon with this type of brain injury. Doubtful that she'll remember this morning's conversation by tomorrow, but I'll ask you, Dr. Lawrence, to be liaison with psychiatry. Ask Dr. Spencer to do a consult evaluation, please, and do a written analysis of his report. Be sure to discuss the crying episodes and unrealistic expectations. Any questions or comments, doctors?"

No, all the residents got the picture.

• • •

Dr. Captain saw Mom stepping off the elevator and walked toward her. He talked about my demand, and she nodded.

"Dave and I would like her to see a physical therapist if she wants to, Dr. Bonner."

"Mrs. Jamron, I've been chief of neurology here for years, and I've never seen this type of paralysis reverse. I'm so sorry. There's simply too much damage."

Mom silently stood her ground, the regal tilt to her head natural and powerful, tears sitting still in her eyes.

"Well, perhaps someone from PT can meet with you and your husband. I've spoken with their director, though. He looked at her [prehistoric] brain scan."

"She wants to try. Her father will be back from Kiamesha late tonight."

"Very well. I'll see both of you tomorrow, and we can talk more. I'm truly sorry about your daughter. I ordered a psychiatric evaluation. I will assign a resident to re-examine the PT issue."

He nodded and joined the lab coats in the next room. Mom walked into the room and sat near my head. I felt the presence but didn't acknowledge it. She brought my favorite, a vanilla milkshake from the Shake Shack, but the offering was predictably ignored.

• • •

Fiercely determined, I had not spoken a word for two days when a man with a casual, confident air came in and walked directly to my bed. A Mount Sinai ID tag was clipped to his shirt pocket. Serena watched him; Jenny was packing her bag again. He announced that his name was Thomas and he was from the Physical Therapy Department. I took a deep breath and smiled.

"What a relief. Let's get to work. I have things to do."

He grinned with his eyes, this Thomas fellow.

"Fine with me," he said. "Rumor has it that you're ready to get up."

"I am."

Eye grin. "Great. Do you mind if I examine your arms?"

I looked at my arms. They remained flexed at the elbow and rigid. I was mildly surprised, quite removed from that body I so sorely wanted to heal.

"I don't mind anything."

Thomas held my clenched right fist gently in his hands, and as I watched, he tried to gently coax it from its locked position. I was rapt. The arm didn't move. My eyes focused on the stubborn elbow.

My level of understanding was odd. I appeared to be talking and interacting, yet I had very minimal awareness. Awareness is in the soul, and the soul is outside the physical body. It's a relationship that is far too complex for science while being completely logical and practical when viewed from a spiritual standpoint. *The arm. Back to Thomas and the arm.*

"Just pull it down," I offer as he walks around to the other side of the bed. He tries moving the left arm, but it also remains flexed and clenched. He examines my legs and returns to the right hand.

"Pull it. It'll go," I tell him.

"You're a spunky one, aren't you? That would be awfully painful, young lady." When we look at each other that time, we feel the connection. We smile knowingly.

Quietly, intensely, "Pull it, Thomas. It wants to move."

Thomas is a healthy, strong guy, probably just shy of six feet tall, thirty-something. His slacks hang loosely on his hips. The white shirt is unbuttoned at the top with a dark brown tie loosened in the vicinity of his neck. The sleeves are rolled up to reveal muscled forearms, and the nametag clipped to his pocket, though crooked, clearly says he is a physical therapist. Gentle eyes.

"I don't want to hurt you. Your body is extremely rigid."

"Please pull the arm down, will you? Please?"

His eyes acquiesce. Holding the entire fist, he tenderly asks the arm to move at the elbow. I feel an intense stab of white-hot pain but will myself not to show it. The elbow gives way a barely perceptible millimeter as I urge him to continue, refusing to let him see my agony. He stops and moves to the left side. He does something with my legs that I can't feel, and then he's back to chat.

Before he can say a word, I tell him, "You're the only hope I have, you know. I can do this." My intensity hits him between the eyes.

"You didn't fool me. I know that nearly invisible arm flexion movement hurt like hell. You're tough." He has my chart on his lap and is examining it. He looks at me. Reads. Looks at me. Reads. Rubbing his forehead, he leans back in the chair and closes his eyes for a moment. "It's going to take a tremendous amount of painful hard work, and I can't make any guarantees."

"Okay."

"Your neurological team believes the paralysis is permanent, you know."

"I know. They're wrong."

"No promises, but I can commit to a week-long regimen and see what we can accomplish. You have to understand, though, that it might not be all that you want."

"Got it. Thanks."

"You're very welcome, Hilary. I'm going to talk with all the teams and your parents, do some paperwork, and will be back before dinnertime. Okay?"

"Thank you."

• • •

It was late, the lights were out, and the hospital was quiet. Jenny had been persuaded to stay one more night, and Serena slept on her side, holding on to the rail of her bed. She lay silently, listening to the usual hospital night sounds. The door opened ever so slowly with a sound that was different from a nurse. As I looked into the night, a figure appeared in the doorway and waited as if adjusting its eyes to the darkness. It moved very slowly across the threshold and looked at Serena sleeping.

"Sis?" It was a whisper.

I moved my head, saw him, and that familiar moisture was soaking my face again. Steve. Hair past his shoulders, big green backpack, scruffy jeans, and tennis shoes. My big brother.

"You came."

"So I got off the plane from Athens a few hours ago, came into the city, and got mugged. It's too late for visiting hours, but I snuck in and found some back stairs, up eight flights, and here I am! I came as soon as I could, Sis. You okay?"

A sight for sore eyes. I adored my big brother. "You got mugged?"

"Yeah, but I told the guy I was on my way to see my little sister in the hospital, gave him my watch and cash, and asked him to take it and leave me alone. The mugger cracked up laughing, took my stuff, and walked away."

We talked through the wee hours, and the morning shift found me sleeping peacefully with a scruffy, long-haired hippie guy holding my hand, dozing in a chair beside me.

Family Divide

I essentially raised myself after losing my parents when I was twelve years old. I never felt badly about it; I guess I didn't know the difference between my parents and those of other children.

• • •

While I was in Mount Sinai Hospital, my dad made sure I had the best medical care in the world and every opportunity to recover. My mom was mostly lost in her own world. I know she loved me, and I understood later that she could never quite wrap herself around the role of being a parent or caretaker.

When my mother, brother, and I made the big move to South Beach, my dad went back and forth to New York doing his own thing while making sure we were well provided for. Dad always had charisma and a lot of secrets. I never questioned the shoeboxes in the closet or anything else. I knew better.

Though Mom's health had been poor for as long as I can remember, she always managed to maintain her dignity, her glamorous appearance, and — once we moved to Florida — her private social life.

My brother, Steve, also drifted away in Florida. We really loved each other, but we led very different lifestyles. After he graduated college, Dad used his

Living in Miami Beach

Southgate, Miami Beach, where we lived.

Across the street. Dark place; dark people.

Rat Pack. Fun fair, Miami Beach, 1968.

Ida M. Fischer Jr. High, Miami Beach, Florida.

My brother and me in good times.

connections to get him a teaching position in the Virgin Islands. Steve soon married. With Dad's help, he bought a house and went into real estate as a career. He has lived in St. Thomas ever since and, to the best of my knowledge, remains very successful to this day.

• • •

The next big move found my parents putting the family photo albums in the back seat of their car and heading west, settling in San Diego, California, in 1974. Dad traded his shoeboxes for a condo with a pool. My parents were warm, comfortable, and close to the desert area where I lived at that time. Thus, we were able to visit often.

Dad's propensity for being different blossomed in San Diego. He became somewhat of a colorful character in his later years. After a lifetime of forcing himself to conform in order to support his family, he grew a beard, dressed in colorful thrift store styles, and roamed the beaches chatting with himself and anyone who crossed his path.

In 1982, Dad was diagnosed with colon cancer. He refused treatment and passed away six weeks later. My daughter, Misty, was two months old at the time.

I barely recognized my brother, Steve, as he swooped into our lives once again, quickly and efficiently handling Dad's estate and tossing me a bank bag filled with pennies. Just as quickly, he flew out of our lives, leaving our mother and I to manage as best we could.

• • •

While Mom's health was even more fragile after her third heart surgery, she seemed renewed as she fell madly in love with her granddaughter Misty. Not long after Dad's passing, Michael, Misty, and I had packed up our meager belongings and returned to Idaho. When we got there, I became aware that Mom could not manage on her own. I sent for her and her belongings and moved her into our glorified trailer house, easily coaxing her through mild protests with the lure of her beloved Misty. I was not able to provide for her as well as I would have liked, but just as she had done — just as we all want to do — I did my best. My brother, Steve, remained mostly invisible to us. I survived by remaining always close to nature.

• • •

Death is a fascinating concept. Death and I are old friends. My parents and brother had, for all intents and purposes, witnessed my return from the Other Side. Yet each of their lessons regarding death ran far deeper than I could understand and embrace in that moment of time.

It is believed we each go through five phases as we become aware of our impending death. I feel that holds true for those who are unable, through their own belief systems, to realize that death is only the beginning of a new life.

Both of my parents lashed out at me with harsh, angry words before they passed. I looked at each of them in turn, held their hands, and told them how much I loved them. Their anger was based in their fear of death, that great unknown, that unfathomable place where I felt most at peace. Anger is a mask for fear. Fear is a barrier that prevents us from learning, loving, and growing.

When I informed my brother of our mother's passing, he ran. Steve is a gentle, loving soul who is very afraid. When I informed him of my second husband Ron's passing, he vanished again. Perhaps he has been running from death since the day he sat at my bedside in Mount Sinai. Perhaps my death and return affected him so deeply that he is inconsolable, so he consoles himself in the material world he has created. When I hear from Steve again — if I hear from him again — I will welcome him with open arms. I hope he learns a little something every time he faces death, for one day, it will be his reality.

Death really isn't scary, big brother. Really.

Walking

Slowly and painfully, the elbow gave in to my will. The stubborn fists ceased their grip on death, and the fingers hesitated, then emerged. Searing pain and physical exhaustion were constant companions while emotions maintained a safe distance. It's amazing what a body can withstand as an entity unto itself. Speech meant not only finding words but also learning the intricate ways to move tongue, mouth, and lips in order to speak them. The eyes look at a spoon knowing that the complexity of holding it and using it to eat are mountains to be conquered. The mind recalls that pencils make marks on paper, that with Herculean effort those marks become letters, then words.

Muscle memory fights its way to the surface while a telephone lies in a crib with the curly black stringy thing. Knowing that it's all okay, that Roz or Mary or Tink is there to help.

Knowing that falling is merely a prelude to getting up.

In the weeks that followed, Thomas coaxed my legs from their prisons and persuaded them to flex, to loosen. As body functions returned, there was no surprise, even in the recesses of my mind. Lacking the cognitive awareness to question, I moved forward on automatic pilot. *Coax the spoon to the mouth, connect the thoughts and images of efficient movement to the disconnected but eager body*. Exhausting concentration. Iron will. Learning came clumsily at first, with ultimate perfection the only acceptable goal. I was on speaking terms with Team White again.

Days into weeks into months. At long last came the proclamation that it was time to get out of bed and walk. The announcement, made without emotion, elicited significant team jaw dropping and eye raising.

"Okay. Tomorrow morning, Hilary."

• • •

I wait for Thomas. I plan to jump out of bed and hit Madison Avenue running, opening two hospital doors at once while raising both arms to the sky in a triumphant Kodak moment. I have no concept of how thin and frail I am. My behaviors are not questioned. I am Determination without the distracting extravagance of feelings. With energy at a premium, every bit is focused on healing the body.

Separation of church and state. Separation of body and spirit.

When Thomas walks through the door with a cheerful smile, I see that he is tentative and instantly nod reassuringly.

"Hey, Mr. T. I can *so* do this."

Yep, I am the body. Still, the bookies aren't giving the walking thing such great odds. Thomas and I are alone in the world.

"I know you can. You're too stubborn not to."

Thomas sits at the foot of the bed, helps me to a sitting position, and we look at one another with mutual respect.

"I'm going to stand in front of you, hold your arms, and help you stand up, Hilary. Ready?"

Of course.

Thomas gently lifts me to my feet and holds me firmly, calmly. My face glows with victory. "You can let go. I've got it."

By George, she thinks she's got it.

In the instant Thomas begins to loosen the hold on my arms, rubber-leg knees buckle, and I head to the floor. He holds me up.

"You're weak; that's all. Let me hang on to you, okay?"

Despite the grumbling, I agree that I don't want to fall on my first day. He helps me — carries me — a few steps toward the door of the hospital room.

"I won't be making it to Bloomingdale's today, will I?"

My eyes reveal pain as they beg that I be returned to my bed. Thomas gets it. Thomas gets *me*.

Encouragement and accolades follow, assurances that I will build strength and blah blah blah. Back on the bed, my born-again arms hold me in a sitting position for less than a moment before the body tips over and takes itself to safety. I hear nothing beyond my own mind screaming a single word:

"YES!"

Keenly focused, I have two jobs.

I will heal the battered body.

Team White, I remember, had the audacity to tell me I would never walk again. Team White was mistaken.

I will also continue to gently cajole Jenny back into her hospital bed every afternoon. When the suitcase comes out from under Jenny's bed, I will talk the silver-haired woman into staying with me just one more night. Alzheimer's, in retrospect, was brain deterioration shrouded in mystery back then.

• • •

Detached and confused, I was vaguely baffled by my body's lack of cooperation. I did not have a realistic concept of my situation; existence is entirely concrete, black and white, void of feeling. This delicate existence used my confusion to its advantage as I worked until I dropped from exhaustion only to get up and begin again. The youthful body and resilient brain struggled to keep pace with unrelenting demands. Legs remembered their muscles and grew stronger with every leg lift; hands remembered how to write, how to use a spoon, how to hug. Emotions would come later, when there was strength enough to cope.

• • •

A willowy body follows a sturdy metal walker down the hospital hallway heading to the nurse's station. My brother firmly and tenderly holds my arm as I walk through the excruciating, inconsequential pain. All that matters that day is reaching the nurse's station fifteen yards from my room. The feet stumble and lag miles behind, but I understand that they need encouragement and practice.

Abruptly, I stop in the hallway and look up at my brother.

"Steve?"

"Yeah."

"Steve, which comes down first, the heel or the toe?"

"Heel," he told me.

I nod, pause, enter the data, and we continue on our way.

• • •

My brain had been ravaged, abilities and information eradicated. Fifty years ago, I would have been declared dead when Joey found me in Monticello. Studies of consciousness being done today continue to prove how little we understand.

It's working for me, so who's to argue or question the methodology? I'm walking when I wasn't supposed to walk; writing when I'd been doomed to clenched-ness; moving the entire body with increasing ease, strength, and control. Yes. I can do the feeling later. Right now, I am nothing short of a medical miracle to be written about in scholarly articles of medical journals.

• • •

Months of grueling therapy went by as each word and movement was celebrated. Mount Sinai had New York's finest medical care and the latest technology, but still, the intensive work, frustration, heartache, setbacks, and successes were exhausting.

The level of sophistication in terms of understanding the brain was far different in the early seventies than it is today. There were no MRIs to show precisely what areas of the brain had sustained the most damage. Mount Sinai, using one of the first CAT scan machines in the country, scanned the brain, and the results of that long-extinct machine were interpreted as being "normal." Physical, occupational, and speech therapies were in their infancy compared to where we are today.

It was still the best medical care available at the time, and the outcome was miraculous. I walked out of Mount Sinai with a poor prognosis and a sturdy, four-legged metal walker that supported my weight and my outlook.

Mary

The drive to the Catskills was stunning. The cool, crisp air blew life back into my heart and soul as I looked quietly out the open car window. I was going to stay at my parents' house in Kiamesha while I did physical therapy and built up enough strength to travel. I was still in a haze, but I didn't know that any more than I knew that my prognosis was "poor."

I had only one thing on my mind: to thank Mary. I was going to the Monticello Hospital to find her, and I could barely wait. I needed her to know, as I did, that without her I would not have survived.

The hospital in Monticello was a small one-story facility. I knew Mary worked in the ICU, so I went in the main entrance and approached the information desk. When the attendant looked up, she did a double take, smiled, and rose to her feet.

"Hilary! My God, look at you, you're okay and you're walking!" Tears came to her eyes as she walked around the counter to embrace me. I had no idea who this woman was, but I hugged her and thanked her.

"Wait till I tell everyone," she said. "You did it!"

I leaned on my walker and smiled, grateful for the genuine warmth. I snuck a look at her nametag and told Brenda how glad I was to see her again. Little did I know that I would be sneaking looks at nametags to jog my memory for the rest of my life. Damage to specific parts of the brain's temporal lobe have been linked with permanent difficulty with facial recognition. My brain has a permanent short circuit in that department as well as several others. If and when people are out of what I perceive as their usual context, they are complete strangers to me.

"Brenda, I want to find Mary and thank her for taking care of me in the ICU."

Silence. Eye contact.

"Can I get a look at the nurses' schedule? Do you know if she's working today?

Brenda paused and spoke slowly and deliberately. "You must have the name mixed up, Hilary. I can't think of a Mary in the ICU."

I wasn't fazed in the least. "Oh, sure. She's about 5'5" or so, kinda thin, green eyes, in her fifties, probably. Her hair is shortish and mostly gray, bangs. She always wears the kind of white nurse shoes that don't have any laces — clogs. And always a white nursey dress. Have you seen her around today?"

"Boy, I sure haven't. Have a seat, and let me go ask around for you." She gestured grandly toward the dated, empty waiting room, smiled, and disappeared through the swinging doors behind the counter. My walker was both cumbersome and comforting. I still needed to put all my weight on it. Most of my weight wasn't much, though. At 5'9" I was down to 120 pounds. It had taken a while for me to get back on solid food. I'd forgotten how to eat, in fact — just as I'd forgotten how to walk, talk, and write. But I remembered now, and here I was, just as I'd promised Mary.

The doors swung open when Brenda came back accompanied by two men. One was in scrubs, the other wearing slacks, a light-blue dress shirt, and a tie.

"Great to see you looking so well, Hilary!" The scrub guy spoke as if we were buddies. "Boy, it was touch-and-go with you for a while. You look wonderful — and you're walking! Congratulations."

What does one say to someone who may have saved her life?

"Thank you for saving my life." Then, "Is Mary around?"

"We don't have a nurse named Mary in the ICU. In fact, we don't have any nurses named Mary, and the description you gave Brenda doesn't sound like anyone I can think of. You were a little out of it when you were with us, Hilary. You may have been confused, but we have all the records and know exactly who was working with you. So we'll figure it out and find her. Okay?"

"Sure, sounds good to me. I'm positive I'll recognize her."

They looked at me expectantly and hesitated.

"I'll look into it. Do you want to stop in tomorrow?" the man in the tie offered.

"No, I'll just sit right here and wait, thanks." I had no intention of leaving until I saw Mary.

"We'll have to check records and back schedules, and I'm really sorry, but I can't do it right now."

"That's not a problem! In fact, I'll just go around back and find the staff entrance. That way I'll see her during shift change. What time will that be?"

"Oh, not until 3:00. If you just come back in a few days, it would probably be a lot easier for you."

"Thanks so much, but I'll wait. I've been indoors for a long time. Aren't there benches out back?"

"Yes, there are, but we can't tell you anything right now about who exactly you're looking for or when she might be coming to work."

"I understand that you're busy, really. I've been looking forward to this for a long time, and I'm totally happy to sit and wait. I guess it's possible I got her name wrong, but I'll certainly recognize her in a heartbeat. I'll wait around."

They looked at each other and hesitated. The two men said they would see what they could do and disappeared through the doors. Brenda fidgeted behind her counter. I thanked her as I got up, arranged my walker, and turned to leave.

"Hilary?" She spoke my name in a clipped tone. I stopped and looked at her. "You could be sitting on that bench for a long time, and it's cold outside. Why don't you just let us do some record checking?"

I smiled and laughed quietly. "I guess because I'm so damn stubborn, Brenda. But then again, they tell me that's what's kept me alive." As I left the building, I felt her eyes follow me until I rounded the corner and was out of her sight.

I moved slowly, very slowly. My mind was flooded with memories of a little girl growing up on Chestnut Street. Memories of Mary tenderly washing my hair. The Catskills were still beautiful, and they still felt like home.

Behind the hospital were several benches and a few picnic tables where staff had their breaks and lunches when the weather was good. A few uniform-clad employees sat at one table smoking cigarettes and talking. I made my way to an empty bench and arranged the walker as a footrest. Leaning toward the staff table, I asked whether anyone knew the ICU nurse named Mary. None of them did, so I took a book from my shoulder bag, leaned back, put my feet up, and prepared to wait for Mary.

Cars began pulling in to the back lot by about 2:15 as doctors and nurses arrived for work. There was a lot of greeting, chatting, and activity. I heard people talking about their kids, the new fourth grade teacher in town, weekend plans. I heard one of the nurses say that shift report was at 2:30. I closed my book and tucked it away, preparing to focus my attention on the departure and arrival section. It was entirely possible that Mary would be either finishing or starting her shift! I was hopeful, excited, on full alert. I moved as close as I could get to the doors.

Some of the shift arrivals greeted me, a few by name. Clueless again, I was friendly and grateful. I knew how small towns worked. They had probably all heard about me, and some of them had been involved in my care. I put on my best version of a "born again" smiley face and nodded my best hello nods. Whenever anyone slowed down or veered toward my bench, I asked them to please tell Mary that I was looking for her. Most nodded and smiled. The last two women I'd spoken to were doing that "cover your mouth while you're gossiping in your coworker's ear" thing. I knew I was officially the town DRUG ADDICT, and frankly, I didn't care in the slightest what anyone said, thought, or did. I wanted to see Mary.

By 3:30, activity in the parking lot had stopped. I'd not seen a glimpse of her yet, but I wasn't discouraged. Counting on my fingers (the ones that knew how to move), I figured that the next shift change would be the night shift, probably 11:00 or so. I'd come back.

When I checked with Brenda on shift times she discouraged my vigil and reminded me that "they" were looking up my records. I thanked her again before I left. *Sure. Thanks. Right, Brenda,* I thought.

What part of "I'm going to wait here until I find her" was complicated? I didn't have her name wrong, in the first place, and I *was* going to find her. Hospitals, I knew, were like any other bureaucracy. Employees were just employees, and some of them came and went — especially in a resort town and especially in the summer. But Mary lived in Hurleyville, so she was a local.

Back at my post on the bench by 10:00 and bundled up for the chilled mountain air, I didn't want to miss anyone showing up early. Given Mary's conscientious ways, I expected her to arrive early in order to keep up with her patients. I had a little bag of cashews and some juice, and I was ready.

About half an hour later, one of the staff doors opened, and a tall, plump brunette came out. Her shoulder-length hair was in a pageboy cut. She wore a nurse's dress that reached to her knees, a white cap, and thick-soled shoes. She looked at me, paused, and headed directly toward my bench. She had a crisp, efficient way about her — her uniform, her walk, her manner. She approached me and asked if she could join me for a few moments. *Of course.*

"My name is Anne, and I am the head of the Nursing Department," she said.

Whoop-dee-doo, I thought.

"Hi, I'm Hilary Jamron." I extended my arm to shake her hand, acutely aware of what a miraculous and complex feat hand-shaking was. Anne shook my hand lightly while staring intently.

"I know you from when you were here in our facility. I'm glad to see you doing so well."

I didn't like her. I tried to think her away, but that ability, by this time, was completely gone. Though I could still retreat into myself, the better dimension was getting increasingly difficult to access. *Darn* — it had been so useful. Anne sat on the other side of my bench. The parking lot lights cast a glow on her left side and accented her already angular features. When she spoke, her voice was soft, calm, brusque, and businesslike. It felt as if she were trying to be warm and fuzzy without knowing how.

"I understand you're looking for someone. Is that right?"

"Yes, that's right. I want to thank Mary. She was my nurse during my coma in the ICU. Is she around? You know, about 5'5", short gray hair, lives in Hurleyville."

"No, she isn't around. And we don't have a nurse with that name or description working here, at least not in the nine years I've been head nurse."

What an idiot, I thought. *Well, I beg to differ and I'm going to sit here until I find her if it's all the same to you.*

"We have pulled your records, and I know exactly who worked the ICU during your stay here." She pulled some papers from a pocket and unfolded them. "The schedule was fairly consistent. A male nurse named Don had most of the day shifts. Swing was Judy — early forties, blond, heavyset. And graveyard shifts … let's see … split between two other nurses, both young. Sarah is a tall, lean redhead, and Michelle is a petite Hispanic woman. That's it. No Mary, no one even remotely fitting your description." Her gaze shifted from the papers to me.

I didn't respond. Though she was grossly mistaken, I was not inclined to argue with this woman. I met her gaze with confident, calm defiance. I took a deep breath and gave her a classic teenage "you're a complete idiot" look.

"Well, thank you, ma'am. I'm afraid you're mistaken, though, and I think I'll just wait around. I *am* going to thank Mary."

"Suit yourself," she muttered as she stood up and strutted back toward the hospital doors.

She's an idiot. Small-minded, small-town bullshit. I know *how this works, and I know they would much rather I disappear and never show my face in Sullivan County again. Well, fuck them. I worked my ass off to get back here, and I'm not leaving until I've done what I came to do.*

The next shift wasn't until morning. I was weak and exhausted and knew I needed to get some sleep. I would go back to the house, sleep, and come back in the morning.

I waited at the employee entrance to the hospital for two more days. When it snowed, a doctor let me come inside and sit on a bench facing the door. I felt Mary's presence with every fiber of my being and thought I caught a glimpse of her once or twice.

I left Monticello Hospital only after I came to terms with reality.

• • •

I sit at a picnic table as a light snow falls through the sunbeams of the perfect mountain day. On a high branch of a nearby chestnut tree is a beam of light that flickers and moves with the breeze.

The source of that light is Tinkerbelle, the part of my soul that refused to come back.

My Tink is real.

She shines her light gently on Mary, who relaxes easily at my side while we review lessons.

Mary has always been my guardian angel and always will be.

Mary is also real.

Welcome to my reality.

• • •

Tears flowed as I left the hospital grounds. I stopped for a moment to silently thank Mary for saving me, knowing with absolute certainty that she was listening. As I watched myself leaving, it never occurred to me that watching oneself from above or outside the body was the least bit unusual. Nor did I question the realization that washed over me:

"Never give up, no matter what. The only direction is forward."

I planted my feet firmly on the ground and, without realizing that this conviction would define the rest of my life, I leaned on my walker and moved forward.

• • •

My recovery period left me redefining myself. Wherever I went and whatever I did, I fit in only with those who did not fit in with any "normal" part of society.

Not only had my dad arranged for me to use the Concord's Olympic pool for therapy, but he'd also arranged for a friend of his to work with me in the mornings before the pool opened to guests. At the entrance to the lavish recreation center, a redheaded woman in crisp white tennis garb introduced herself and welcomed me graciously. My awkward walker and I struggled through the doors while Rebecca assured me that I'd find my trainer to be fabulous. I thanked her as she led me to the Olympic pool and unlocked the doors. Sunlight streamed through the windows that enclosed the room. High above the pool was an observation deck, a glass balcony spanning the width of the room. When I looked up, I was not surprised to see Mary smiling down at me while the darting light that is Tink flitted about.

With Thomas's list of pool exercises in hand, I gripped the rail by the kiddie section and took my first tentative step into the water. I looked up and saw a man leaning casually against the side of the shallow end. I gasped and instinctively tightened my grip on the railing when he looked into my eyes. Water glistened on the rippling, deeply tanned muscles as he strode toward me through the thick testosterone and held out his powerful hand.

"Good morning. I've been looking forward to meeting you."

I must have nodded my head.

"I'm Buster Crabbe. I've known your dad for years, and when I heard what happened, I offered to help out with your physical therapy. Swimming is the world's best exercise, Hilary. You're going to be strong in no time."

I must have nodded my head.

He took my hand and helped me into the pool.

Concord bar. My dad, *background*, Gerald Ford, *foreground*.

Concord Hotel, Kiamseha Lake, N.Y.

Room where I worked my last night.

I must have followed him. Who wouldn't?

Buster Crabbe, movie idol, was an Olympic gold medalist swimmer and the Concord's swimming pro. He was also Tarzan, King of the Jungle, Buck Rogers, Flash Gordon, drop-dead gorgeous, and my new personal guide.

My daddy loved me.

The gentle resistance of the water became my ally as time flew by and my body healed. Tarzan and I developed both an unspoken bond and a grueling daily workout routine that left me exhausted, aching, and always ready for more. Muscles replaced atrophied limbs as I swam and moved more easily with each passing day.

He never faltered, and the sparkle in his eyes became as contagious as his confidence. When frustration ran high, Mary faded in and out beside him, calming me with her presence. She came to me as I slept.

The puzzle that was my body learned to bend and flex and run and twist and stand, to make letters and write, to engage in all the complexities of functioning that we take for granted. I progressed to a cane after less than a month and was rapidly building muscles and confidence. My gait was awkward, but even if I'd realized it, I wouldn't have cared. I approached rehab with intense single-mindedness.

The inconvenient encounter with death had changed my plan to travel with my friends, but what was left of my mind knew I would still travel. It also knew that with Mary and Tink on board, I would never, ever be alone.

My People

I got a job as soon as I could and began to save the money I needed to move forward with my life. The small-town gossips held an emergency meeting after my vigil at the hospital. They determined that I was not only a drug addict but delusional and obsessed with an imaginary friend. In their worlds, Mary was not real, and I was damaged. The truth was that I was a lost little girl with a fierce determination to survive, a jigsaw puzzle of a person with pieces scattered throughout space, time, and levels of reality. From that time forward, life would reveal itself in front of me, and I would simply step into my future. Decisions would be made without fear or hesitation by an unconscious multidimensional consensus, and I would survive.

Part of survival meant understanding the person who came out of the coma. This person has multiple vantage points from which to view the world. One is the view from inside the body looking out, which I guess most people have. There's also the view from above through Mary's eyes.

Mary lives at the height of pine trees in an Idaho forest. I can always summon her closer when I want to. She not only watches me, but she also watches Tink watch me watch the world. Tink is perpetually visible in the periphery of my vision. A tiny gnome-fairy-leprechaun dressed in colorful, sparkly clothing and pointy gnome shoes, I've always found her completely adorable. In her mischievous, impish way, she dashes hither and yon just above my head to the right. I used to assume that everyone had a playful little gnome-like friend running around the periphery of their awareness. I'm told that's not the case.

My arrangement with the universe, I've learned, creates a unique, dream-like brand of consciousness. I liken my awareness to kayaking on a misty lake early in the morning. With the world shrouded in mystery, I trust that it's safe to blindly paddle through the haze, knowing that unstoppable forces guide my path. I trust completely in powers greater than myself — powers that I have never, ever questioned. I'm guessing it hasn't always been this way. I'm guessing this is a perk I brought back from the Other Side.

• • •

I cringe at the sight of anyone's blood but my own, but when I see someone whose soul is aching, I feel completely capable involving myself. Had I not died, I would certainly be different. I came back with Mary's essence guiding me from within. I don't "see" her or "hear" her; she is inside of me in all her stunning glory. I feel her ebb and flow, step forward and hold back, always with gentle grace and perfection. Intrinsic in my world, Mary, Tink, and a lifetime of being labeled taught me to honor uniqueness.

The remote rural county in Idaho where I lived and worked covers about 4,000 square miles, much of it wilderness. The population averages two people per square mile. Such an environment affords its inhabitants the freedom to do as they please and behave in ways that could be labeled odd, even unacceptable, in places where people are closer together.

My Michael, the artist, knew that in the West Central Mountains he could find the solitude and peace he needed for his creativity to flourish. Tender, talented people with too much innate sensitivity to survive elsewhere find solace and like souls in the splendor of untamed wilderness.

The area was home to an intensely unique blend of inhabitants, including perhaps more than our fair share of people with chronic, severe mental illnesses. Fragile souls seem to intuitively know that in places where acceptance is the rule and being different the norm, they are apt to survive. There may be two people per square mile, but those two people, I guarantee, are interesting.

From the nearest city, an 80-mile drive on a treacherous, windy road takes you to a world of tiny mountain towns where winters are harsh and people maintain a fiercely independent mindset to make it their home. Such a rugged, rural area tends to draw people who may not fit in elsewhere, for in a vast wilderness, there is little with which one needs to conform. People who are different are the norm.

• • •

The State Mental Health Clinic where I worked was housed in the Health and Welfare building a block from Payette Lake. Child Protective Services, Medicaid, and other public programs worked side by side to meet the basic needs of a diverse population scattered throughout a region roughly the size of Connecticut.

We were not there to provide marital, family, substance abuse, or other forms of counseling that could be addressed by traditional community counselors. The outpatient mental health clinic was an overcrowded landing strip for men and women completely unable to navigate this world.

The vast majority of our patients were labeled as "indigent, severely, chronically mentally ill." Most would have been relegated to institutional settings without the support and treatment provided through our rural outpost. Only with consistent advocacy, medication monitoring, and life assistance could they maintain independence and a reasonable quality of life. We took the time to coordinate resources, find subsidized housing, and involve ourselves in every aspect of patients' lives in an effort to keep them in the community.

These are folks who might need a hand to survive, people who have spent years in psychiatric hospitals or shelter homes and are eager to do whatever they can to maintain the most basic kind of freedom.

For over twenty years, I worked with Dr. Johnny, a psychiatrist transplanted from Texas, a brilliant, gentle man with the demeanor of a cocky bull rider and the soul of a newborn lamb. Rather than opting for a comfortable practice treating white-collar professionals with depression or anxiety, he had chosen early on to work in the trenches and has devoted his life to the sickest of the sick, the craziest of the crazies, the hopeless, homeless wackos of the world. Dr. Johnny drove the 200 miles roundtrip from the city on a regular basis to see patients, listen to them, and offer a superb level of care and medication management.

After spending thirty years in the trenches, he possessed an unequaled base of knowledge, a finely honed level of skill, and a sincere love of working with patients. When Johnny was with a patient, that person had his undivided attention. Never rushed and eternally behind schedule, he came to know his patients from the outside in. He took great care to prescribe combinations of medicines custom-suited to the wiring of each patient's brain.

He taught me subtleties of behavior and barely perceptible cues to side effects along with the impact of each and every drug we used. He taught me what was required to keep patients from suffering manifestations of their illnesses by careful, consistent monitoring. I learned to recognize that a tremble, facial expression, or voice tone might warrant a medication review. Johnny showed me nearly invisible nuances that indicated when someone was losing ground. Their suffering broke my heart and brought me to my knees, and most knew instantly that I was trustworthy. Without that, I wouldn't have lasted five minutes. We wanted to keep them out of the hospital and, given the severity of illness in our population, did a damn good job of it.

It didn't take long to establish myself as a known and respected professional. When Mary plucked me out of Palm Springs and transported me to Idaho, she was giving me the opportunity to utilize experience and skills I'd spent my life collecting. She gave notice that I was a woman of my word who would teach by example and open minds to new ways of viewing the world and its inhabitants. I came to know patients' families, friends, and neighbors. They nicknamed me "the Vault" because people knew that their secrets were safe with me. They knew that I listened without judging and had no goal beyond easing suffering and pain.

• • •

When we look inside of ourselves, most of us know what it's like to feel nervous and depressed. We've had unreasonable fears or embarrassing quirks, but few of us let on when we suffer this way. Many of us avoid dealing with psychiatric patients because we don't want to look at behaviors in others that we secretly see in ourselves — vulnerability, weakness, confusion, fear. Experiences with psychiatric patients bother us; they force us to look at gateways that might suck us into a vortex whirling toward a frightening loss of control from which there may be no return. To be mentally unable to advocate for yourself while suffering severe mental pain is no different from lying on the ground alone in the middle of nowhere with a bone protruding from your leg. It's just that spiritual-mental-emotional-psychiatric suffering happens to be invisible to the untrained or naked eye.

In our culture, the mentally ill are demonized and shunned, ostracized and marginalized because of our own innate fear of going bonkers. Despite the multitude of examples of "crazy geniuses," we ridiculously tend to assume that nuts are not as bright as normal folks. Most of us keep our distance as if mental illness is contagious, perhaps transmitted through dark, mysterious ways known only to the afflicted: "Stay away. You'll catch 'crazy.'"

Psychiatric illness has a stigma like no other. As we rush to help someone in a wheelchair stuck in a doorway, we turn our heads and become silently terrified of the twenty-two-year-old college student at Starbucks insisting that tiny devils are coming out of that straw the barista just put in her latte.

Oh, we've come a long way. We need only look at ads on television to see that medications will cure our depression. Side effects are spoken in tones so expertly modulated they make the risk of heart attack, stroke, kidney and liver damage, and death sound delightful compared to being depressed.

We do well until we remember old Aunt Joan who lived in the little house out back and talked to plants but not people. Or until we hear about the night that the neighbor, a fifty-three-year-old respected construction foreman, loaded his Dodge pickup with thousands of dollars' worth of tools, locked $185,000 cash savings in the glove box, and slipped quietly out of town so the FBI couldn't get him. He drove seventeen hours to hide his treasures in a locked room in his son's garage, then turned around and went home, where his odd behavior escalated. This upstanding member of the community with a lovely home and model family certainly doesn't sound like a mental patient. It wasn't until he'd been peeking out windows through closed blinds with doors locked for several days that his wife realized he was "off his rocker."

What would it be like to realize that the world's water supply was drying up and you must fill every container you can find? How would you feel when the weight of all that water caused the floor to give out, and you landed in the drenched living room of the apartment below? Can you imagine voices screaming profane insults and commands in your ear? Evil, threatening gnomes running around your neighborhood, taunting you until you have no choice but to let loose with your shotgun? What might it be like to find yourself in the county jail because you ran through town wearing nothing but a Batman cape and combat boots?

We all have reasons for doing the things we do.

We all have our own realities.

It is my blessing to have more than one.

• • •

I have always been drawn to the fringes of society, to people who are shunned, tossed away, discounted, ignored. I find kinship with the lonely souls inhabiting the suburbs of mainstream society: hippies, gypsies, wanderers, rebels, desert rats, farmworkers, mountain folk, addicts — those whose brains cause them to be labeled as mentally ill, schizophrenic, loony.

Societies categorize living entities, organize us in a way that is conducive to placing each of us tidily into a suitable box. For most, it is easier to be part of the Box World. In Box World, people know where they stand, what is expected of them. You do X and you will receive Y and live in the land of Z. That is, as long as you follow the rules of that particular box. There are many boxes, each with its own set of rules and rewards.

Americans have the American Dream box that goes something like this: birth, childhood, school, job, marriage, kids, debt, house, car, work, retire, die. Each society has its own sequential version of life events and a script/path to walk in order to achieve that culture's version of success. Though ours is silly, I have no doubt that there are lots of other ridiculous versions of the "good life" around the globe.

Outcasts come in all shapes, sizes, and varieties, from all walks of life. In the world of box-less outcasts, labels are useless, judgmental, annoying, and frequently hurtful. Hippies defied boxes — those of us who were smitten with leather, fringe, sex, love, and rock 'n' roll. We did precisely what we wanted to do when we wanted to do it. We created realities and defined a generation. Some of us sailed through those days riding magic carpets across the sky. Some traded tie-dye for BMWs and prestigious careers. Others passed through hippie-ness and chose a box. Some of us walked the hippie path a few steps too far and paid with our health or sanity, some with our lives.

There are those of us who meditate or spend time on soul journeys, transporting ourselves to other realms. Outcasts, we reality explorers move through the universe to spend time where souls are at ease and lessons are learned. There are places where outcasts congregate, out-of-the-way places where out-of-the-box people go to live in peace. The deserts, stark and barren to some, exquisitely captivating to others, are where desert rats congregate, people who happen upon vast expanses of sand and cactus and stay still long enough to learn a lesson or two from the tumbleweeds.

Prisons are filled with outcasts — men, women, delinquents, unable to live by acceptable rules of society, who commit crimes that cause them to be locked away. Certainly some people do cause harm to others and need to be isolated. Perhaps, though, many others are outcasts who, because they are unable to find a safe haven where they can fit in, are locked away in very tangible boxes, the kind we can see and touch.

Many boxless ones want little more than the sounds and sensations of nature. I understand the hermits living with their trusty dogs in old log cabins high in the hills and tented ones in isolated jungles far from the distractions of society. I have lived lives as a hermit, a monk, a cave dweller — but not this one. This time, I function in a time and space where I embrace humankind in a unique manner.

Through the years, I learned that people with mental illness are special souls who inhabit a fringe of boxlessness of their very own. These special souls are often shunned, feared, mocked, medicated, confined, and hidden away because society's responses to their differences tend to be based in fear and ignorance.

Schizophrenics are often intellectually very bright people — witty, well read, educated — from every socioeconomic part of society.

Clinical depression skews reality until negativity and emptiness are all that's left.

The roller coaster of bipolar illness has Mary Poppins flying with her umbrella to magical places before she crashes into the Grand Canyon, bruised and broken.

A psychiatric patient in the midst of a delusion is certain that her perceptions are true, and anyone who disagrees is sorely mistaken.

Drunks tend to be steadfastly adamant about their versions of reality. Not only do they know they're right, but they repeat it over and over, embellish it, and bore us to tears until they pass out.

Every drug takes us to a different place. Hallucinogens, prescriptions, cocaine, meth, heroin — it isn't the drug that matters. What matters is that the takers of the substance believe wholeheartedly in the space and time to which they are transported.

We have a tendency to believe ourselves. Altered states of consciousness begin with a whirling dervish of a child turning herself in circles until she gets so dizzy she falls on the lawn, lying still until the world stops moving. Are we hard-wired to expand our minds?

Timothy Leary's acid brain.

Summer. Town beautification project with patients!

Across from my office, 2004.

The teachings of Don Juan.

Meditation.

Religious ecstasy.

Reality is always in the eyes of the perceiver.

Labels are useless, judgmental, and annoying to the boxless of the world. We exert tremendous time, effort, and expense to isolate outcasts. Might they cause us to question the validity of the "norm"? Might they laugh in the face of boxes and thereby rebel against all that is "comfortable"?

Yes, indeed.

Those of us who are different are clearly labeled in our society. We either fit in or we are outcasts. Being labeled all my life for one reason or another taught me that being an outcast isn't necessarily a bad thing, though for some it can be lonely. At work I strove to do more than keep crazy folks out of institutions. Most of us strange ones tend to isolate ourselves as a defense against being shunned or ridiculed. When outcasts have a chance to meet under the right circumstances, however, friendships can be forged.

• • •

At work we made an effort to educate the "regular" folks. We showed the wary and frightened that schizophrenics are not freaks to be feared and locked away but human beings with a treatable illness. In order to accomplish this goal, we created opportunities for positive interactions in the community through our presence at local parks, coffee shops, and other places where we had formerly been shunned. Most of our people had little or no social life and little reason to feel joy. We began having small gatherings, bringing patients out of hiding with a glimmer of hope. I labeled the gatherings as "therapy groups" to make them sound official, but what I was really doing was handing out smiles. Soon we were a familiar sight around town, going to parks, having picnics, fishing, doing all kinds of "normal" things. A core band of enthusiastic oddballs eager for better lives banded together. Our outings and adventures were, for many, the high points of otherwise mundane lives. There's not a lot of fun in existing day after day with the singular goal of making it through without a psychotic crisis.

When outcasts are with a group of other outcasts, we are no longer outcasts. We transition into members of a group, and that, for many, brings newfound self-worth, identity, and joy. We can laugh at ourselves, talk about our alternative universes, voices, or new medicines with complete transparency, knowing that we are a family of special souls.

I remember one very special Thanksgiving when, against every rule in existence, I welcomed a troupe of patients into my home for a full-blown family style Turkey Day. With a simple invitation into my world, a bunch of crazy folks suddenly managed to organize themselves into a grateful, cooperative family. A group of outcasts gathered together to give unconditional thanks for the lessons we had chosen this time around.

On my wall is a photograph taken at a picnic area on Payette Lake. I am surrounded by a group of patients, and I'm holding a cake with the words "thank you" written in chocolate frosting. Everyone is smiling (except Teddy, who had managed, with the support of the group, to show up despite his agoraphobia), and a light of joy is shining as brightly as the summer sun. The photo is mounted on a weathered poster that a patient gave me, one that proudly proclaims that "People With Mental Illness Enrich Our Lives." The rest of the poster is filled with names of famous people who made significant contributions to society despite/because of their uniqueness. People like Winston Churchill, Beethoven, Ernest Hemingway, Michelangelo, Virginia Woolf, and Isaac Newton.

We are all valuable.

Including outcasts.

• • •

I leaned back casually in my office chair, feet on the desk and coffee in hand. I worked at a substance abuse facility, and I was talking with Clayton, the director of the county's mental health clinic. He was a tall, brawny teddy bear of a man with a neatly trimmed beard and mustache and a sparkle in his eyes. We were both dressed quasi-professionally, which in McCall meant any attire other than jeans and a sweatshirt. We frequently collaborated on patients with dual diagnosis, that winning combo of mental illness and substance abuse. Clayton was offering me his job. He was done with the fishbowl existence of being a single professional in a tiny, remote town.

My work life had always been something of an expedition. I'd been a garbage woman, hanging off the back of the truck, hopping off to empty trash cans, running to keep up with the musical pace of trash, and banging lids to the beat of a different drummer. I'd waited tables in the ballrooms of renowned resorts and the wannabe fancy Donnelly Club, with its kitchen two flights of stairs down from the dining room. An ancient dumbwaiter that used to serve as a food elevator now sat idle and bored, fixable but for the apathy of the owners. I had countless fleeting careers learning not so fleeting lessons: substitute teacher, convenience store clerk, landscaper in Palm Springs, social worker, bartender, security guard on a marine base, intake counselor for arrested juveniles, paralegal in a legal aid office. I spent a time devoted to driving my yellow VW pop-top van along the California coast with a portable, never-boring-for-a-minute smoked salmon stand. I spent years as a member of the elite 1970s band of California moccasin makers who crafted custom-fitted works of art made popular through customers like Jerry Garcia and Grace Slick. I could go on, but I won't.

Ever the chameleon, I fit in wherever I went. All I had to do was think a reality, and Tink would set about making it work. Delighted with theatrics, Tink adored finding just the right outfit, accessories and mindset for every occasion, every persona.

Oops — took a detour. But I'm back now.

As Clayton was offering me his job, I was telling him a bit of my personal history, explaining that after drinking over a fifth of Jack Daniels a day for years, I had quit drinking on the pink-sunrise desert morning when I found out I was pregnant. "No," I told him, "I didn't go to rehab or AA." My methods were far too simple and infinitely too complex to explain, so I chose not to try. Discussions involving my guardian angel and spiritual guide are intensely personal. Mary, Tink, and I live quietly in a private world.

Sobriety gave me the best high of my life, I explained, so I went back to school for a bit and decided to help other people get straight — people unaware, who thought that they didn't have a Tink or a Mary and had gotten lost stumbling about in search of their own brand of magic.

Clay and I recognized that this geographical area was definitely a perfect haven for anyone unable or unwilling to fit in elsewhere. We laughed at the irony of our own choices knowing full well why we were where we were.

He felt too isolated and had to move on, he explained sadly. He was being summoned to meet both professional and personal challenges. He had a chance to implement an innovative mental health program on a larger scale and hoped to slow the prevailing revolving-door treatment that had become the State's way of dealing with an overload of patients. He was also in love and wanted to get married.

Clayton had enjoyed two years in this special place. Two years was the usual clinician limit, and it was his time to go back to the other world. He was to create a lasting professional legacy. He was to marry his sweetheart, and they were to buy their house in the suburbs. He was also to suffer a massive heart attack and die less than two years later.

Before he left, Clay taught me everything he could about the job I eagerly accepted, including tips about:

- men and women who live in other galaxies
- fugitives protected by aluminum foil headwear
- recluses, mountain dwellers, royalty, and gun-toting alien fighters
- nature lovers, cattle that bore women's faces, and monster hunters
- hiders, warlocks, weirdoes, and dragon slayers

"Yes," I proclaimed, "sign me up!"

They did. And absolutely nothing could have prepared me for the work I would do over the next twenty years.

Joey

"Your first real, live schizophrenic, Hilary. Name is Joseph Martin. Eighteen years old, multiple hospitalizations. Nice kid. Auditory and visual hallucinations as well as a history of elaborate delusional systems. Take a few minutes to look at his chart while I go have a smoke and get him. Oh — one other thing: Never, ever, seat a patient between you and the door. Remember that." Clayton looked at me over his glasses, eyes serious, face smiling.

A longhaired boy with sandy blond hair came back with Clayton. Joe was 5'9", lean and lithe. He was disheveled in what could have been sixties hippie style — hair falling softly around his face and shoulders in soft curls, torn faded jeans, tennis shoes, and a denim jacket. His hair wasn't combed, but he and his clothing looked clean.

Clayton introduced us and explained that he was moving away and I would be taking over the clinic. The same psychiatrist would be making the biweekly journey to see patients in McCall. Joseph's eyes were captivating; a glance grasped my essence just long enough for us to connect on a level that transcended my job and his illness.

"How has your week been, Joseph?" Clay began after the formalities.

"Okay."

"Are you taking your medicine?"

"Uh-huh."

"Every day?"

"Uh-uh."

"Is that a no? Not every day?"

Joe shook his head as if to wake himself up. His hair covered one eye, the other one focused now on me.

"I take it when my mom reminds me or I remember to. I'm taking a judo class."

"We need you to take your meds every day so they can help you, Joseph," Clay reminded him for the umpteenth million time.

"Uh-huh. I have this really cool book. It's really cool. Daniel and I are both reading it. It has recipes on how to make stuff. It's cool. You can look at it some time if you want to."

"What kind of recipes?" The first words I spoke to Joey. There were to be millions more.

"Oh, pipe bombs and stuff — to blow things up." Clayton gave me a knowing glance, one that said, "You will never, ever be bored here."

"Joe, tell Hilary a little about yourself, okay?"

"Yeah, I used to live with Dan, but now I'm living with my mom. I like my real dad. I used to live with him, but he doesn't let me anymore. They make me come here but I'm gonna build a cabin way up on top of Banner Mountain. Then I can do just what I want. Like, then I can do my judo too. I'm into martial arts a lot but when I practice, Curt says I make too much noise. He yells at me, and then I go to my grandma's 'cause he just keeps yelling at me. I lived with my real dad before but he doesn't let me."

"Joe, Hilary is going to be taking over for me starting next week when Dr. Ekman is here. She'll walk out with you and schedule an appointment. They'll review your meds, and you can all get to know each other. Sound good?"

"Uh-huh."

Clayton stood up and seemed to tower over the fragile boy. He shook Joseph's hand, held it for a moment, and wished him all the best.

• • •

Martha knocked lightly on my office door and poked her head in. "Hilary, Deb just called me from the school and said she's seen Joey's truck driving back and forth in front of the Mission Apartments for the past couple of hours. She just wanted me to tell you because she thought it was kind of strange."

I looked at her with a grin. "It is, don't you think?"

Martha was in her midsixties and had been the real boss of the Health and Welfare Office for thirty years. She had five or six grown kids, a herd of grandkids, and a totally charming, gruff façade. No one messed with Martha. She flashed a smile and rolled her eyes. "Could be, couldn't it?"

I laughed as I closed the file I'd been charting and grabbed my car keys. "Well, golly gee, I feel like going for a little drive. Be back in a few, and thanks."

I pulled out of the lot and took a back road to Mission Street, avoiding the school kids out for lunch hour. All twelve grades were in the same building with separate areas. The little ones at recess were whooping and climbing. The snow was mostly gone now, and spring was being greeted with open arms. I stopped at Mission Road and looked up and down the street. Tink chuckled as she darted through the air above my head. She had become my smile, my link to the glittering dance of time.

Joe had taken up residence in a soft, mushy part of my heart. *No truck.* Turning left, I headed toward the dated apartment complex and drove slowly through the school zone. A row of trees hid the building from the road, so I pulled into the driveway and stopped in the small parking lot. I turned off the engine and stepped out in the sunshine. When I heard a truck tailgate close, I followed the sound toward the back of the building, kicking crunchy snow and sticks to make myself heard. Several mountains of snow were piled behind the complex by town plows. Joey's pickup emerged slowly from behind one of the piles, and when our eyes met, he hopped out of the truck to greet me. He did so without surprise, speaking as though continuing a conversation we had left off five minutes ago.

"So, it's all here, Hilary. I'm just getting the fuses arranged."

"Good, Joe. Want me to check anything else for you?" My favorite man-child opened the door to his reality and invited me to cross the threshold. I seamlessly traversed. Such crossings had become an integral part of my life and daily work. Operating from multiple realities gave me enough perspective to maintain both safety and respect in our tiny corner of the world. Plus, it was never boring. Joey was soaking wet, hands and face smudged, clothes covered with dirt. He moved quietly, furtively, purposefully. He came toward me and stood still by my side, shaking his head. When we looked at one another, our eyes connected in his world.

Wild.

"How can I help?" There was no way of knowing what the purpose was, but clearly there was one.

"Okay, Hilary. Wow, I can sure use some help."

"Just tell me what I can do, Joe."

He brushed his hair from his eyes, took a deep breath, and I felt his energy relax. "Here's the deal. They're gonna come up about five feet to the left of that highest mound of snow by the building." He led me farther from the road as he talked. I nodded and followed. "So over there is where we need to finish setting up. We still have some time but not much. We have to finish burying the dynamite next. I've got a good start on it."

Dynamite? Bury? Okay. I spoke slowly, deliberately. "Joey, you know how slow I am. Let's go over the whole plan from the beginning again. I just want to make sure I understand it all. So we're sure they're coming up here?" *They? Up?*

"Okay. Sure. So the ninja sewer rat king in New York telepathically confirmed that the tunnel is getting close. That it's time."

"Tunnel from New York."

"Right." He nodded vigorously, glad that I got it. "Yeah. That band of ninja rats that have been digging? Well, he told me that the tunnel is going to end up right over there. When it does, the ninjas are going to come up armed, take over McCall, and move on from here. It's my job to stop them. I *have* to stop them."

"Got it. Do we have enough dynamite?"

Joey led me to his truck and lifted the tarp in the back. The bed of the little Ford was filled with neatly tied bunches of explosives. He put the tarp back down and looked around. "Man, I've been digging a long time. This is a big job. Got to dig around the whole back here." His shovel rested in the hard dirt, still partly frozen. We looked down at the trench he was currently working on: forty feet long and about a foot deep. He was doing precisely as he was being instructed. I was at his side, resting easily on his shoulder, an honorary member of Joseph's "blow up the tunneling evil ninja tunnels" club. *Big job, huge responsibility, saving the world* — especially with the school across the street and the apartment house occupied.

I looked through his eyes. The ninjas were two feet long, green, and I thought they resembled iguanas more than rats. When they stood erect, I saw that they had muscular arms with webbed hands that allowed them to dig very efficiently. Thin legs, long tails, reptilian faces with piercing, dark eyes. Two of them menacingly slithered toward me, oozing evil. I stood my ground and met their gazes as they silently challenged me. One of them stood up in front of me and hissed. I looked away in disgust, refusing to engage.

"Gigantic job. Geez, Joey. As cold as this ground is, do you think we could use some more muscle?" His eyes were glazed. He probably hadn't slept for a few days and clearly hadn't taken his meds.

"Well … yeah. I'm pretty tired. Was digging between communications all through last night. If I could thaw out the ground, I'd be finished, but man, the cold sure is slowing things down. I don't know who we can trust."

"Do you have any ideas at all?" I asked. In his world, he gets to be in charge. Silence as he searched his mind. I watched the blue eyes travel a steep, narrow trail around his head and get lost in the forest.

"Noooo, I can't think who to trust. Can you help me out here, Hilary?"

"I'll sure try — let's see … hey, Joseph — how about Tom Branton?" Tom Branton was the chief of police, a kind, fair-minded, robust man in his early fifties.

"Tom! We can trust Tom. Where is he?"

"Don't know, but I'm sure I can find him if you want me to."

"Yeah."

"There's no one around. Want to come with me for a few minutes?"

He hesitated. "You think it's safe? Wasn't easy for me to get all that dynamite, you know."

"It'll be okay. Let's just go to my car and try to call him."

Get him away from the fuses, I thought as we walked toward the car and cell phone, but he immediately became agitated. We didn't want that.

"Think you can watch your stuff better if you stand at the other end of the lot? If Tom needs more information, I'll tell you."

"Yeah, my stuff is super important. " He calmed as he positioned himself more strategically.

"McCall Police Department."

"Hi, Shelly. This is Hilary. I need Tom, please, and it's important."

"Hang on. I'll find him." It didn't take long. It was well known that I did *not* abuse the word "important."

"Chief Branton."

"Hi, Tom. It's Hilary. I'm at the Mission Apartments with Joseph Martin. Can you please come help me out? We might be needing an involuntary admission to Saint Al's psych."

"Of course. Can you tell me what's going on?"

"He's off his meds and has a truckload of dynamite." I could hear his eyes roll back in his head. My people.

"Three minutes."

I was back at Joey's side when Tom pulled up and got out of his car. A second police cruiser was cresting the hill, and I heard the unmistakable horn of a fire truck leaving the station. In another reality, dynamite could explode. As Tom sauntered toward us, he reached out to shake Joey's hand. When I stepped aside, Joe hesitated, then leapt into a Judo stance with his arms raised as I gently left his world.

"Joey, the sewer rats are not real. You haven't been taking your medicine, and you're sick right now. There is no tunnel from New York, and we aren't going to be blowing anything up. It's not real."

Tom gently turned Joey around and handcuffed him as two other officers got out of their vehicle. Joe's eyes remained fixed on mine.

"Am I going to the hospital?"

"You are, Joey. The sewer rats are not real, and you need to get back on your medication. Dr. Ekman will be there to meet you."

Now Joe began to straddle realities. Part of him began to remember that he was sick. He wanted to hug me. He wanted to kill me. He looked at me in silence as he was directed to the back seat of the police car. Given the level of imminent danger to others and mass quantities of illegal explosives, there would be no flight risk allowed. They would drive him the two hours to Boise. I'd walked into his world and left without him. Tears overflowed from my heart and welled in my eyes as I returned to the world of the "system" to make the calls, do the paperwork, and let his family know that he was safe.

• • •

Joey's family had lived in Valley County for generations and were model citizens. His mother, Annie, worked at the Smokejumpers Base on a highly trained team that dispatched firefighters, planes, and supplies. Annie was a contradiction; tough as nails and highly regarded in her job, she was otherwise quiet and mild mannered. She spoke only when she had something to contribute (a quality that I admire, by the way; I strive to be succinct).

The family lived in separate mobile homes on ten secluded acres along the river. Annie lived with her second husband, Curt, who had no tolerance for Joey's constant problems or disruptive behaviors. Joey's older sister Julia had joined the Navy and left as soon as she could. She was married and came and went with her husband and two young children. Grandma Emma, in her eighties, was a wisp of a woman, maybe 5'3", all fire and spunk. She was Joseph's rock. Her depth of awareness let her love Joe unconditionally. Her soul "got it." She got Joseph. She got me.

He had lucid times. Joseph knew that I loved him. He knew that he was far more than a patient. His soul knew when his brain could not. We communicated on a level that transcended my job and his illness.

• • •

I had a phone line in my house for work. It was easier that way. I could screen calls, and I knew when to respond. I chose to be available after hours in ways that I certainly could have avoided, a choice that put me on call 24/7. But if I could minimize crises and suffering with a five-minute phone conversation or a quick home visit, why would I *not* do that?

Emma left a whisper of a message one night: "Hilary, I don't want to bother you, but Joey is in my bathtub, and, you see, he … well, he says there are demons coming out of his …. penis. He was screaming in there, Hilary. I've managed to get him out and wrap him up in bath towels, but he's shaking and terrified. I don't think he's taken his medicine, Hilary. He's so scared."

I was carrying an armload of firewood in when I briefly heard her voice followed by a soft click as she hung up. I stoked the fire, tossed the rest of the armload in the wood box, and called her back.

"I don't know what to do," she said. "He's shaking, scared, and afraid his stepdad will call the police."

"I'll be there in half an hour."

They sat side by side on the battered couch, little Grandma's arms around big boy Joseph, who cuddled into her warmth and love, quivering. I sat next to Grandma Emma. No one spoke for several minutes. Then Joey turned and looked at my heart. His gaze told me everything I needed to know. With his eyes, I saw them clearly, crowding the room. Humanoid reptiles filled with hatred, blood, and pus, drool covering their faces while their eyes mocked and taunted. They reclined on the chairs, hovered in the air, three of them directly above Joey — upside down, sneering at him, smirking. From inside Joey's gentle blue eyes, I saw terror and suffering, and I ached.

"Demons," he whispered. "They've come out of me, and they're everywhere now."

What was this boy here to teach, to learn? What could this level of awareness, this degree of suffering possibly accomplish? How could it be okay? I didn't know. All I could do was be there and ease his suffering by helping him banish demons and monsters. I touched him gently on his shoulder, helped him to his feet, and hugged him. He dressed in the clean clothes Emma brought him.

"Hey, Joey, I thought we agreed you'd take your meds. Remember, you said the Clozaril was a demon killer?" He was coming back from that day's version of hell when footsteps approached the trailer. Annie came in and looked at her son, then at me.

"Curt wants him gone."

"He'll be okay now, Annie. He missed some meds. We can stabilize him and monitor him closely. That's what they'd do if we admitted him to the hospital. How about if I call the doc and talk to him?"

Her eyes let forth the deafening shriek of a mother's anguish.

• • •

Given his circumstances, lack of medication compliance, the severity of his illness, and his propensity to add beer and street drugs to the mix, stability was not Joey's strong suit. He did have an enduring friendship with another of our patients, a local he'd known since childhood: Daniel, who also had a schizophrenic illness. Unlike the majority of our patients, Dan was not intellectually bright. This difference rendered him less functional, and he kept to himself for the most part, isolated with his accusatory voices. He and Joey were roommates off and on as their paths crisscrossed in strange and unusual ways. Joe and Dan liked to drink beer together. Lots of beer. Enough beer that I recall a time when I literally shoveled empty beer cans into 30-gallon black trash bags in an effort to see the floor. The friendship was one made in heaven; companionship sometimes eased the drive through hell. The two did their best to help each other, but the definition of "help" was an ever-changing work in progress.

When Daniel phoned me one day, there was uncharacteristic panic in his voice. "Hilary, Joey's scary. He's been in the garage for days. Won't let anyone near him. He's been screaming out there."

Dan perceiving Joe as scary instantly had my full attention. When I turned onto their street, I prepared to look for Joe in the place where consciousness shifts. They were living in Cascade, a small mill town 25 miles south of McCall. Many of the streets were dirt. The houses were cookie-cutter basics built for workers by Boise Cascade. Joe had moved in with Dan and Dan's brother, Jeff, who had inherited the home when their mother died. It was unkempt; the inside had "the smell" — the stench I associated with sick people unaware of their surroundings, the smell of tobacco, dirty laundry, rotting food, and people who are unable to care for themselves on the most basic level.

The detached garage doors were closed. Dan, who had been pretty stable, was standing in the driveway when I pulled in. His arms went up in a helpless gesture, and there were tears in his eyes. "I can't get near him. I don't want him to die in there, and I'm never gonna call the cops."

Putting an arm around his shoulder, I assured him that calling me had been the perfect thing to do. Approaching the garage doors, I heard nothing. I tapped lightly on the door.

"Hey, Joe? You in there? It's Hilary."

No answer.

"Joey, come on, let me in. I drove down here to see you, man. Danny's worried about you. Come on. Please? Open the door."

Nothing.

"Joe, you know me. Hilary."

I waited several minutes, giving my words time to travel. Then, "You gonna make me stand out here in the cold, Joey? How about it?"

A few minutes more, then a lock clicked. He opened the door just a crack and peeked out. I caught a glazed blue eye making an unsuccessful attempt to focus. At Joey's, there was nobody home, and the lights were dim.

"Let me come in, buddy. Open the door."

He threw the door open and moved quickly, cat-like, to the other side of the big garage. He sat on the floor, leaned against a commercial sanding machine, and resumed watching a movie on the invisible screen on the ceiling. Small paper bags were in a pile next to the bottle of whiskey beside him. I moved slowly across the room and sat on the floor five feet from him, mirroring his body position, hugging my knees and curling into myself.

"Thanks for letting me in."

He rocked silently.

"Joey. Yo."

Ever so slowly, his head turned toward me. The long hair covered most of his face. His clothing was torn, the jean jacket covered with dirt and paint. It took what seemed like several decades for his eyes to find mine. When they did, our souls met for a fleeting instant. I tried with all my might to stay with him in that moment, reached and shifted and called out every tool and helper I had. This time even Mary's energy couldn't do it. I watched Joe's consciousness move, saw it flying around the garage, lost and frightened, angry, frustrated, haunted.

"What do you want?"

"To say hi and see how things are going."

The vacant eyes met mine in a faraway place.

"I'm making a bomb."

He was serious. Books were scattered about, instruction manuals he and Dan had collected.

"You're certainly smart enough to make whatever you want, Joe. How long you been working on this?"

"Awhile." He'd been in the garage for two days. "I have to finish this before they come take the house. They're gonna throw us out, and I can't go live with my dad. I'm gonna protect my friend so we can live here."

"You're a true-blue guy, Joey."

Time passes slowly, ever so slowly, when words must traverse worlds. *Shift. Tiny quake.*

"Hilary."

"Yup. That's me."

"Oh. I've been drinking. Huffing some paint and glue too. But I took my meds a few days. You remember, I took them when I used to take them and lived with my dad."

"Good job taking meds."

"Hilary?"

"Right, Joseph."

"What do you want?"

"How about you let me help you clean up a little bit?"

He was moving in and out and up and away, his mind and body separating, reuniting, his brain a scramble of firing neurons, wires, glue, and alcohol searching for a place to meet. "I don't want to. And I can't leave till I'm finished."

I nodded in agreement as our eyes tried, for a moment, to find one another. "Okay. How about we look at what you've done so far?"

He picked up the whiskey bottle and took a long draw. Suddenly, he stood up. He was unsteady on his feet. His consciousness had gone to a place I couldn't follow. Joe turned toward me and spoke calmly, resolutely.

"I've gotta finish this bomb, and you're not going to stop me. I *said* I'm gonna finish this to help my friend, and I am. You're in my way, and I'm gonna have to fucking kill you."

I believed him. He'd moved far, far away to the paranoid section of the garage where he had a parking spot reserved. He took a judo stance, glaring in my direction. I stood slowly. The good news was that I'd heeded Clayton's first and strongest rule: Never, ever let a patient between you and the door. Joe remained where he was, teetering on his feet, then reached over and pulled a small pistol from behind a stack of boards on the workbench.

As he did, I followed my second strongest rule: When all else fails, run away. Reaching my car in record time, I paused just long enough to let Dan hop in the passenger seat. As we drove away, I watched Joey in the rearview mirror while he stumbled outside and got in his truck. He started it up and was backing out to follow us.

"Whoa, this is not good, Dan. I have to do what I have to do, you know."

"Yeah."

I never hesitated to call police when death or destruction were involved. The Cascade Police coordinated with the Sheriff's Department when I told them that Joseph was psychotic, high, armed, and dangerous, that he was in his vehicle, hunting. For me.

"Hilary, keep driving. Just keep driving. We'll call your cell when we find him."

I dropped Dan off at his uncle's house and, with a knot of fear in my heart, headed to a favorite area at the south end of the lake where a washboard dirt road led to an isolated camping spot on the water. I am always safest in the arms of nature. Word came several hours later that Joe had been picked up by a deputy. A petition for involuntary admission to the psychiatric unit was being filed; Joey was unquestionably an imminent danger to both himself and others.

When I drove into my driveway that evening, my husband, Michael, was in front of his studio. His AK-47 was strapped over a shoulder, and he had clearly fallen off his wagon. He'd been drinking again. Though I didn't consciously realize it at the time, I knew that my husband was every bit as unpredictable and potentially dangerous as any of my patients. Random knots of fear and scary behavior had become so familiar to me that I felt little beyond annoyance at having to deal with him being drunk again.

By the time I finally had to let him go, his essence was fading, and the alcohol had all but destroyed his life. I later recognized that I had allowed my parameters of what was acceptable and normal to stretch far beyond any reasonable line of sanity.

The last time I saw Joseph, he was in a psychiatric hospital, extremely medicated, emaciated, and disoriented. When my soul reached out to him, the flicker of recognition was fleeting, a shooting star in the night.

The last time I saw Michael, he was drunk, emaciated, and disoriented as well, fighting an imaginary war with his own demons.

Sophie

In the waiting room of the mental health clinic, Sophie paced slowly, spasms contorting her every movement. When I came out of my office to meet her, she was talking with conviction to both herself and Martha, the office boss/receptionist/manager/matriarch. Martha stood up and brushed past me with a wink. The office staff had told me that Sophie would be "a challenge." A good-natured bunch, they assured me that she didn't like anyone and was volatile, unpredictable, difficult, and crazy. Then they all smiled and wished me luck.

I wandered into the waiting area, said hello, and nodded politely as Sophie looked me up and down with a disdainful, intense gaze. I sat in one of the quasi-comfy, state-issued blue chairs, away from the other waiters. A powerful presence, Sophie was definitely unique. She moved slowly with deliberate effort, her energy angry and guarded. I sat quietly for a few minutes, giving us both time to see how we fit in the same space. When I felt Sophie move toward me, I looked up, introduced myself, and asked her if she wanted to join me. She stood still holding her ground, sizing me up, knowing that I was the new "mental health" person.

"So — you're Hilary." Hostile edge to both her tone and manner.

"And you're Sophie. Glad to meet you."

"My sister told me about you. You're new."

I let her words hang in the air for a time.

"Well, aren't we all at some time or another? We have to be new so we can hang around long enough to be not new, and then we become old before we go somewhere else and be new again." I hesitated. My words were not coming from thoughts; they were just coming. Prepared to dislike me by virtue of the history of her life, Sophie was as surprised as anyone else when she plopped down in the chair next to mine and burst out laughing. Her energy was contagious. When our eyes connected, we laughed even harder, neither of us noticing that we had already bonded. It's funny how two souls sometimes wrap around each other backward, forward, in and out, and right side in and inside out as they recognize lifetimes of familiarity.

Our combined energy immediately left the room and took us to a place where we were walking along a deserted beach together collecting elegant shells, rocks, and life leavings. A precious miniature castle rose between us as we wordlessly shared resources and ideas. Our world was filled with knights on horseback, drawbridges of driftwood, carefully sculpted windows, doors, tiny people made of abalone lounging on starfish, a tower or two with conch shell tops, a bridge to everywhere, and a rocky stairway to the heavens.

Rapunzel showed up in the highest of the towers, her face peeking out through the white-pink curve of a smooth shell, and — wouldn't you know it? — a handsome prince (on cue) cried out, "Rapunzel, Rapunzel, let down your hair," and the damn rubber band got tangled in her golden locks.

"OUCH!" she screeched. "I've done this billions of times. It's supposed to be tied with silk, not this newfangled crap that's pulling my hair out. Hang on, Handsome Prince. Just press pause, and I'll be with you in a minute."

This time, Sophie and I laughed until our bellies ached and tears flowed down our cheeks. We came back slowly as the scene faded. I stood up and leaned my hands on my knees, trying to regain a semblance of composure.

"Wanna go in my office?"

"Yes," she said. "I'd like that."

• • •

In her early fifties, after a Herculean lifetime effort, Sophie had at last worked her way from the back wards of Bellevue Hospital to sharing a subsidized apartment with her mother, Amelia. They did their best to care for each other as they each tried to keep tabs on reality enough to make it work.

Amelia, an aging, schizophrenic, New York-Italian matriarch, was both demanding and disagreeable. She had alienated herself from her brood over the years, and though alliances shifted, love and history ultimately bound them together. She'd not been able to parent any of her kids because she lived in a revolving door.

You've seen them — the revolving doors that have four or five sections. As a kid, I'd sometimes make a game of staying in, going round and round and round as others got off and on. It reminded me of the automat for some reason, where you take a sandwich out of the little box and another appears — on and on, endless revolving sandwiches, endless revolving lives.

Sophie and her mother didn't have the luxury of revolving until they wanted to stop. Instead, they were unceremoniously plucked out by a hospital attendant, slapped in straitjackets, and dragged to psychiatric facilities where they were subjected to unthinkable atrocities.

Sophie was sixteen years old the first time she was admitted to Bellevue Hospital's Psychiatric Unit in New York City. That was in the early 1950s, prior to the introduction of psychotropic medications. Treatment options for mental illness were limited and barbaric. Sophie was schizophrenic, the doctors said. She would be confined and would receive the very latest care regimens available. And so it began.

Insulin shock therapy involved repeated injections of large doses of insulin in order to induce "therapeutic" comas. Patients were kept in comas for about an hour each day. During that time, they experienced seizures as their bodies spasmed and thrashed uncontrollably. After the prescribed period of time, comas were terminated by the administration of intravenous glucose. Sometimes electroconvulsive therapy (ECT) was administered during the comas.

ECT was done without anesthesia or muscle relaxants. Patients were strapped down, electrodes were attached, and electric shocks were administered. An effective treatment for some patients, ECT is still used today with the game-changing humane addition of muscle relaxants and general anesthesia.

There was also hydrotherapy. Though it may invoke notions of privilege and luxury today, it was far from therapeutic in Sophie's time. One "treatment" involved wrapping the patient in towels soaked in ice-cold water. Another involved the patient being restrained and continuously submerged in a cold bath for hours or days, allowed out only to use the restroom.

Sophie was repeatedly exposed to these modalities as well as others. She remembers them well. She described what it felt like to be forcibly placed in a straitjacket and taken to a filthy, dark room where she was beaten with a chain or leather strop. In painful detail, she talked about having experienced the inhumanity of a system that could do little more than keep the oddballs of the world confined.

Sophie's life has been a revolving door in and out of hospitals, shelter homes, and hidden back wards. When she was discharged, she would go home to her schizophrenic mother. Her siblings were frequently left to care for one another and fend for themselves as best they could. The scar that runs along the front of her torso is a reminder of the time she plunged a butcher knife into the left side of her stomach and cut up to the right hara-kiri style until her intestines came out. "Nutty thing to do," they said when they locked her up that time. Is it crazy to want to escape from the life she was living?

She loves poetry, classical music, literature, and theater. She recites Edna St. Vincent Millay, E. E. Cummings, and Shakespeare with depth and understanding. Her intellect is clearly not impaired; she is a brilliant, loving woman with a chronic, severe mental illness.

Tardive dyskinesia, a permanent, irreversible side effect of neuroleptic medications, causes her to walk with a shuffle as her tongue and face involuntarily move in spasmodic, jerky ways that often frighten people. Children point and laugh or scream and run away. Grownups whisper, cross the street, avert their eyes. People tend not to see the kindhearted, good-natured, sophisticated woman with a quick, witty sense of humor. They see "weird."

• • •

In the small town where we lived, I met several of Sophie's relatives before I came to know her. They are a colorful crew. They are also a crystal clear example of the power of genetics. The eldest sister, Alberta, was the one who discovered McCall while traveling with her children in a tie-dyed VW van. Over the years, other family members moved from New York to Idaho.

Alberta was the town witch. She lived in the "castle," a cavernous, rambling, ramshackle building across the road from Payette Lake. There she made soaps, lotions, and potions, which were packaged and sold in local shops. She seldom left her house, and people avoided her for fear of being hexed.

When I was introduced to her at a boutique one day, she crooked her right index finger, pointed at my face, and nodded her head. "I know about you," was all she said. Her wry smile told me that I was probably not going to be turned into a toad that day. She held out a tiny, round, elaborately wrapped bar of soap and pressed it into my hand, holding both my gaze and my hand for several meaningful moments. I felt her energy with a jolt. A physically slight woman with angular features and a huge presence, her long, wavy hair flecked with gray was escaping wildly from a quasi-ponytail.

Dino, Alberta's son and Sophie's nephew, told me that he had been separated from his team, the New England Patriots, while traveling to an away game. A tall, stocky twenty-five-year-old, he was grandiose, a bit bizarre, and seemed to be responding to internal stimuli as his eyes darted and his head tilted toward the perceived source of voices. His speech was fragmented.

A few months after our first meeting, Dino took a Greyhound to Boston, stole a Patriots uniform, and joined the game. He was taken off the field at Gillette Stadium in a straitjacket. Our office was contacted by the hospital once he was stabilized and able to provide contact information. Alberta bought him a bus ticket back.

I met the brother, Anthony, in the context of a discussion about our mutual history of heroin addiction. Having just moved from New York to Idaho, he was interested in local support systems and resources. Strikingly handsome, the tall, dark Italian New Yorker fascinated me. He had cleaned up, gotten a divorce, and followed his sister to Idaho where he would raise his two sons. Other than a few psychotic episodes, including a naked romp around Idyllwild Airport (now JFK) in his early twenties, the "crazy" gene had been kept at bay in Anthony.

Lisa escaped with an eating disorder and a lifetime of depression, though one of her daughters is known to have a case of the "family flu." (That's what they call it. Really.)

Maura, forever manic, sells real estate, coffee, pizza, and lives in terror of losing her mind.

Mom Amelia and Sophie share an apartment. Mom cooks meals with invisible pots, pans, and food, smokes heavily, and has a problem with accidentally starting fires.

• • •

Martha put the call through. I knew Sophie well enough that her tone and rate of breathing told me how she was. This day, the words came in gasps, as though she were fighting to the surface of the ocean, drowning, trying to survive long enough to get the words out. Terrified. Angry.

Her house had been burglarized, she told me, and "they" were on the grounds of the apartment complex still, waiting, lurking, menacing. She had already called the police but now didn't know whether to open the door. People lied, you know. She didn't live far from the office, so I told her I'd come over between appointments. When I drove into the apartment complex parking lot, it was a scene of controlled chaos — the drama created around mentally ill folks living in community settings. Two police cars had their lights flashing. Neighbors were gathered and huddled together, some still wearing robes and slippers. I knew most everyone, and scenarios were hurled at me — one after another, each version more dramatic than the last.

She had reported that the burglar had a huge rifle.

She had been attacked physically — that's why she was screaming.

She'd run out of her apartment door naked and twirled in circles, chanting incomprehensibly.

She had opened her door and stood with a carving knife, defiantly, demanding that her stolen property be returned.

She was scary.

Officer Dave shook his head slowly as he made his way through the crowd. When he approached me, he sighed deeply.

"Your people," he said.

I looked at him as I always did, offering no response; rather, I nodded my head knowingly. Situations resolved more smoothly when I agreed with every version of every story and every opinion, acknowledging that each scenario was someone's reality.

There was no hurry. I listened patiently. When at last there was a community moment of quiet, I asked gently if the neighbors would please disperse and give me a few minutes. Muttering and grumbling, they did. One police car left, and Officer Dave agreed to wait outside until he could get close enough to take Sophie into protective custody and get her to the hospital. I moved slowly and spoke quietly. My manner was subdued as I thanked them.

I turned and walked toward Sophie's door, lifting myself in the air toward Tink a tiny bit in preparation to switch realities. If Sophie would let me, I would join her. I tapped very lightly on her door, doing the first six knocks of the universal eight: Doo-doo-doo-dee-doo-doo (doop doop, as we all know, are the last two). A whisper from just across the universe. Her eye, I knew, was to the peephole.

"Hilary?" Her breathing was labored. I could feel her through the door sucking deeply on a Marlboro. Whatever comfort her cigarettes gave her, she needed that and much more.

"Yes, it's me, Sophie. You called. Would it be okay if I come in?" I waited silently as she considered my request. Two deadbolt clunks were followed by the door opening at the speed of global warming and her face appeared in the space still separating us by the chain lock. When she was satisfied that I wasn't an imposter, she closed the door, released the chain, and opened it just enough for me to get in before quickly re-securing the locks.

I said nothing. When she politely motioned for me to have a seat, I went in the living room and sat in my customary spot on the couch. She paced slowly, chain-smoking deeply with gusto.

"You called saying there's been a burglary, Sophie. Quite the town happening in the 'hood here. What can you tell me about it?" As she paced, her legs jerked in spasms, her tongue darted uncontrollably, her tortured face twitched with the never-ending signs of tardive dyskinesia.

"They're all out there, and one of them is the culprit."

"No doubt about it."

Inside her fortress, the walls were yellowed with the remnants of thousands of cigarettes, the air thick with schizophrenic oxygen. The kitchen looked like a tornado had passed through. Ashtrays overflowed, a burned pan of what used to be food was simmering on the stove. Her eyes beseeched me to join her, to understand, to help. With the guidance of my history, I dove into myself and did as she asked.

"What did you notice first?" I needed a place to land.

"First, it was my royal-empress-red nail polish. Gone — along with my whole pedicure kit. Then one each of three pairs of warm socks. After that, they got my waffle iron. *That* I keep in the bottom-left cupboard right in here."

She spoke much as she moved — slowly, in spurts, words getting out between the endless spasms. I was on my feet, following her. I flipped her CD player on, knowing that Elton John's *Lion King* would start up, volume low. I'd just made the cassette for her last week, aware that his music soothed her. It soothed me too. Then on to the kitchen, fully engaged. I turned the burner off, removed the charred pan, and got on my knees. I searched the bottom cupboards thoroughly. She was right. No waffle iron.

"It started early this morning, Hilary. There were footprints in the snow when I let Pookie out at about six. *Then* somehow they got in here and stole my telephone."

"You called me on your telephone," the other reality whispered in my brain. *"From here, half an hour ago."*

"So I called the police."

"Good. What happened next?"

"My neighbor Rachel banged on my door, and when I opened it, she made Pookie run out and oh my GOD we have to find my sweet Pookie kitty, Hilary!"

"We do, and we will."

"They're outside and they're after me and I won't let them." She paced, smoked, and talked in gasping bursts, distracted by the ever-present voices and music in her head. The apartment was morphing and shrinking, closing in on us, becoming a prison cell and refuge at the same moment in time. She alternated between rage and terror as I followed her, feeling the sting of emotion. I listened as Sophie railed with passion and bemoaned the persecution she was experiencing.

I listened as sneaky little rogues and thieves darted about the apartment, moving things around, giggling, knowing that they were the source of chaos. These were not evil entities. They were mischievous, impish troublemakers who meant no harm. They expected that I would find them amusing.

They paused and listened when I explained that there was nothing remotely funny about causing Sophie to suffer. They understood. With their little gnome-like heads bowed in embarrassment, they rectified what havoc they could and apologized. When I opened the cupboard door, Sophie's nail polish was back where it belonged and her phone was lying beside the pedicure kit. Pookie meowed and scratched on the door to come in.

No need for further intervention, no more need for neighborhood drama or police. Sophie came back with me that time. She sat down at her old, green, upright piano, closed her eyes, and began to play.

• • •

Sometimes I don't follow rules. Well, hardly ever, actually.

Sophie, in addition to being schizophrenic, had a significant bipolar illness. She tended to know when she was getting manic during the early phases. Her intelligence and humor united with mania and carried her through the sky, darting playfully in and out of reality. At those times, her energy was contagious. Thoughts and ideas flew at her wildly, filling her with notions that she couldn't possibly keep to herself. They were far too fascinating, far too important, and far, far too amusing.

In the local hospital where everyone knew everyone, the medical staff certainly knew Sophie. They knew to call me when she showed up, and they knew that I could bring her back sometimes. Sometimes I couldn't.

She presented in the emergency room one autumn night after having phoned to see which physician was on call. When she'd learned that her favorite doctor was working, she decided to walk the mile or so to the hospital. She was a familiar sight in town with her distinctive shuffling gait, but even after twenty years, few people stopped to offer her a ride. She knew that she would see the doc and knew that he would call me. She did, and he did, of course. Small towns are comfortably predictable. I was buzzed in through the back door, a familiar and welcome sight to staff who preferred blood and guts to suffering souls.

"How do you do it? She's *so* outrageous." The ER nurse, Marian, ushered me to one of the exam rooms where the door was ajar and Sophie was singing to herself. A consummate New Yorker, she was in full-on show tune mode — *West Side Story* this time. Her voice was raspy as she sang out of tune and moved in fits and jerks. When I walked in and saw her doing a rendition of "I Feel Pretty," it was perfect. Charming, believable, and real, I could tell that she did indeed feel as pretty as the essence of her soul.

She stood 5'6", weighed 160 pounds or so, and kept her hair to her shoulders and dyed various shades of red. She brought a rather cosmopolitan sense of style to the traditional McCall jeans and sweatshirt uniform. A jaunty hat one day, a feather in her hair, sash, scarf, a treasured offbeat sweater she'd picked up at the thrift store. Her long tweed coat hung on a cupboard door. Her shoes, damp from early snow on the ground, were set neatly under the exam table. When she saw me, she smiled and stood still. I take photos in my head. Despite what's defined as a memory disorder, the photos I *do* have are crystal clear. Like this one:

Sophie's arms are raised joyfully to the heavens, her head tilted slightly back and to the right, eyes closed. She was managing with her entire body to incorporate the involuntary movements of tardive dyskinesia with the graceful dance of Maria in the dress shop, innocently and classically in love with Tony. The humor was evident to me the moment I saw her. She was draped in an exam gown using props from the cupboards and sashaying around the room.

I saw her beauty and spirit that evening. I see it still in my photograph.

When she held her hand out to me, I took it and joined her in a bit of "pretty and witty and gay."

Marian peeked in, shook her head, and looked at me. "The doc is at a school meeting. He'll be twenty minutes or so." The exam room door closed gently.

Tink has a tendency to show up at times like this, sparkling in costume, playful and joyous in her lighthearted way. Tonight she wore a long, glittering gown that flowed gently through the air as she gracefully flew above us, singing along. Tink too felt pretty. Tink too has an irrepressible sense of humor.

When the soundtrack ended, Sophie saw me for the first time as we stood there together. Again we met in that place where humor rules, where laughing is akin to breathing. I broke out in uncontrollable belly laughter; hers was the comedian knowing how funny she was. Fully aware that she could launch into a rendition of "The Jets" or "Cabaret" at any moment, I sat on the rolling chair, shifting the energy ever so quietly.

Sophie danced a few more steps in perfect time to the music in her head before rewriting the lyrics:

"I am manic. I am manic.
Can't stop talking or thinking at ALLLLL.
And I pity every ONE who's never felt SO GOOOD.
Could be trouble. Am too perky —
and I KNOWWW I need a tune-up sooon."

She tossed the exam gown over her shoulder with dramatic flair and then stumbled into the gurney. Belly laughter erupted again.

We sometimes referred to inpatient medication adjustments as tune-ups; she knew she was manic and wanted to have her mood regulated before she lost control. Being manic is a bit like being Mary Poppins flying through the air with the umbrella — it can be fun. Most people with a bipolar illness don't want to give up the highs. Sophie's combination of diagnoses meshed with her intellect in a way that worked. More than anything, she wanted to be able to function in the world and manage her illness responsibly. Really. She didn't want to be crazy.

The doc came in a short time later. Munchler was a tall, handsome guy who truly enjoyed working with psych patients. Most of our people chose him for primary care for precisely that reason. Sophie had a total crush on him. She sat on the exam table as close to Munchler as she could get. They chatted for a bit, he examined her, and when she agreed to a voluntary admission to Saint Al's psych unit, he asked me if I could make the arrangements.

A family member or friend could drive voluntary patients the 100 miles from McCall to Boise once the admission was arranged. Saint Al's staff knew Sophie well; she was a regular. Rather than go through the on-call psychiatrist, I had the privileged luxury of simply calling Dr. Johnny on his cell.

"I'm in the ER with Munchler and Sophie, John. She's manic as hell, and we're thinking an admit to Saint Al's might be just the ticket."

"Voluntary?"

"So far."

"Who can transport?"

Having been on the phone for half an hour before calling for admission approval, I had confirmed the availability of a bed and spoken with everyone I could think of who might be willing to drive Sophie to Boise. No one in her family was willing, and despite the fact that she did have friends, they were all predictably unavailable. They like her company when she is here, but one step away into another reality sent them scattering.

"I can do it, John. She's just manic, and I have a friend I've been wanting to see down there anyway."

"Hilary, we're not supposed to do that."

"Your point? If you have one?"

"What the fuck," he said gently, *"am I going to do with you?"*

"We can be there in a few hours. The roads aren't icy, and she's compliant."

"All right, I'll have Dr. Leon do the admission, and I'll see her first thing tomorrow morning."

"Oh, she'll like that. Max is *so* good looking. Seriously good looking. But nowhere as handsome as you, of course. It'll be about two-and-a-half hours."

Munchler chatted with Sophie while I ran home to pack an overnight bag, and then she was discharged from the ER. She was not a danger to herself or others nor was she gravely disabled at the moment. Those are the only criteria for detainment. She was delighted to ride down with me. Against all the rules, as usual, I would take my own car rather than a state vehicle so that I could stay the night with friends. Forty minutes later, we were on the road.

Highway 55 is the only north-south route in the state of Idaho. It is a windy, steep two-lane affair that runs along the Payette River. Most years, there are more accidents between McCall and Boise than the rest of the state combined. Steep drop-offs can send a vehicle flying 100 feet down into the river at some corners, deep rocky canyons at others. It's dangerous.

Sophie was glad that we would spend the time together. I expected a smooth drive. I plugged in an Elton John CD, we fastened our seat belts, and off we went into the wild blue yonder. Again. About twenty miles south of town, the hairpin curves begin in earnest. As we drove into the canyon, I intuitively felt a change. Hoping I was mistaken and needing to concentrate on driving, I glanced over at Sophie. She was quiet now. Too quiet. I followed her gaze to a corner of the dashboard where I saw nothing unusual. When I looked at her face, though, I knew that she did. She curled into herself, hugging her knees, and grew silent.

"Hey, Sophie, want to hear that new Eltee song again?" The reminder of a shared affinity for Elton, unanswered, sat heavily in the air. "Yo — you're in charge of entertainment here."

Silence. Uh-oh.

Forty miles of Highway 55 has no shoulders, few guardrails, and is so narrow that vehicles have to slow down in places just to be sure they can both make it. *No passing, just drive … and do it carefully.*

Five miles into that section, I knew the hallucinations had begun. The dash was no longer a dash in Sophie's mind. I kept talking, trying to bring her back. I couldn't go to her because driving and space travel don't mix. Without warning, her arms and legs began to flail dangerously as she fought off a monster. Her fist accidentally hit me while I tried to hold her still with one hand and drive with the other. As the little Subaru swerved into the oncoming lane, I managed to avoid the logging truck. Her voice got louder as she kicked and punched to defend herself against large insects.

I knew there was trouble right there in River City.

Well.

This was a stupid idea.

Having driven the road a gazillion times, I knew I could pull over at the next wide spot just past the "falling rock" sign a little way down. I spoke calmly, but it made no difference because she was gone. I turned on the hazard lights at the wide spot, breathed a sigh of relief, and looked over at my passenger.

"The HUGE SPIDERS, they're flying all over your car, and I'm going to get them!" Her eyes were wild now. We'd been separated.

"Sophie. Sophie." I put my arm around her quaking shoulder and felt her terror. "Sophie, we're going to Boise. There are no spiders in the car. They're not real. I promise. Not real. We're driving to Boise and that handsome Dr. Maxie is waiting for you." I spoke with calm firmness, touching her gently to give the words sensation. She stilled some, looked at me doubtfully. "Really. Please, Sophie, we're going to get in a wreck. Spiders not real. You're with me, and you're safe."

From the other galaxy, her eyes tried to make contact with mine, but she remained a ways off.

"Will you please do something for me?'

"What?" Flat now, Sophie showed signs of dwindling mania taking her who knew where.

"Will you please sit in the back seat with your seat belt on till we get down the hill? Come on, we can play chauffeur. I'll be the chauffeur, and you be the boss."

A smile cracked, briefly, almost invisibly but not quite. I got out, watching carefully for speeding flat-landers with no road respect. I opened the passenger side door and dramatically bowed as I unfastened her seat belt.

"Madam."

Thankfully, she followed me. Throwing her scarf around her hair she became the entitled princess.

"Yes, Jeeves."

"If Madam will be so kind."

She took my proffered hand and stepped out of the car. I folded a blanket neatly and set it in the back seat on the passenger side, as far from me as I could get her. She obligingly and regally sat down, accepting help to belt herself in.

"If it pleases Madam," I said, "we shall resume our journey. We will arrive at our destination in approximately forty-five minutes." I had to hope and pray this was going to work; there was no cell reception, no 9-1-1. She miraculously acquiesced. I got back in, arranged the rearview mirror so that I could watch her, and pulled slowly back onto the highway.

Two minutes passed in silence.

"Sweet, sweet …"

"Sweet, sweet memories she gave-a-me."

Oh dear lord, thank God — singing is GOOD. When I looked in the rearview mirror, Dean Martin sat with his arm around Sophie's shoulder, singing softly in her ear.

"Take — one sweet and gentle kiss."

I was wordlessly elected to sing background.

"Sweet sweet — memories she gave-a me."

"Add ... one stolen night of bliss."

"Sweet sweet — memories she gave-a me."

My heart was pounding. This one was close. I'd misread it — screwed up and put a lot of people in danger. Mania is not a predictable state of being. As I watched in the rearview mirror, I saw and felt Sophie's struggle to stay in the car. When I caught Dino's eyes, he smiled in his suave, sexy way, blew me a kiss, and crooned on.

"Don't — forget a small moonbeam ..."

"Sweet, sweet — memories she gave-a-me."

"Fold in lightly with a dream ..."

It was one of those times when I called on Mary, Tink, and my own power to make things work. Tink swayed sensually in front of Sophie and Dean, a fine impression of Rita Hayworth, martini in hand. We arrived at the hospital safely an hour later. We sang of memories neither of us remembered — perhaps memories of past lifetimes that led to our surviving the perilous drive down the mountain that day.

That was fifteen years ago. Our paths were crossing as clinician and patient with unspoken knowing that each time was but a shift, new meeting, and new lessons, new crossing of old paths.

The bond we formed was strong and true. Her depth of wisdom never ceases to amaze me. Her intensity comes through always, and there are but a rare few who do not find her disarming.

Sophie will never give up, much like me in many ways. Regardless of how sick we may get, despite petrifying delusions and debilitating pain, beyond the sadness inherent in knowing that we will never be "cured," we tenaciously struggle against all odds. Quality of life is in moments of joy. Above all, the lesson we share has been the ability to laugh at ourselves within the absurdity of the big picture.

Michael

Within the box-like setting of pursuing my professional career while being a wife and mother, it was easy for life to complicate itself. In order to maintain my sanity, I journeyed far from the beaten path to places where I happily indulged in lucid memories of the past, memories of truth, nature, and simplicity.

My fondest memories are times when I was as far as I could get from the American Dream.

My Michael and I lived in a tipi in the wilderness of Idaho. We did what needed to be done to make it through each day: hauled water from the creek in buckets, split wood for the fire that warmed our bodies and cooked our food, swept snow off the tipi, adjusted the smoke flaps according to wind direction, remembered to pay attention to miracles.

Thanks to the wisdom and ingenuity of Native Americans, when temperatures plummeted to twenty or thirty below zero, our tipi fire maintained the inside at a comfortable 55 degrees. While the never-ending pot of beans cooked in the Dutch oven, we worked tirelessly on bath day to turn snow into hot water and fill the metal sheepherder's tub, to share, to laugh. Looking with our eyes was but the first step to seeing our surroundings. We became our surroundings. Michael and I were of the forest and its inhabitants, those nights so clear and bright with stars they made our love brighter, and fairyland mornings when ice crystals made the world sparkle — pure, unblemished, untouched paradise. Simplicity, tranquility, and peace, hearts filled with love, grateful for each and every moment.

He teased me when I amused myself with a quest to find out who the president was in November of 1980. With snowshoes and a daypack, I made my way across the tree bridge early one morning to the nearest facsimile of a road (a glorified, rutted dirt path that could accommodate only the most rugged or beat-up vehicles). After three days, a Paul Bunyan sort of logger friend drove by. He stopped when he saw me sitting in the snow with a book and, when I asked, told me that Reagan had won. It wasn't the knowing that mattered — just the quest.

I smiled when Michael cooked me frog legs and trout for dinner or when he knelt beside a deer or rabbit he'd shot with a bow and arrow. We bowed our heads together in prayer, respect, and gratitude to the universe for our sustenance.

The man I'd met in Palm Springs was now in his element. I suspect that was the happiest time of his life. Society and its complexities are too much for some tender souls to handle. Our daughter was to be born with such a fragile, tender essence. Her and her fathers' hearts and souls are far too fragile to manage a life within any semblance of a box. When they must function in society, such entities suffer unimaginable pain and heartbreaking internal chaos.

For Michael, tipi life was perfection. For me, feeling his soul smile was my joy. One of the greatest honors of my life was being chosen to live that incredible lifestyle with my Michael, to wake up every morning in the world's purest cathedral and lie down snuggled into his body and a bed of furs at night. So many stars shone through the flap opening that some nights we knew that the show was for us alone. We needed nothing, no one beyond our tiny piece of the world. When survival is a full-time job, the lessons are truth, gratitude, love, and purity.

It was said by those who knew us then that wild horses couldn't tear Michael and me apart.

It was true.

Michael and I were unboxable. Unstoppable.

Irene

At least one morning a week, I went to the office at six — when not a creature was stirring. Without bodies around to muddle the energy, I was able to feel more clearly and catch up on paperwork. Early birds occasionally saw my car and came to the back of the building to tap on the sliding glass door of my office. One summer morning, I looked up to see a tapping deputy sheriff named Victor with coffee and a bag promising baked goodies. He told me of an eviction notice that his department had been trying to execute for the past several weeks, explaining that the occupants were completely uncooperative and irrational.

Would I check them out?

Of course.

Did I want him to go with me for protection?

Of course not.

Later that morning, when I pull into the long dirt driveway, I see that the house, weather worn and unkempt, was once a beautiful place. I knock politely on the door and am answered with a firm, "Go away. Leave me alone."

I don't go away. I spend half an hour charming the voice into opening the door just a crack, and once I have eye contact, I cajole her into letting me in. Her name is Irene, she says, and she doesn't know why she is being harassed.

She's lived in this, her house, for over twenty years. She's a wealthy divorcee, and she's not bothering anyone.

She has an air of privilege. Probably in her midsixties, she has silky red hair that flows to the middle of her back. She wears a lavender satin robe that drapes elegantly to the floor with matching slippers. The woman has a regal air about her and wreaks of old money and class. I can easily picture her former life of opulence and entitlement. The spacious home is filled with antique furniture, Persian rugs, and winding staircases.

Why in the world would people tell her she has to get out of her own home? The ex-husband, she explains, ran off with a younger woman and is being vindictive and cruel. Their disabled son lives with her. She isn't going anywhere.

I gently ask Irene questions as I step into her mind, her home, her world. She welcomes me and is glad to talk, explaining that no one else has bothered to listen. As she welcomes me into her world, I become an ally.

The windows are covered with aluminum foil. Honest. No foil hat with antenna to help communicate with Martians, so I'm pretty sure I haven't been transported to a 1950s B movie set.

Piles of stuff are everywhere making it difficult to navigate around the place. It's a huge house, three stories, on five acres of land. Her forty-year-old son, Colby, is in town with a friend. He does little to help with the house, she explains, and has difficulty managing his own basic living needs. *Poor Colby*, his father refuses to even help him pay for his medications. As she talks, I walk and look around, taking stock of her living conditions.

"I bet the foil on the windows helps." I have no idea what it's helping with, but surely it's there for a reason. *Her foil, her world.*

"Yes, it certainly does. How did you know that? No one else knows that. I'm in a lot less pain since I put that over the windows."

"I'm sure you are. What can you tell me about that?" Changing realities is second nature to me; my ability to travel is as real and effortless as the way Tink moves with me in space and time.

"It's those people who live up the hill. Well, it's not really them. They're gone, but their house has been taken over by the bunch that's after me. They've been shooting me with their electric shock guns, and when I get hit, it hurts like hell. Then they laugh, and I hear them telepathically. I don't know what they want."

"Damn. Well, I sure don't blame you for staying indoors. There's something not okay going on. What did the cops tell you?"

"They said my ex-husband wants me out of here. He's the one who ran off five years ago, for heaven's sake. I don't think he has anything to do with the shooters, but that's not the point. This is my house, and I will *not* leave."

There is a valid eviction notice, though, and Irene has been getting warning letters and notifications for nearly a year. It's come down to a twenty-four-hour notice now, so if she doesn't get out, she will be forcibly removed. She's disoriented, frightened, suffering.

Irene beckons me to the kitchen. She carefully moves the aluminum foil aside from one of the windows. At the same time, she takes a small case from the pocket of her robe and opens the snap. "From Sharper Image catalog," she explains. "It measures the strength of electrical alien rays."

As we walk close to the uncovered window, the device beeps like a metal detector, louder and faster in certain spots. "They're shooting from the other house," she tells me. A moment later, Irene doubles over in pain and sinks into an antique velvet lounge chair, writhing in agony.

"They hit me again," she says with tears in her eyes.

I believe her. Her pain is as real to her as her reality. Through all this, she maintains her air of dignity, old money, and entitlement. Oh, and a haughtiness that is not particularly endearing.

The alien zap gun is destroying her body and mind. With great effort, she pushes her ample body out of the chair, eager to show me more. As we walk around the house, I marvel at the efficiency of the alien detector as it beeps sporadically, and our bond intensifies with every moment I spend in her section of the world.

When we hear a car heading down the long driveway, I see both resolve and terror in her eyes. I protectively put an arm around her shoulder and tell her she doesn't have to talk to them. She sighs and moves to a couch, reclining with the drama and stage presence of Sara Bernhardt in her prime. She breathes deeply and relaxes when I assure her that I will deal with whatever is approaching. *Gotta feel for this woman with all my heart.* I walk out the heavy double doors to the front porch and see two police cars approaching. *Four uniformed officers for one harmless sick woman? Okay.*

"She has to be out, Hilary. We've tried to talk to her, and this has been going on for weeks. We can't take her on a mental hold because she's not a danger to herself or others, and she's not gravely disabled. She manages to take care of herself, but her neighbors are fed up, and we do have the legal eviction paperwork. She's out of time and has no intention of going anywhere. We've been trying to talk to her, but she wouldn't answer the door until you came."

"Come on, guys. We'll work it out without you having to handcuff the poor lady and drag her off."

Time to navigate.

My lessons learned from Mary are now put to good use, understanding that there is not one definitive reality but many — a clear knowing guiding the gentle chameleon in and out of parallel worlds and teaching them to exist in harmony. Each reality is validated as it must be, and I am honored to orchestrate the cosmic dance.

In Irene's world ,I can talk about both realities while keeping her safe. *Yes, this sucks. But it's what we need to do for now.* We need to pack up her most important things, get them to a storage unit, and arrange a place to stay while all this legal stuff gets worked out. *Yes, it may be the ultimate travesty, but it is what it is, and we're out of options.*

"We." Magic word.

In law enforcement's world, their court order is the only truth. By speaking their language fluently, I manage to negotiate an additional forty-eight-hour delay.

Everyone is right, and everyone agrees that they are right.

We are granted seventy-two hours to help Irene maintain the dignity and grace that she needs to define herself. Seventy-two hours to somehow sift through a 4,000-square-foot house filled with a lifetime of possessions and rescue essential treasures, seventy-two hours to comply with a court order.

Can do.

For two days and nights, we work tirelessly, sorting through the house and outbuildings. The story that is revealed layer by layer evokes memories of Turner Classic Movies. An entire room is filled with evening gowns and furs hanging on store-like racks, another with shoes and handbags piled to the ceiling, a third with mountains of makeup and hair products. Irene claims to need everything, but I am lucky enough to find the one small upstairs room that she actually lives in and pack a few boxes from there.

Once circumstances are known, help comes in the form of friends and neighbors with trucks, muscle, and compassion. Her behavior becomes increasingly bizarre and disorganized. She is overwhelmed, despondent, and wounded. She hasn't left her house in months and is unable to grasp what's going on or why, but she trusts me.

• • •

When her ex-husband stopped supporting her, the resourceful woman had simply continued to write checks from his account. Marshall was a wealthy man and not unkind. He let things slide until the amounts escalated as Irene spent more and more money while steadfastly refusing to reason with him. When he eventually pressed charges, Irene was legally charged, convicted of forgery, and put on probation.

Ben, the local probation officer, later made it a requirement for her to engage in mental health treatment. Irene did not comply with taking oral medication but did agree to weekly injections of an antipsychotic medication called Prolixin. Her mental status improved during that time.

Most of our people at the clinic, even the sickest ones, gained some level of insight into their differences and the options available to help them function in society. Most realized at some point that compliance with the right kind of support clearly improved their quality of life. Irene was one of the few who never did. We managed to house her until we could get her disability benefits and find her a place to live. She was difficult to deal with, given her sense of entitlement combined with circumstances that were unacceptable in her mind. She tended to be rude, petulant, and aloof. When she and Cleopatra the cat moved into a one-bedroom apartment, her monsters came and went. She heard them through the walls and felt the familiar stabbing pain of alien laser guns come and go.

She ultimately refused to leave her world of entitled opulence, despite the stark reality of eventual destitution. She spends her days watching a Turner Classic Movie of her life on the big screen in her tiny subsidized apartment. Aliens roam a nonexistent attic, and foil covers the tiny kitchen window.

I'd been able to easily walk into her world of aluminum foil laser guns and take her hand. For years, she followed me to the outer fringes of that other world, but she never left it.

All soul lessons are unique, of course.

I don't get to get it just because I want to.

Ted

Ted was raising a bit of a ruckus at the police station, reporting that he'd been the victim of an elaborate robbery. He was explaining that he used to be an ironworker in LA and had $750,000 in a pension fund. He claimed that his brother, Howard, had stolen his money using a combination of fraud and lies. Ted was agitated and adamant, demanding that they help recover his money and telling them that I would vouch for him.

When the police contact my office, I confirm that I will indeed vouch for Ted. I assure the officer that he is our patient, likely off his meds and delusional, and that I will be over to intervene. When I arrive at the police station, Ted launches into his story.

Ted is thirty-four years old and has schizophrenia. He's a big man, 6'2", 280 pounds, scraggly black hair past his shoulders. We have known each other for years, and I have rarely seen his innocent blue eyes so intense.

He explains the problem and assures me that several of these plots were reported on network television this morning. He provides specifics in terms of the name of the ironworkers' union in LA, the type of pension fund, and other detailed information. He hates his brother and will kill him if the money isn't returned.

That's when it's good to work in a small community and have long histories with patients and their families.

Ted's father is a retired ironworker who lives on a small ranch a few miles outside of town. Ted lived with him until just two years ago when we were able to stabilize his medications enough that he could manage his own apartment in town. His dad had difficulty understanding Ted's schizophrenia but was always polite, supportive, calm, and willing to help his boy. The other son continues to live on the ranch, works, and helps with the horses and chores.

Ted's father confirmed that Ted was indeed an ironworker in Los Angeles for a few years before he got sick. He had an episode 600 feet up on scaffolding, though, and nearly caused several deaths, including his own, before he was sent for an evaluation by the company. He never worked again after explaining that small creatures in the sky held workers up with ropes that were invisible to human eyes.

If the "Bahdoos" were angered, the ropes were instantly severed and the worker fell to his death. Mostly the creatures were helpful and reasonable, but occasionally they would get out of line and want a worker harmed or pushed.

I genuinely like Ted. He believes 100 percent in what he is saying, and the delusion gets more elaborate as the story unfolds. With a history of violence, he's not a guy I want to see angry, especially when we're alone in my office.

Yes, I have pepper spray in my desk.

Yes, I have a button to signal 9-1-1.

No, I don't want drama. I just want to help this gentle man with his illness.

"Okay, Ted. What do we need to do to resolve this?"

"Call LA to the ironworkers union." He provides a phone number.

I call.

Ted did have a small pension fund, but he had emptied it years ago. There is no money. But you never know. When you believe in everything, anything is possible.

Last I heard, Ted was apprehended in a bar with the help of a huge fishing net because he was psychotic, armed, and dangerous. He has been in a state hospital ever since.

Mountains

My respite from the complications of the world was the beauty and solitude of the unblemished wilderness that surrounded me. My piece of heaven was the small ranch I'd bought when I picked door number two during a game show moment in life. The nearest house was barely visible. I was surrounded by thousands of acres of ranch land and pastures.

In my spare time I was an aspiring hick studying mountain law with a Donnelly rancher and neighbor named Dwight. He taught me that the rules in our neck of the woods are about handshakes, integrity, and remembering that "do unto others" is the accepted way of life.

One winter day, I strapped on a pair of wooden bear claw snowshoes and walked toward the nearby hills with my faithful Blue Heeler, Molly. I walked with purpose and direction yet without a conscious destination in mind. Several miles past the dam, I was drawn to an invisible trailhead at the base of a snow-covered mountain. I claimed it as my own. It's easy to claim a mountain when there's no one around.

The Gold Fork wilderness went on forever. Snow-packed dirt roads led to hundreds of miles of nothing and everything, depending on your point of view.

Once I'd claimed the mountain, I often drove the few miles from my house and parked next to a huge boulder that marked the entrance to my kingdom.

Mountain Living

Views from my ranch house.

Front yard. Neighbors feeding cattle.

Boulder Lake is on mountain range, far left.

I dressed comfortably with snow pants over my jeans, a down vest over a tank top, a neck warmer, and the warmest gloves on the planet. I'd sit in the snow and throw sticks for Molly as I strapped on the snowshoes. She was ready for anything, excited, always reveling in our adventures. When I grabbed the ski pole, she was at my side and we were off.

White. No one. Nothing but white, silence, breathtaking serenity, like walking in a cloud. I had no idea how far or how long we walked because it didn't matter. I knew that mountain before I ever hiked it. The pure, untouched wilderness was ours and ours alone. We never saw another human being there, which was just the way we liked it. Molly and I ventured farther and farther into our kingdom as time went by.

If it was daylight and I had free time, we were there. If the moon was full and we could see our way, we were there. If it was dark, my headlamp had a battery, and we were feeling outdoorsy, we were there.

But nothing was more glorious than the sunny winter days I still see clearly in my brain's photo album. Or are the pictures in my heart? No matter. The pristine snow glistened, ice crystals filled the air, and the sky around us sparkled.

We would stop when we felt these magical moments, Molly and I, and stand still. Molly sat on alert, barely moving a muscle. I would close my eyes and raise my arms to the heavens, allowing the power of the universe to fill my body and soul to the brim. An intense physical sensation, warm and peaceful, charged my cosmic battery. A spiritual orgasm filled my soul with love, gratitude and the power of a thousand lifetimes. Those were the moments I lived for. That is the feeling that has always kept me strong and true.

• • •

Then came the day when I pulled into our spot and we were not alone. No more than six feet in front of the car lay a cougar, feasting on a deer so fresh that steam was still rising from its half-eaten body.

Quiet. Molly didn't say a word, just let out a very, very, soft whine. We both sat still and looked on in wonder. No fear. Awe. The big cat slowly raised her head and looked directly at me. I briefly made eye contact before averting my gaze as a sign of submission and respect.

Languidly, slowly, she pulled herself to her feet, sated from her meal. She stretched gracefully as she stood, then turned her head and casually looked over her shoulder at us before wandering into the forest. I sat where I was, honored that this magnificent creature had blessed me and grateful that we were safe. As she disappeared into the dense brush, my heart soared.

Molly understood. Of course.

After a time, I instinctively turned the car around and headed home down the snow-packed road. I strapped on the holster that held my .44 Magnum and returned to the trailhead. The deer carcass was still steaming when we got back. Getting out of the car, I loaded a round in the chamber while Molly covered her doggy ears and put her head under the seat.

I felt that we had intrusively walked into someone's home without knocking, and I wanted to make it right. As a sign of respect, I stood and shot a round into the air. The sound reverberated for miles in the tranquil wonderland. Echoes told me the gesture was understood. I put the gun under the seat. I strapped on my snowshoes, put the Camelback water pouch on my back, coaxed my courageous companion from the car, and walked into the forest.

From that day on, it became a tradition to shoot a round in the air as my way of being courteous enough to knock on nature's door.

The cougar, the mountain, and I had an understanding.

Silly, worried people repeatedly assured me that I would die out there. Friends begged me to carry the gun or not go alone or snowshoe in the park where it was safe.

Silly.

Worried.

People.

Hep C

My physical body began its rebellion a little over ten years ago. I am unaware of having done anything offensive to spark this process.

I'd had to divorce Michael and his liquor.

Our tender-souled daughter, Misty Dawn, had left the mountains for the big city down the hill in search of herself.

Molly and I were living in the Donnelly house, the isolated paradise surrounded by postcard-quality 360-degree views of mountains, pastures, and ranch land. Following a brief moment of profound loneliness, I'd kicked up my heels and done a driveway jig. I was going to love the newfound solitude.

I did.

Until the mysterious revolution began.

Usually brimming with energy, I felt myself being slowly enveloped by a heavy shroud of weariness. With no obvious medical explanation, I came to the reasonable conclusion that I was simply exhausted from all the years of work, life, and stress. Understandable. I hadn't had a vacation in .... let's see ... that would be ... ever.

A trip to Mexico. Yes. The sun, ocean, a lounge chair, and a book were what I needed.

Before long, my friend Maggie and I were leaving our snow boots in the car and laughing our sandal-footed way through the snow to board the plane. Within ten minutes of landing, I decided that Cabo was not for me — crowded with loud, obnoxious tourists who did little but exploit the locals in any way they could. Worse yet, the tourists were clueless about the culture that had been destroyed and mutilated by their invasion. The first night, I watched an American couple at the next table posing for souvenir photos with two barefoot five-year-olds dressed in rags and selling Chiclets chewing gum. The wide-eyed children appeared to be brother and sister, and when I looked up and down the street, I saw the mother, holding an infant and watching the photo session with ancient eyes and a heavy heart.

This was not a vacation spot. It was a travesty.

Maggie went out dancing and didn't come back. I spent the night in the hotel room we had reserved and hit the beach at sunrise the next morning, walking directly into the water to renew myself with the feel, taste, and smell of the ocean. I absorbed power and energy, hungry for renewal.

Then I walked into town, rented a little white convertible VW bug, and drove it to the hotel. When Meg showed up raving about the guy she'd spent the night with, I told her that I wasn't staying in Cabo. I was glad that she had fun, and I was packing my bag and leaving.

She and I had forged a delightful friendship based on hard work and irrepressible, frequently dark humor. Younger, smarter, and infinitely more energetic than me, she laughed and asked where I thought I was going.

"I have absolutely no idea," I told her, "but I'm leaving as soon as I get some breakfast."

"I'm going too! You're the one who speaks Spanish. Even though I don't need language to find good-looking men, I wanna go too! Where we going? Let's go!"

"North, because there is no south from here. Come if you want to, your royal slut-ness."

We burst into laughter, loaded the car, and forty-five minutes later were driving in circles trying to find our way out of town. Not surprisingly, we found ourselves lost on dead ends several times before we found the one that actually went somewhere. The dusty, desolate roads boasted an occasional cow or small shack with large families and small armies of hungry dogs wanting to eat us. We spun the little bug car out of places we didn't belong, raising dust, driving fast, and laughing until our bellies hurt.

Finally, many hours later, the road hugged the ocean and we saw buildings off in the distance. I was wiped-out tired as we checked into the Palma de Oro, a quiet place in a small fishing village. When I lay down by the pool that time, getting up was no longer an option. I was sick.

Maggie was a nurse practitioner and leapt into action. She leapt as far as the local pharmacy to get a Z-pack. We decided that I had a sinus infection and she would take care of me. The good nurse brought the antibiotics with a huge cup of warm tea. I thanked her and lay back to read as she took off in search of men, liquor, and her version of fun. At least it was quiet here, and off the beaten path.

As days went by, I became increasingly weak until, despite the powerful antibiotics, I could barely move. Something was wrong.

• • •

When we got back from Mexico, I had no choice but to solve the mystery of my declining health.

I saw specialist after specialist, each with a different answer and most with a different antibiotic. Frustration peaked when I was diagnosed by a pulmonologist as having bronchiectasis, an evil something in my lungs that was planning to kill me within the next five years.

Nothing you can do?

I'm going to die of lung something?

I don't think so, dip-wad.

The gods love Idaho enough to have blessed it with incomparable beauty, but there are lots of places to get better medical care. Most places.

I did a Google search for the finest diagnostic facility in the country, and up popped a place I'd never heard of: National Jewish Research and Medical Center in Denver, Colorado. *Colorado? Who'd have thunk it?* I picked up the phone and scheduled an evaluation.

These people didn't mess around. Their evaluations lasted five full days. I was on a plane to Denver two weeks later. My doctor, a gentle man sporting an understated halo, assured me that they would find an answer. I believed him.

Testing involved scans, breathing tests, at least half my blood, tubes stuck down my throat, hoses going everywhere, and forms of exploration I suspected were developed during covert military operations on other planets.

At the end of day five, I sat with Dr. Mathews in his small office as he finished studying the extensive results of all the scans, labs, and tests. He scooted his rolling stool close to my chair.

"Well, this has been quite a week for you, Hilary."

I nodded. I liked him.

"The good news is this: You definitely do not have bronchiectasis. You do, however, have a severe sinus infection that appears to have been with you for a long time. You're going to need sinus surgery."

"That's fine."

"I had some special blood studies done because we had a lab result one number above normal range. Normally one point isn't a concern, but I figured we needed to be diligent here. Turns out, Hilary, that you have hepatitis C."

Images of South Beach thirty-five years ago, friends whose eyes and skin had turned yellow and friends who had died, sharing needles because we didn't know any better.

Though death is familiar — even comforting — territory to me, I knew it was not yet time for me to go back. His halo twinkled softly, and I took a few deep breaths.

"Hep C? Didn't see that one coming. I'm not letting it kill me, so what's next?"

Dr. Mathews gently touched my arm.

"There is treatment, though I'll tell you now that it's pretty rough. Let's be glad we found it, Hilary."

Yes indeed.

A liver biopsy confirmed that the hep C was stage three-and-a-half on a scale of one to four. I am convinced that the one point above normal had been overlooked, brushed off, and ignored through many years of routine lab work.

Hep C carries an interesting stigma in that it exists in a unique, isolated, contaminated box.

People with hep C are dirty.

You? Hep C?

Is that the one from bad food?

Oh, a mosquito bite. Doesn't that kill you?

People with hep C are dangerous, aren't they?

Don't drink from her water bottle or go too close because it's highly contagious, you know.

What about the bodily fluid thing? If you cry on my shoulder, your tears will seep into my pores and infect me.

Oh my God. How did you get that?

How long do you have to live?

I'd been a teenage heroin addict, I assured the world. I'd paid some dues, but apparently not enough.

Without fear of hesitation, I decided to start treatment, though I had no idea what that meant. I just knew that I was being confronted with a hoop to jump through, so jump I would.

And jump I did.

There was a grand total of one treatment option. I would inject myself with Interferon once a week for forty-eight weeks in addition to a twice-daily dose of Ribavirin. I would be monitored, have regular blood draws, and I had a 40 percent chance of successfully clearing the virus. Those odds were better than no odds, so off I went. I could do this, and it would work. I would keep my job and health insurance.

Not for a moment did I doubt that the virus would clear and get rid of this pesky illness. My approach was clear, determined, and certain. Sure, treatment was awful, but it would be well worth the price.

I operated on autopilot, doing what I had to do — a way of functioning that had grown familiar to me. I once again watched myself from outside and above as I set about each day with the guidance of my higher power. My coworkers set a chair in the hallway between my office and the restrooms because some days the 300-foot journey was more than I could manage.

Me. Climber of Mountains. Hiker of the Wilderness. Conqueror of Kingdoms.

Whooped.

• • •

One of Mary's most impressive embodiments was joining forces with Dr. Johnny. He is my very best friend and angel on Earth. Johnny increased the time he spent at the clinic during my treatment, making the 200-mile roundtrip drive more often regardless of weather or road conditions. He triple-checked my work as the chemo-like drugs slowly but steadily diminished my already compromised cognition. He constantly monitored my mental status and prescribed the medications it took to keep me at my job. More importantly, that man called to check on me every day for 336 days.

I love him.

He always knew exactly when to call, and he always did. Still does.

"F-Squared," he called it. "Fucking Friday," the day I injected myself with the Interferon after work, down for the count all weekend only to crawl back to the office on Monday morning. As my hair thinned, I found colorful scarves and delightful hats that kept me from looking like a patient. Having a psychiatrist as a best friend is obviously another part of the synchronicity.

I was a regular at the emergency room (lovin' the small town thing). None of that "checking in" stuff for me. I staggered or was carried in the back door, went into a vacant exam room, and lay down until the on-call doctor came by and took care of me.

Dangerously low white blood cell count, headaches that only unconsciousness would ease, dehydration. Through it all, I never for an instant doubted that I would clear the virus.

• • •

Wendy was the not-both-feet-on-the-ground nurse at my hepatologist's office. We all know that Wendy and Tink go way back to Neverland, but that's another story. Wendy held my hand throughout the year of treatment, encouraging me with her knowledge and compassionate understanding.

After only four weeks of treatment, blood tests showed that the viral load had gone from 2.5 million to under 50,000. At that time, under 50,000 was considered the best possible outcome — I was a "responder," and I was winning.

On occasion, Wendy and Tink invited Peter Pan and his friends to entertain me as I lay stuporous on my couch. The visits often turned into adventurous outings as we held hands and flew effortlessly to Neverland. Peter showed me how he rescued Tiger Lily from the clutches of Captain Hook, shared his antics, and charmed me with his unaffected ingenuous ways. These were joyous times of escape, trips that freed me from my body. Peter said I got to go because I believe in everything and part of me already lived in Neverland.

• • •

Billy Franklin, nicknamed Uncle Woogie by his niece, was one of my great Neverland friends. He was always there when I needed him, shoveling snow, chopping firewood, and doing grocery shopping. He carried me into the emergency room when I was too weak to walk, and he was gone when I needed to be alone. Tall, lean, and athletic, with a winning smile and carefree demeanor,

Woog had been delivering firewood for years. He stopped by often after my drama-filled divorce to have coffee or offer to help with chores. One summer day, I came home from work to see his tanned, muscular body in a tank top dancing gracefully on my roof.

Woogie.

Because I tend to think in music and old show tunes, my *Fiddler on the Roof* impulse had me scanning the fields in search of the historical exodus of my Russian ancestors. There was no fiddler to be found, and Joe Edwards, not Tevye, was working the nearby fields.

It turned out that Woogie was painting the roof of my shop. One hand lightly held a rope, and his body swayed rhythmically with the paint sprayer. He smiled, removed his sweat-stained hat, and did a theatrically exaggerated bow. Here was a pure essence of light and playfulness, completely delightful. I laughed out loud.

As time went on, we spent time together hiking with our dogs, playing in the lake, and exploring vast expanses of wilderness and remains of mostly abandoned towns where his forbears had mined gold long ago. In time, I realized how strongly I was drawn to this man of light who was fifteen years my junior.

We looked at one another differently the morning of the first big snowfall, and with dogs bounding around us, we fell to the soft ground and were consumed by passion. That passion continued to consume us for many years to come; we had a grand time and perfect understanding.

Inevitable gossips did what they did, of course. We wished them well and went about our lives walking in fields of smiles. They lost their footing when met with unapologetic honesty.

"Right, he's really young," I'd say. "Great sex — lots of great sex. And your point is?"

Label, label, label.

Woogie came complete with a cosmic creature in the form of a dog named

Snoogie. He had a blue eye, a brown eye, a short spotted coat, and was as irrepressibly joyous as his person when he wagged his entire body rather than live in the box where dogs wag only their tails.

Snoogie was secretly smitten with my mature heeler, Molly, who enjoyed his boyish antics but gave him the requisite snarl every so often for good measure. It's true — Snoogie and Woogie. Honest.

Angels.

• • •

Forty-seven weeks went by. My blood work remained stable, and I miraculously still had my job. Congratulations were in order when the last blood test was drawn at the lab in McCall. Woog drove me down the hill to the hepatitis specialist in Boise, where I would be certain to get a gold medal or plaque suitable for framing. No, more likely it will be that sword-on-the-shoulder thing that King Arthur does with people he likes. In the grand scheme of life and time and musicals, Lancelot and Guinevere had not yet sung "I Loved You Once in Silence," which meant that Camelot was alive and well.

When Wendy summoned me from the waiting room and I looked in her eyes, my heart stuck in my throat and I couldn't breathe. She led me to the room where Dr. Jensen waited, and I broke down before a word was spoken. I sobbed quietly, and my skeletal body curled into itself, slumping toward the clinic floor.

"The virus broke through, Hilary. I've never seen this before."

Oh dear God, NO.

Negative at three, six, nine months — negative, negative, no trace of the hep C virus. Until yesterday.

"I'm so sorry. No real point in trying again. Your side effects were too severe. Go get strong."

NO WAY. HOLY SHIT.

I boarded the plane to Zihuatanejo, Mexico, two days later and ordered a margarita.

What the hell.

At least I looked good in a bathing suit. Strength returned slowly as the tropical breezes coaxed the cobwebs from my brain. Long walks in the sand reminded me that the ground beneath these feet is as temporary as a lifetime, to be washed away with the next tide. The Spirit of Oceans remembered my name — knew me as a child, a wayward teen, a woman, knew to lovingly remind me of the many lessons I had learned on her shores.

I remembered. I would just keep going, that's all. Move forward without fear just as I always did.

I'd come to Mexico to recharge my battery. I'd flown down with my friend Barbara, who wanted a break from the snow and had been planning this trip to help me celebrate the successful year of treatment.

Yes, I do think I'll lie here on this lounge chair under the palapa and order a piña colada while I read my book, thank you very much. After the warm shower in the four-star hotel, we can walk the few blocks into Ixtapa for dinner and drinks.

I know, Barbara — how about if you go shop while I sit by the ice cream vendor's cart and speak my long-ago Spanish, because I want to talk with the little children whose mothers sit down the street encouraging them to ask tourists for money? The tiny ones with liquid eyes, dark-skinned, barefoot, scraped knees, long hair, bringing pesos to mama so they can have dinner.

"Hola, hijita. Hello, little one. Will your mama mind if you talk with me? Do you go to school? What must you think of us, the foreigners who throw pesos to the wind when your little brother is hungry? Tell me, little one. I care about you. Yes, I still care. I still believe that I am here to reach out, to stretch beyond my limits in order to understand humanity. Si, mi niño, you have far more to teach me than I you. I will fill your pockets with gold. Tell me something of your world if you can trust me enough to speak."

What hypocrite can feel love for beggar children of the night and wake up in a crispy white hotel suite for another day of lazing in the sun?

Me.

I may be honest about it, but it's still hypocrisy.

• • •

Back in the snow and back to the office. I was weak, but tanned, rested, and finished with Interferon. The rest of the winter would fly by, as I was able to exercise again and get the poisons out of my system. When I shook my head to clear the haze in my office, it was actually in pretty good shape, especially given the fact that I'd been gone for almost a year.

Dr. Johnny, my cosmic psychiatrist angel, was around with his gray, curly hair and boisterous, self-important drawl.

Billy the Woogster flashed his charm as winter turned to spring and shoveling snow transitioned to slogging-through-mud season. He remains a smile disguised as a man-child.

• • •

The year of brutal hep C treatment had bashed me about and left me fighting against a wind so powerful that when I tried to move forward, my body was held up at an impossible angle. I knew that I had to fight until I summoned enough strength to put one foot down in front of the other. There in Limbo, I recalled the hurricanes of my youth when the wind had been my ally, and I trusted it to take me where it would.

In this new scenario, I willed the Interferon to leave my body and brain, release me from its grip, and let me continue my life. I expected that any day now I'd be back to my old self. Because the well-being of our patients was partially dependent on my ability to function both professionally and intuitively, I tried with all my might to make my way out of the fog. Try as I might, though, my office became a cave where I often sat, head pounding, wearing sunglasses as I tried to do paperwork using the 20-watt bulb I'd put in the desk lamp.

Interferon is known to cause extreme fatigue, body aches, and nausea along with changes in cognition and mood. The side effects most often go away once the drug is withdrawn, but we slowly recognized that having gone into it with compromised cognition, the side effects might well be permanent. I wasn't bouncing back, and I wasn't going to.

For many years, I'd had the blessing of loving every minute of every day of my work. Now John and I realized that I could no longer effectively manage the responsibilities of my job.

I had to stop working.

For the second time in my life, part of me hadn't come back.

That realization was one of the saddest moments of my life.

I cried.

He hugged me.

I was officially "disabled."

Molly

The plane touched down. Aunt Kathy would be doing her drive-bys around the front of the terminal. The Boise airport was familiar — off the plane, short walk to the escalator down, and at the curb in two minutes. When Kathy and her car stopped, I opened the door, tossed my small bag in the back seat, and got in beside her.

"Thanks again, Kath. I appreciate you, you know. And I like your hair." She looked over at me and smiled.

I'd met Kathy twenty years ago when Michael and I were living in the tipi outside of Idaho City. Our ex-husbands had been best friends since the third grade. Taller than me, at 5'11", Kathy kept her hair short in various shades of blond. With a bird-like quality about her, she moved quickly and flitted about, never quite landing.

Molly had stayed with Aunt Kathy while I was gone. I was seeing Ron in Seattle and had gone back and forth several times during the past few months. I didn't like leaving Molly, but she and Kathy had known each other forever, and I knew she was safe, loved, and spoiled. Kathy asked about Ron, about Seattle, and we talked easily as she headed down State Street to her place.

As she unlocked the door, Molly looked up from the comfort of her doggie bed in the living room. I set my bag on the floor and went to give her a hug. Molly didn't get up to greet me, but her eyes held mine tightly. When I

Molly.

sat on the floor, she reached over with her paw, touched my arm, and settled her head on my lap. Something was very wrong.

Kathy was bustling about in the kitchen. I could already smell the french roast brewing.

"What's been going on here?" I asked Kathy and Molly at the same time. I looked over at Kathy since she was the human and allegedly had better communication skills.

"Oh, Miss Molly has been a little tired. She hasn't wanted to do much — goes out back, does her business, and lays on her bed. I figured she was depressed because you were gone."

With Kathy's answer spoken, I turned to Molly. She and I had been inseparable for eighteen years.

"What, baby girl?" Lounging on the dog bed with her, I picked up the slightly overweight blue heeler and put her on my lap. She snuggled into me with all her might and wagged her stub of a tail. I held her and rocked her for a while before telling her about Ron and apologizing for leaving her. I had been gone four days. When I tenderly lifted her chin to look into her eyes, I saw tears. We sat on the dog bed holding each other tightly.

Molly was articulate and spoke far more clearly than anyone I'd ever known. Kathy stood in the kitchen looking at us, saying nothing. She handed me a cup of coffee. Tears filled my heart.

"I'm gonna go to Misty's, Kath. I haven't seen her for a while, and I want to catch her before she goes to school or work. "

I went outside, unlocked the Subaru, and threw everything in the back. Then I carefully folded the blanket I kept in the car and laid it gently on the front passenger seat. When I went back in, Molly hadn't moved a muscle. When she looked at me beseechingly, I thought I felt my heart crack. Without hesitation, I walked over, picked her up, and hugged her close. I carried her out and laid her on the folded blanket as I told her all about going to see Misty, having a boney, and driving home. A hug and another thank you to Kathy, and we headed toward Misty's place.

When we got there, Molly looked out the car window and saw Misty through the sliding glass door. Her little stub tail did the wag and she insisted on getting out on her own. She took a few labored steps, did her doggy duties, and the three of us sat on the grass in the sun and visited awhile. Misty couldn't remember much of her life before throwing tennis balls for Molly. She'd been five when we got her and would soon turn twenty-three.

"Is she okay, Mom?"

"I don't really think so, sweetie."

Another heart crack. Two, I counted, as I felt Misty's do the same as mine. We talked about school, work, life, men, friends — everything but Molly. As the sun went down, we went inside. Each step Molly took was painful to watch, but she would have none of that "being carried" business now.

Doug, Misty's husband, got home. I liked this man. My daughter had married him on a whim, thinking that marriage was a club she wanted to join.

I sat on the couch with Molly on my lap. When she moved to get down, I helped her. As her feet hit the floor, she immediately lay down and began a series of coughing and choking spasms. They went on for a minute while Misty ran to grab Molly's water bowl and set it in front of her. Molly thanked her, took a sip, and relaxed her head on Misty's foot. We sat like that, and ten minutes later the spasms started again, this time more violently and urgently.

My daughter and I looked at each other. We didn't need words. I held my best friend until her body calmed again.

"How far?"

"Four minutes."

We moved quickly, then. Silently. Misty pulled her little purple car to the front door, jumped out, and opened the passenger side as I got in holding Molly. Misty shut the door, and within thirty seconds, we were driving 70 miles an hour to the vet, screeching to a stop at the entrance.

"I'll be right in."

"Okay."

It was a new clinic, well appointed and shiny. I was in a trance. I waved off the usual greetings, forms, questions, and announced the biggest emergency in the history of the world.

"Molly is sick."

We were ushered into one of the rooms as soon as I pulled a credit card from my wallet, and Molly was on one of those cold steel tables being examined within a few minutes — not even her customary "I don't wanna see the vet" protest. Her brown eyes bored into me as I held her on the table. The on-call doctor examined her and then said she'd like to do an x-ray and some blood work.

"Of course, whatever she needs."

"Okay, will you please wait in the lobby? We're going to take her back to another area. I'll come out and get you."

"Of course, whatever she needs." Misty watched me stumble out of the exam room in my trance. "She's okay. They're just doing some tests," I explained.

Misty and I sat side by side in a corner of the lobby in silence. We both knew better than to look at each other, because all that was left were lies. When the reception person headed toward us with a clipboard, Misty reached out and said that she would take care of the forms. Name, rank, and serial number. Done and done. She returned it to the desk.

After a very long time, the vet came out. An attractive young woman, long blond hair framed her face with loose curls, and her eyes were filled with compassion. Her name was Lillian.

"Come back," she invited. Misty and I followed her together, and Molly was relieved to see us. I sat on the exam table and lifted her onto my lap.

"She should stay here tonight. The x-rays don't show anything, but I can't get the blood work results until the morning. We may need to do more tests when the lab gets those back to us."

"I'm taking her with me. I'll check in with you early."

We went back to Misty's. The convulsions had stopped now. Molly took a few sips of water and lay down. A few minutes later, she threw up the water. I went into the bathroom with her, and we lay on the tile floor. Blankets and some pillows appeared as Doug and Misty went about the business of turning their bathroom into a hospital room for Molly. I thanked them from Trance Land.

We lay awake all night, Molly and me, talking, hugging, laughing about old times, saying our goodbyes without either of us admitting what we were doing. We had a blanket under us and one wrapped around us. Our heads shared the pillow. We were at peace. No more spasms, just us.

Doug and Misty used the neighbor's bathroom.

• • •

As the sun came up, we looked at each other and Molly told me it was time for us to go. I got up quietly, wrote a "have a nice day — we'll be fine" note, and snuck out before anyone woke up. We easily made our way back to the clinic, and I carried her in the door.

Incredibly, the kind blond doctor was still working. She opened an exam room door, and we went in. I laid Molly gently on her blanket and settled in beside her.

"The blood work shows liver damage. Severe liver damage. Unusual for liver disease to get to such an advanced state without warning signs. I'm so sorry."

Several months had passed since I'd finished my year of hep C treatment. That year Molly was the only one who stuck with me every minute of every day, lying on the couch with me when I was unable to move. Through all the hospitalizations, pain, work, and drugs, Molly had watched me every minute, silently offering the support I'd so desperately needed. We had laughed and cried together, crawled to the kitchen to feed ourselves, waded through snow, reveled in sunshine. Together.

I'd been devastated when the virus had broken through at the end of the year. Crushed. When Dr. Jensen explained that another liver biopsy was the only way to clearly assess how the treatment regimen had impacted my liver, I'd decided to have one. The procedure had been done just before I'd left for Seattle. The results would be in any day.

I looked at my friend, then leaned over so we were nose to nose, eye to eye. "Molly," I whispered, "what is this all about? I'm the one with liver damage, silly girl. Not you."

Barely able to move, she held my gaze, smiled sadly, and managed to wiggle her head even closer to mine.

I knew.

She knew.

She had managed to take on part of the illness that threatened my life, to give me the ultimate gift. She had chosen to take the agonizing pain and debilitating weakness in order to give me a chance to live on more comfortably.

Animals understand life on a level far deeper than most humans. They give unselfishly, love unconditionally, and, when we let them, teach us to take love to a higher, purer level. As Molly snuggled me with all that was left of her, we vowed that we would never part.

"What do you need from me?" Lillian asked quietly.

My head was down. I nodded, still in the trance. "We'll need a few minutes."

"Of course you will." She left the room.

Here we were, Molly and me, on the floor together again, loving each other. I whispered to her quietly. I don't know if I whispered words or thoughts or feelings. I was holding back the floodgates.

The exam room door opened without warning, and a young woman barged in and stood over us. "I'll need a credit card."

Really. That's what she said. I felt my blood boil. I didn't move, but glared up at this fool and struggled to keep my tone level.

"You *what*? What the holy living fucking hell is wrong with you, you goddamn idiot? You *fucking* insensitive bitch. How fucking *dare* you come in like this when my friend is so sick?"

I didn't want an answer. I just wanted her to go away and die of heartlessness. I reached across the floor for my purse, took a credit card out of my wallet, and threw it in her general direction. "Take the mother-fucking thing and get out. Now."

She did.

I resumed the position with Molly, which actually hadn't changed much in the past twenty-four hours. After another fifteen minutes, there was a light tap on the door. Dr. Compassion opened it a crack and asked if she could come in. I nodded, exhausted and beaten. She had "the needle."

No words again. Lillian looked at me. I looked at Molly, then turned back to the vet and nodded. She joined us on the floor. I held Molly tenderly while clutching her heart in my hands with all the strength of my being. She looked me squarely in the eyes, completely alert and aware. As she held my gaze, my heart was reflected in her eyes. She neither broke the gaze nor flinched as the needle was injected.

When the storm blew up in her eyes, I saw an instant of surprise followed by love, gratitude, and relief. All of that passed between our knowing in less than a second.

Then I cried. Sobbed. For weeks. Months. I cry as I write this, nine years later. The picture of Molly's eyes is as clear to me today as it was the day she left. A profound moment of energy shifting. I believe she saw All That Is before she closed her eyes.

• • •

I would pick up her ashes, I told them. We would take one last hike to

Boulder Lake. When I walked out, the bright sunlight hit me, and I moved quickly to hide from the light of day. I started the engine. The furry blanket was still folded on the seat next to me. I instinctively turned on the CD player. Ron had given me some CDs, and Misty had loaded them in the player. The sleepless night and grief intensified the trance as I sat alone in the parking lot with my shattered heart.

The music engulfed me, and I slumped over the steering wheel. Molly's voice was cleverly disguised as Bono of U2 fame, reminding me that she was still with me:

"I see seven towers
But I only see one way out,
You got to cry without weeping,
Talk without speaking,
Scream without raising your voice."

"Just like you always did, baby girl. I'll do my best," I told the music.

"You know I took the poison
From the poison stream
Then I floated out of here
Singing … la la la la de day
La la la de day
La la la de day,

"And the storm blows up in her eyes
She will …
Suffer the needle chill
She's running to stand …
Still."

That's exactly what happened.

When I picked up her ashes, I was told that the final labs showed that she had end-stage liver disease, that her liver was almost fully consumed with dead tissue.

The next morning, Dr. Jensen phoned to tell me that though my hep C virus had broken through, the biopsy showed that my liver condition had dramatically improved from stage three-and-a-half to an entirely manageable stage one.

Thank you, Molly.

There was snow at Boulder Lake when Molly and I headed up together for

Molly and me at Boulder Lake.

the last time. Boulder is where the spirits I have loved the most gather, where I am closest to my source and essence. I didn't need snowshoes yet, not like when our pilot friend Ernie died last winter. I stood at the edge of the pristine lake and spread Molly's ashes with her song playing on my headphones. When the bald eagle soared overhead, my knees buckled. I dropped to the ground on the muddy shore, my hands in the icy water, touching Molly one last time.

• • •

Eight years passed before Alfie won my heart. Though I'd already had the perfect dog, there was something about this breeder's throwaway that made his way to my core.

Alfa Romeo Pellegrino (pronounced like the car and the water), aka Alfie, has charisma. He is an Australian labradoodle — a newfangled, expensive designer-mutt breed — but his fur does not meet "breed standard," so he is therefore an outcast. While his littermates sold for $2,500, little Alf was going to be tossed away. The breeder clearly told us that she "could not have her customers see *that*."

At the time, I was working with a service dog agency to acquire a dog for assistance with mobility. I could get rid of my cane and use a dog for balance and stability. I'd been introduced to no fewer than ten potential doggie partners with whom I did not connect. Perhaps I'm picky.

When my second husband Ron and I went to see this outcast pup, he made my entire being smile. Still does. He is absolutely an old soul with an uncanny ability to read my mind, anticipate my needs, and keep my brain from exploding.

I'm frequently asked what kind of dog he is. Tired of the world of doodle snobbery with its endless conversations about the five breeds that make up this third-generation Australian labradoodle, one day I simply answered the question with, "He's a Smile."

That has been my answer ever since, and not only is it true, but it makes people nod their heads and smile. Always.

Mary and Tink sent Alfie. Definitely.

I took the caramel-colored, smoke-eyed puppy to the lake near my house the day we met. Springtime mud surrounded the water that beckoned me and my yellow kayak to paddle away to peace. In the lake, I renew myself and my spirit is most alive.

The pup ran through mud puddles with abandon, a run for his own sake, for the sheer joy of being a puppy and being free. Alfie found the deepest pile of mud and dove in: "Yippee, I'm full of mischief and trouble!" I watched and shared his glee, laughed aloud at his antics as my heart warmed despite the biting wind.

I looked at the mountains and thought of Molly. When I dropped my eyes to the lake in front of me, a brand-new, shiny tennis ball drifted near the shore. No one in sight, not a soul.

Thank you, Molly, for dropping that bally. Thank you for your blessing and for the speckle of soul you saw fit to share with the silly little Alfster. Thank you for bringing me this wise old soul.

I know that your spirit lives both in my heart and in this world of nature that we both love.

I know that my daily routine is but an illusion called "life."

It is here in the natural world, here, at the shore of this spectacular lake, that reality begins.

Ron

Ron and I were familiar and comfortable together from the moment we met. We shared a New York something, and I knew that we had laughed and loved in other lifetimes in other places. We had much to learn from one another and, unbeknownst to us, we were not to have nearly as much time together as either of us would have liked.

• • •

I met Ron at an Indian casino the summer I finished Hep C treatment.

I played the poker machines on occasion, and he was playing the machine next to mine one Saturday afternoon. A random drive had landed me there. Molly was waiting outside the door. Molly knew it never took long for me to lose the $25 limit I set for myself. I'd chosen a row of machines that allowed her to see me, so she would sit there until hell froze over.

Ron's heavy New York accent took me home and reminded me of my past. When the server came by, he came over and asked me if I wanted anything from the bar. *Big accent, big man, big attitude, big charm.*

"I'll have a Diet Coke, thanks."

As we continued to play the machines, we began to talk. He lived in Seattle and was some kind of mucky-muck money guy doing stocks and bonds

Ron.

and other stuff I didn't understand. His easy manner and quick-witted New York edge had been tossed in the blender of my childhood and was familiar and comfortable. When he realized that the dog sitting at alert and staring intently through the glass doors was mine, he began to fret about her, asking if she was okay, worrying that she would run away, that she needed a drink, or that someone would steal her.

"She's fine. She knows I'm in here."

"But-but-but-but-but what if she … how can she …?"

Soft heart, I thought. *Good man.* "She's fine."

We exchanged emails and phone numbers.

Disabled

Disabled.

The dis-ability needed a proper label in order to fit in the disabled box that pays money. It was apparent that the year of hep C treatment had taken a toll on my ability to function and that I was unable to continue working.

Given my New York history of a hypoxic brain injury, I was referred for extensive neuropsychological testing. Such testing provides information about cognitive, motor, and executive functioning and includes evaluation of memory, thinking, and attention. I spent two frustrating (and at times tearful) days trying to fit square pegs into round holes, counting backward, and trying to remember various lists and stories, mostly to no avail. The results, combined with an MRI of my brain that clearly showed an enchanting arrangement of inappropriately placed white streaks, resulted in the official diagnosis of "organic brain syndrome with cognitive impairment." In other words, it was scientifically proven that my residency on this plane of existence was definitely tenuous.

Bingo.

The label made no difference to me. The bottom line was that I'd landed further away from this realm than I'd been before. The further away one lives, the more difficult the commute.

Grasping the whole "disabled" thing was a challenge. What does it mean? "Not able"? Not able to what? Not able to tolerate absurdity or societal bullshit? Discombobulated? Doomed? Blessed? Terminally unique?

"Dis-abled" — not able to function in my bureaucratic job despite the post-first-treatment perk of having landed a few feet farther from the ground, allowing me to connect and communicate with crazy people with greater ease? Though connecting is not the part that brings in the paychecks, is it? We must do the paperwork and document journeys to other realities in clinical terminology in order to justify our work because helping crazy people love themselves unconditionally and live a reasonable quality of life is not measurable treatment.

I realized that my brain might be a mess, but I still had my body. I packed up my life; set aside my beloved work, my wannabe hick life, and my forever love affair with Woogie; and moved on. Having been properly wined and dined by the charming New Yorker, Ron and I had decided to build a future together. I headed the U-Haul toward Seattle. Ron was magnetically extraordinary and gently powerful, confident within himself and decidedly sophisticated. I deserved a man with brains, strength, and tenderness as I took this next step forward.

The luxury of time was new to me; I had the freedom to do as I pleased. It pleased me to walk; it pleased me to wander the waterfront and ride my bicycle and be with a man who treated me like a queen. It pleased me to be a walker in her walking world singing loudly and out of tune, moving to the beat of a different drummer.

My always magical headphones afford me the privacy that precludes small talk and other distractions. I'm in charge of what, if anything, I choose to let in. I like that. I stop to talk with people at times — street performers, downtown loners, meth addicts. I step inside the shoes of invisible companions speaking with their creators, the lonesome souls of the sidewalks and parks who wear the "mentally ill" neon blinking placard that keeps most people away; I remain still and was always drawn to my brother and sister outcasts.

• • •

One day, I fell down on the sidewalk.

Hard.

With no warning whatsoever.

I got up, bought some Band-Aids, and kept going.

The next week I fell harder. I fell forward on the concrete and ended up lying face down, scraped, bruised, and bloody on a busy sidewalk. People gathered around, kindly asking what they could do to help.

"Stay away," I thought. "Stay away from my blood. If you get near my contaminated blood, you will be infected. I may look innocent, but I am a murderess in disguise." I politely declined help, sat on the bloody sidewalk, and called Ron on my cell. He was there in a heartbeat. I was hurt. It was time to go to a doctor.

Let's get a couple of things clear:

I have not a stoic bone in my body.

I see no nobility in suffering.

I am not afraid of much, including death.

I have, in my entire life, had but one memorable fear.

What I know of fear is to honor it.

I'm going to share my memorable fear because I want to.

I lived on a mountain in Idaho for over twenty years, and the entire time I was terrified of driving the 80 miles of curvy highway to Boise during the winter months. Unconditionally petrified for no logical reason. Rather than having to come up with an excuse every time I needed to go to the city, I implemented a rule: I don't drive the canyon in the winter. Period.

You don't have to give a reason if it's a rule.

When I felt fear, I simply honored it before it had a chance to consume me. Perhaps my intuition has gained strength because it appreciates being honored. Not once did I drive the treacherous road in the winter. Ever.

Twenty years in the mountains. Geographically isolated, yes, but circle-of-life boundaries pulsate, morphing their limits so that they may gather that which will be useful at another time, on another ride.

Falling down wasn't frightening. It was interesting from all of my perspectives. Falling down was the catalyst that brought me back to my circle.

• • •

I know that I digress. I leave gaping holes in my story. This is neither intentional nor unintentional; it is simply my way. Inner dialogue flows easily through my fingers whereas I struggle in vain with any attempt to be linear. I am digressing again, but I must in order to connect some important points of my story.

• • •

Through a series of "nothing is random" events, Misty was diagnosed with Fetal Alcohol Spectrum Disorder (FASD) when she was eight years old. At that point, we became involved in research studies being conducted at the University of Washington's world-renowned Fetal Alcohol and Drug Unit.

There was a working definition: FASD is an umbrella term describing the range of effects that can occur in an individual whose mother drank alcohol during pregnancy. These may be mental, behavioral, and/or learning disabilities with possible lifelong implications.

I have an intensely personal knowing that has become valuable on both a personal and professional level. As a birth mother and professional, I was a rarity, as the majority of affected children are either adopted or in foster care. There had been trips to Seattle for testing and evaluations, and we were recruited to participate in a cutting-edge research study.

After a brief period of intense and unproductive guilt, I'd turned it around, devoured information, and become a workshop presenter and resource in the field. It was, at the time, groundbreaking work, and I became one of a handful of respected presenters to conduct workshops nationwide. Experts at the University of Washington encouraged us to educate mental health professionals, law enforcement, teachers, judges, and other parents, helping them to recognize, understand, and deal productively with the fallout from the invisible epidemic. I contributed articles to the few publications dedicated to FASD, organized conferences, and spoke with the knowledge and awareness born of inner knowing.

I attended an FASD conference shortly after my move to Seattle. I was stopped in my tracks during a presentation when, on the large screen before me, I read one of my own ponderings:

"How can a child who gets straight A's in school not understand that when she is rude to her friends they get upset with her?"

ICEBERG FASD Newsletter

University of Washington

Hilary O'Loughlin, 1991

A dilemma I'd outlined in a long ago article had caught the eye of a professor and researcher at the University of California in San Diego and spawned a research study. Scientists were using MRIs to study brain structure and finding

Conquering Obstacles

Dr. Anne Streissguth, angel professor, researcher, director of UW fetal alcohol and drug unit.

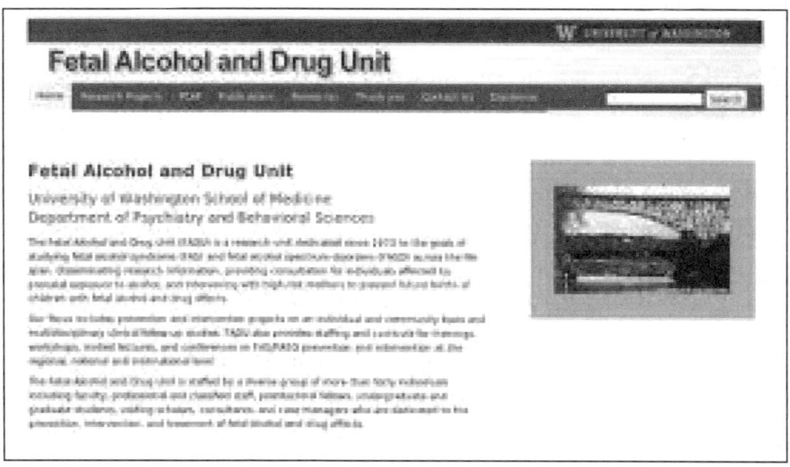

very specific differences in the brain structure of children affected by maternal alcohol use. One example is in the *corpus collosum*, the ridge that connects the left and right sections of the brain. Its job is to quietly network information; it connects the dots, so to speak, thereby providing us the ability to understand such things as the relationship between actions and consequences. Studies show that in children with FASD, the *corpus collosum* is either smaller in size or, in some cases, completely absent.

Circles are Circles are Circles.

From a traditional mental health vantage point, Misty was labeled with a myriad of psychiatric diagnoses and had fourteen involuntary psychiatric hospitalizations between the ages of fourteen and twenty-two. Tremendous efforts were made to place her in a box, any box that would provide explanations and a direction for treatment. Bipolar disorder, major depression with psychotic features, borderline personality disorder, schizoid with FASD, and the list goes on and on. Medications were ordered and treatment protocols implemented. Every effort was made to manage her inner nightmares, all to no avail.

Today, Misty Dawn struggles with might and power. Her superior intellect combined with behaviors and perceptions that are painfully different cause her to be labeled "mentally ill." While Tender Hearts are honored in other cultures, they suffer unfathomable pain when society tries to smash them into the limited boxes of American culture.

Misty Tender Heart's "disabled" label doesn't suit her. She is quite able. She is an old, wise soul born into a body that she is slowly destroying with razors, knives, bulimia, and other unimaginable forms of self-harm in an attempt to ease the intense agony with which she lives. Her body bears the scars of a thousand centuries.

The circle turned as the University of Washington's ten-year longitudinal research study showed that those with the highest levels of intellectual functioning suffer the most significant secondary disabilities. Misty was at the top of that list. Her ability to understand the nature of her difficulties causes a lifetime cycle of angst. The lead researcher and undisputed queen of the Fetal Alcohol and Drug Unit is a silver-haired marvel who has devoted several lifetimes to helping children. Misty Dawn is well known as one of "Ann's kids," and as such, their connection is profound.

Yes, whirling like a tornado, the circle had indeed established a deep connection to the University of Washington, which would play a crucial role in the next step of my life.

• • •

I definitely needed help for what was going on in my physical body. I was at my wit's end, not far from my wit's beginning, and desperate for direction. Fortunately my wit's end picked up the phone and called Ann. Ann had a friend, she said, a psychiatrist who she thought could help me, and she would make a call. Ten minutes later, I had an appointment.

Dr. Conway is a smart, highly respected professor, a key figure at the top rung of the university ladder. She has helped me tremendously. Shortly after our first meeting, as the circle continued its motion, she and Dr. Idaho met at a conference.

Coincidence?

I don't think so.

Their discussion paved the way for collaborative treatment efforts that would not otherwise have come to pass. I was efficiently routed to some of the top physicians and researchers in the world.

Batteries of tests and consultation led me to a neurologist who, it turned out, is an undercover angel. Tricky. Disguised as a mild-mannered neurologist at the University of Washington, Dr. Mannis was immediately familiar. He had a sparkle in his eyes, a melodious timbre to his voice, and moved about with his feet not quite touching the floor.

He was expecting me when I entered his kingdom, the Neurology Clinic. Here I was again, thirty-five years and several worlds away from Mount Sinai, and I was flunking the rudimentary "can you feel the pin?" test. I couldn't feel the pin. No sensation on my feet, ankles, or shins, which is not a good sign. I didn't think it was so bad, though, because it didn't hurt; it was just numb.

"Peripheral neuropathy. How can you walk as you do, Hilary? People with neuropathy don't walk up and down the hills of Seattle all day long."

"Nothing hurts, Dr. Angel," I responded, "except the falling down, which hurts my pride."

I got a cane and resumed my wanderings, albeit with caution, until the day numbness gave way to excruciating pain with every step.

Medical minds were fascinated. Dr. Undercover had to know what was going on — why was there numbness without pain for so long before every step suddenly became unbearable? What do we do when a brain is unable to tolerate any of the medications used to relieve neuropathic pain? What combination of factors makes this body and brain such a challenge to some of the most highly regarded physicians in the country? More tests. A nerve biopsy, a muscle biopsy. A trip in a dark, whirling time capsule that assessed balance while I journeyed to outer space with a brief stop on the North Star. As scalpels pierced my skin in search of answers, my body became exhausted trying to heal from each exploratory expedition.

They told me that I was presenting a complicated and fascinating combination of symptoms. It was as if they knew that I was complicit in their higher cause.

"If my body can help you learn and potentially help others, I am deeply honored." And so the journey continued. In my most intense moments of pain, I longed for ways to move freely, painlessly, in the natural world I love.

Keep moving forward.

Kayak

My daughter Misty came to my rescue.

The Great Northwest is not the ideal spot for being outdoors all year round unless you are a duck.

I am not a duck, nor do I aspire to be one.

I want to be outside and active, but such a seemingly simple desire becomes complicated when a body is uncooperative. My body craves exercise as it craved heroin on South Beach.

Bright and early one Mother's Day morning, my daughter and her boyfriend, Luke, pulled in the driveway.

"Come on, Mom! It's Mommy Day — come with us."

I hobbled outside and got in the car. Walking had become so painful that I avoided every step I could. They drove me the quarter mile to the small marina on the edge of our lake.

"Come on, Mom. You can use Luke's kayak — that blue one. I'll take the yellow one my friend Paul gave me. A Mommy Day mother-daughter kayak! Yeah, let's go."

The sun was out, the lake smooth as glass. I easily slipped on the life jacket and settled myself into the sleek kayak. Luke handed me a paddle, helped Misty into her kayak, and smiled his oh-so-charming smile. "Have fun, you two!"

Feeling Free

Mother's Day kayaking.

Feeling the freedom.

I was off like a racehorse leaving the paddock, never looking anywhere but forward. I headed toward a small island several miles out and south of the marina. The thickly wooded, house-less island was a beacon of mystery in such a densely populated environment. When I reached the island, I paddled around it twice, exploring with my eyes before heading south as the kayak glided effortlessly through the stillness of the morning.

I was free! I felt renewed, strong, and blessed. Energy flowed into my pores with every stroke as I began feeling suspiciously like a human being. *My GOD, this is perfect. This is a way for me to move and be free, to feel powerfully alone in nature with my higher power. YES.* It had been far too long. This was precisely what I'd been missing, craving, needing. My baby-big-grown-up-child-woman-daughter-person understood. So alike in our need for solitude and independence in nature. Misty Dawn got it. Just because my legs and feet have issues doesn't mean the rest of my body should have to follow suit. Two days later, I was in the Costco parking lot watching a bright yellow kayak being tied to the top of my faithful old Subaru.

The kayak has kept me relatively sane for years now. Regardless of what goes on around me, Old Yeller relaxes in her bunk on the kayak racks, always ready and eager to go. The instant we hit the water, I'm free. A smile fills my heart and power fills my soul. Every time. In the middle of the lake, I feel God's presence. Past, present, and future merge to become one timeless, invisible entity, and my senses become vitally alive.

There's always a place.

There's always a way to get there.

How could I have let myself lose sight of that?

No matter, the knowing had returned, and now I would hold on to it with all my might. Misty's Tender Heart understood the moment I paddled past her without looking back. This time, my little love had walked through space and time to remind me that the arms of Mother Nature are always ready to take me in, body and soul, and hold me until I am at peace.

• • •

As I paddled, I seamlessly drifted into the time we know as the past, my own past, and felt myself step out of the kayak. My feet felt the earth of the Greek Island of Ios in 1972. Alfie faded into the future as I stepped comfortably off the ship that had taken us to what was then the next step on my path.

During those times, no decisions were being made; the future was simply laid at my feet in the moment, and I moved forward without hesitation.

When the boat docked in Ios, it looked no different from any of the other isles — same white stone village, same white church with the blue cross. The small island had no roads, no cars, and one mule. The village consisted of a tiny market and a café. Seafood was fresh and sold at a stand in the town square. That was it.

On a stone stool in the café, I traded drachmas for ouzo and octopus. A group of headbanded hippies wandered in and instantly befriended me.

"We have a place," my brand-new friend Annie told me. "We're going back in an hour or so. Why don't you come stay with us?"

"Okay."

Leaving the village, we walked through Sapikota Valley past small groups of stone shelters where extended families had lived for centuries. The island's mule argued with little boys about whether or not it would move. We walked for miles along a windy dirt path that served as the island's main road. Olive trees were as plentiful as the barefoot children playing in the footsteps of their ancestors. Many of the caves dotting the hills had been transformed into homey hippie shelters complete with kerosene lamps and cooking fires. Eventually, a headbanded hippie named Liam took my arm, turned me toward the sea, and pointed at a white dot at the bottom of a steep hill.

"Home," he said.

We descended slowly as the white dot morphed into a stately abandoned villa set on a private beach. People came out to greet us speaking the universal language of friendship, all in their own native tongues.

The villa, like the other buildings on Ios, was made of white stone. It boasted arches for doors, stone floors, a spacious kitchen with a massive built-in (carved-in?) stone table with bench seats that could easily host twenty people. One of the expansive rooms had a tree growing up through the floor with the top somewhere above the roof.

"How respectful," I thought, "the house had chosen to become a shrine to the tree rather than disturb it."

Out the front door, a graceful stone staircase led to the beach where two or three naked bodies lay in the sand. I stayed. The simplicity of island living suited me. Supplies were carried from the village and seafood came from the sea. True to our hippiedom, we luxuriated in the blessings of our paths.

Adonis (yes, really) came from Athens to Ios to see one of his friends, a

Ios, Greece, 1972

The villa on Ios.

Staircase from villa to beach, Ios.

It's all about perspective. Parthenon, Athens: inside looking out.

Adonis.

Greek named Atraeus, who had landed at the villa. He was exquisite. My friends laughed and waved their hands in front of my eyes trying to break the spell. Was he real? Come on — Adonis, Greek island, castle, he and I in one of those Hallmark commercials where the rest of the world fades into a mist leaving only the couple to approach one another with burning passion? He was tall, strong, tanned, broad-shouldered, bearded, and worried, with dark eyes like burning coals. When I welcomed him into my tree room, his gentle Greek god soul held me, his dark eyes shared his deepest secrets, and his powerful body enveloped mine.

We had just over two months together before three men in military uniforms came hiking down the hill with walking staffs, holstered pistols, and serious rifles strapped around their shoulders. They cordially ordered the two Greek men to return with them to Athens, where they would face charges related to their political actions and beliefs. They were rebels against the status quo, and our haven was, for a short time, their refuge and hiding place. Neither man offered resistance. Adonis held me with secret whispers before he faced the soldiers with dignity and pride. Not a glimmer of resistance — I watched five men climb from the valley that day, two of them vowing to return.

I never saw them again.

I watched myself from alternating vantage points and believed that everyone did. I watched my body gain strength, my spirit gain power. I noticed that despite vast quantities of ouzo, I rarely felt impaired. How could I? I wasn't in there drinking if I was watching, now, was I?

We learn from our travels. The Greek people showed me what dignity, pride, honor, and conviction really mean. From treasured children I learned that wealth can be measured in olives, goats, and love. I lived in a fog that was silent and subtle. I heeded whispering voices from beyond, those tender, familiar guides with the road map to my life. After nearly a year in heaven, I boarded a boat to Athens one day heading toward the present.

• • •

The Mother's Day kayak trip sparked a renewed passion for the small vessels bravely maneuvered down rugged Idaho rivers by a younger, stronger me. Now those rivers were a placid lake mostly surrounded by homes and utilized by the citified multitude without a working conceptual understanding of solitude. No matter, I could go to the few private spots, like the tiny island I've claimed (even though it really belongs to a Boy Scout camp). All it took to claim it was a stick, a piece of cloth torn from Alfie's signature red bandana, and an alternate belief system. We paddled to an inlet where no one could see us and proudly planted the stick in the earth like Neil Armstrong planting the American flag on the Moon. "I christen thee … Alf Island."

Done.

And I believe myself.

Once or twice we've been asked to leave by vigilant scoutmasters in (harrumph) motorboats, but for the most part, the teensy area is a playground for me and my Smile (Alfie). We play explorer and say lots of "harks" and "ahoys" and a few "land ho's." He frolics delightfully in the thick forest as I no longer can and makes piles of sticks for a fire in case the weather should suddenly turn and we become stranded. We stash treaties in the dry compartments of the kayak with emergency rations that he fearlessly guards by sitting on the rubber cover of the front hatch. We lounge in the sun; we are transported to other times, other realities.

There we revel in our blessed sanctuary of nature.

It is in nature that I find all that I need. Heaven and earth become one; what is above blends with what is below and all around us. In the natural world, I live in the past, present, and future all at the same time, and I am connected to the awareness that there is no beginning and no end. I am surrounded by higher powers, guardians, angels, and the limitless power of the universe.

• • •

Day-to-day life can take me to a place where I am disconnected from the Essence, a place where I am separated from my protectors and guides. In these alone times, I reflect and remember that I am infinitely blessed. Mary and Tink have, for the most part, arranged throughout my life for my teachers and guides to appear in seamless succession. It is because I am cosmically spoiled that I was surprised several years ago with a loud and clear feeling of stuckness. I felt lost.

It was unfamiliar and uncomfortable, so I decided that I must be found. *Let's see*, I thought, *how does one find oneself?* To begin, one must pose the question. Question posing is similar to prayer when one is asking for guidance. In my world, meaningful prayer is done outdoors and in a proper setting.

Kayaking to Alf Island that breezy summer day, Smile and I had a rousing game of "overboard." That's the one where he pretends to see an underwater monster and ends up in the lake, the monster nipping at his heals as he pleads to be rescued. When I lift him by the handle of his lifejacket, he shows his gratitude by making sure that I am thoroughly soaked. I whack the paddle on the water a few times to let the monster know we'll be back, and we move on. In a secret cove, we maneuver the vessel to a private spot behind some logs and land on our favorite giant lounge chair of a rock.

That day, with laughter in our hearts and the sun on our bodies, the time was right to focus on prayer. I breathed deeply as I prayed aloud with Alfie sitting respectfully still at my side. Of course I was answered. We all are, whether we recognize it or not. Little miracles appear when we least expect them.

Yes!

Land-ho approach to Alf Island.

My kayak, Old Yeller.

Onward

I remembered having met Ariel, an ageless, silver-haired woman, briefly once through my daughter. I easily found her, reminded her of our meeting, and asked quite simply whether she knew of anyone who could find me.

Of course she did.

Ariel gave me the name and phone number of a woman with whom she had been doing spiritual work for many years: Leia. The first time I spoke with Leia, I told her that I was continually being hit on the head with a two-by-four. I explained that I knew there was a lesson to be learned from the repeated blows, but that all I was getting was a headache. In rather short order, Leia explained that I had lost sight of my purpose: to teach and help others. More specifically, she explained that at this point in my life, I was to write. The instant she said those words, the two-by-four splintered before my eyes, the headache subsided, and I recognized Leia as my next guide.

And so it began, this new way of fulfilling my purpose. When I did not know where to start, Leia guided me to the center of my heart. "Begin here, Hilary," she said. "You must stop and reassess, then move onward. In that way you will be able to feel the beginning of your heart."

Stop and reassess? But I've been busy muddling about!

Okay.

Once I did as Leia suggested, I was able to get back up and move onward with purpose.

I knew then as I know now that there are things I need to say. Throughout most of my adult life, I had been a binge writer, creating pieces and middles of this and that. Putting the puzzle pieces together was certainly not something I was able to accomplish alone. I can barely organize myself to get out the door of my house much less organize my Very Important Thoughts in a cohesive manner.

Leia has no computer, no e-mail, no interest in becoming technologically involved with the world. I have mailed sections of my writing to her on paper in envelopes with stamps. I find it satisfying that once the packet is in the mailbox, I have the luxury of not needing to think about what I've sent. It works out perfectly since I don't remember what I've written five minutes after I'm done. Words simply move through me, coming from my higher self, and go directly onto paper. The only part of me that's involved is my fingers because words flow through them. As I write, I am drawn to a special place from which I see and feel where I am now, where I have been before, and where I might be going. These images merge into "now" as I realize that I can be all of this; I can be everywhere at the same time. I am never alone but part of the great universal whole.

Leia is my current guide. Mary, my forever guardian angel, and Tink, my higher self, help me overcome any and all obstacles in my path. I'm pretty sure we all have such entities within us. While mine have never needed an invitation, yours might need to be sought out and nurtured or even given permission to be part of your everyday world.

I know.

But it's true.

I keep saying that because as I write, I have a little trouble believing myself. Then I realize that most of what I write is so outrageous that no one could make it up.

• • •

I know precisely what it is that causes me to be less able. The disability is nebulous in that it is essentially invisible to the naked eye. I live on a platform separated from this existence. I live here with an unreasonably agonizing level of pain and frustration that no one should have to tolerate. I am like a greyhound at the dog track chasing a coveted prize that dangles just out of my reach. I've been on the racetrack for years going round and round, faster and faster, panting, exerting more effort and energy than I ever knew I had. There have been moments when it seemed that if I could summon one more burst of energy, I would catch it; once or twice I might even have brushed its surface, but it's a trickster, this carrot, and it leaps away before I can grab it. It is those times that bring me to my knees. NOOO, I cry, *stop taunting me*.

I can accept whatever life throws my way. If I am not to walk again, then let's get in a wheelchair and carry on. Enigma that I am, though, nothing is certain. It's possible that I could walk again; there's a chance that medical minds could sort out the confusing interconnected diagnoses that render me unable to walk or remember things or tolerate even a moment of stress without my head blowing up. I might conceivably beat the odds and hike to Boulder Lake again. No one can say for certain, so I continue chasing the carrot.

Never give up.

I chase the carrot until I reach my limit.

Reaching one's limit is unrelated to the concept of giving up.

Limits are temporary. They can always be stretched, reshaped, and redefined. The truth is that each of us is as limitless as space and time, with no boundaries, beginnings, or ends. Limits are illusions, delusions, pebbles that we may casually kick out of our way as we move forward. Illness, pain, heartbreak, and life circumstances are all pebbles. There's no point in looking back when we've already kicked our earthly problems off to the side of the road. The kicking is a gentle toss of the foot done in perfect synchronicity to the drumbeat of lessons learned. After that, the only direction is forward. The future is without limits as limits are without limits.

I am clearly not able to do things that I want to do.

Like walk.

Or have thirty seconds of pain-free existence.

Or organize myself in space and time.

I am awakened periodically throughout the night and every morning by pain. When my feet touch the floor, it instantly worsens and continues to increase throughout the day only to reach a crescendo by late afternoon. At its peak, the pain holds me firmly by the back of the neck and repeatedly slams my face into the brick wall of my will. I often storm about the house in my eternal quest to find whatever it is I've misplaced. It's always something — sunglasses, keys, a book, my mind. Storming around means that my body is

Triking on leg braces.

Alfie running beside Trikey near Stickyville.

moving. When my body is moving, my pain is worsening. I rarely stop moving until I reach the limit of my tolerance.

The limit is alive. It beckons, hands gnarled and misshapen, knowing that I am breathing air thick with anger, tears, frustration. Powerful squalls become violent typhoons as energy battles limits of endurance, waging war on obstacles, mightily slaying dragons, shouting battle cries as I fight to free myself from the gnarled hands of limits and the thick, toxic air.

True drama.

I can always escape, though, because I have a secret: I know how to find the rabbit hole to Alice's Wonderland.

Did you think for a moment I wouldn't?

This particular hidey hole is the land of Loudly and Out of Tune. A place, a state of mind, and a haven, it's where I get to go when I turn on my Bose world-canceling headphones. It is where I am afforded respite from this world, privacy in a crowd, and escape from my own often confusing and overwhelming thoughts. Methods of implementation have changed over the years as technology has evolved, but the basics have remained constant. With a conscious decision and the click of a button, I'm transported to my own version of Neverland and become both invisible and invincible. Happily lost, a proverbial ostrich with its head in the sand, I play to my heart's content as I sing along, loudly and out of tune. It's a survival tool that is simple and mostly foolproof.

In the now version, Alfie finds me, battle weary, and draws me to his essence. Sitting before me, leash in mouth, he cocks his head at a seemingly impossible angle and shifts the dark clouds of frustration in a heartbeat.

"Let me in," he begs. "Let me take you far away to Stickyville, where we can frolic and sing Loudly and Out of Tune."

Tink joins in beside him dancing a two-step or the occasional Charleston.

"Yes," I pant, spent. "Thank you. Okay."

I pick up my iPod (or Walkman, or CD player, or cassette deck), grab my headphones, find a jacket, and out the door we go, no matter the weather. The point is to be outdoors and moving. I used to walk to the music. Now that I can't walk anymore, I've been provided with such luxuries as a disabled-people scooter and other forms of movement that substitute for functional feet. The music begins, the volume goes up, and problems and frustrations melt away. It doesn't matter where we go. I am in motion, feeling free, and I am singing Loudly and Out of Tune. I sing to myself, to the universe, to my Smile — my incorrigible, irresistible, old-soul Smile.

As Alfie runs free, he leaps in the air with the joyfulness of being alive to lick my face or hand me a stick. He gives me one end of the stick and, holding the other end in his mouth, he plants his feet firmly on the ground. He tells me to hold the stick, to hang on and not let go. Then Smile moves forward with his end of the stick in his mouth until we are going at full speed. He checks to be certain that we are connected so I can feel the intense pleasure of a physical body in motion. The stick conducts energy. If either of us should drop our end, Alf resets the connection without hesitation. He moves for me, and I feel whole and pain is gone as we romp in that world we have built together.

We play "cowboys and Indians" or "pirate or Superman" games, hiding behind trees together, scanning the hills and bluffs of the prairie (golf course) for invisible monsters, villains, or enemies (golfers) from whom we must flee.

We plan our strategies by disappearing to our fort in Stickyville, a little-known town nestled in a stand of trees just the other side of this dimension. "RUN AWAAYYYYY," I yell from Headphone World, and off we go. "RUN LIKE THE WIIINNNND, RUN FOR YOUR LIIIFFFEE!!"

I never want to stop, for when the headphones come off, the other reality returns. I'm considered eccentric at this point — a polite word for a crazy person who lives in a good neighborhood. If I were singing Loudly and Out of Tune and hiding behind telephone poles, feeling energy through a stick on a street in downtown Seattle, I would be a crazy person, perhaps even dangerous.

My dog angels have traditionally shared in the joy of my loud, out-of-tune singing. Words don't matter. Words are a pain. They can be mis-interpreted, mis-spoken, and a mis-take. Music, though, music for the sake of music that fills my mind, body, and spirit, can block out thoughts and draw me in until I am one with it in another realm. The Loudly Out of Tune world never fails to whisk me away and make me smile.

Magical, mystical world-canceling Bose headphones effectively make me more able and less dis-abled. I have found them to be an unquestionably worthwhile investment in sanity.

• • •

The music ends and I am back in the reality of pain, grateful that it is not my only reality. There is no pain like neuropathic pain. The embers, smoldering, white-hot, searing, and invisible, threaten to set my entire body on fire. It reminds me of being in labor when a woman clenches her teeth and fists, closes her eyes, and holds on tightly, waiting for a contraction to pass. Except this is not labor, and it does not pass — no exquisite miracle at the end of the pain trail. Only a barely traveled path through the desert, and when I look closely, I see that it goes on forever through ancient canyons and past timeless mountains with fading telltale lines that tell us they were under the ocean centuries ago.

Journeys

Though I have searched for stoicism, it was not to be found. When enduring such a high and constant level of pain became unbearable, I was sent to meet with the director of the pain clinic. Dr. Sharret rather strutted into the exam room, shook my hand, and sat on his rolling doctor stool.

"I have reviewed your chart," he said in a familiar thick accent, "and you will have no pain pills from us. You are drug addict. Wait here. I show you."

A spine on wheels rolled into the room in front of him and came to rest at his side. Just the three of us.

"Doctor, your accent — it reminds me of something. Where are you from?"

"I am Russian Jew." A hint of a smile. "I guess is combination of Ukranian and Hebrew. Not familiar, just different."

"My grandparents on both sides were all Russian Jews from the Ukraine. They all spoke as you do. That's why I know it."

"Ah. Well. So you see spine here? Well. This is what we do. We use neurostimulator. So. Battery goes here."

He turned Spiney around and pointed to a spot on the hip just above the butt of the spine.

"We place it here. Then we attach leads, what is word … 'wires.' Yes. Wires go from battery to specific spots on the spine. Pain signals will be blocked this way. So pain signal interrupted does not reach brain so patient does not feel pain. Is best. We do this." He gently rolled Spiney away and scooted himself close to me. "What you think?"

"Yes. I think whatever you think is good."

He was obviously family; I trusted him immediately and implicitly, with his almost brusque but (to me) completely endearing manner.

"We do trial first. We try for one week. You schedule for procedure. If is effective, we do permanent implant. We set up time on your way out at desk, and I see you then."

He stood with the strikingly perfect posture of a soldier.

"You were in the Israeli army."

"Of course. All Israelis in army." His eyes held mine firmly. The right side of his hint of a smile joined the glint in his eyes for a shared instant of celebrated emotion. "Our families have same background, Hilary. I went to Israel, others before me to Ellis Island as yours."

The way he spoke swiftly carried me to the Bronx, back to my grandmother's apartment where the grownups of her generation gathered to cook, eat, drink, and most memorably, dance.

• • •

Tink grabbed my hand. The next thing I knew, I was in the elevator of the grand old brick building. The elevator operator slid the section of the door with the steel octagons shut first and then did his magic to close the outer door. As he moved the lever to the right, he commented that lots of family had been visiting Fanya and Sahkee this week.

I got out on the ninth floor and walked to my grandma's door. Familiar aromas triggered memories of the long wooden table, intricately carved, highly polished, formally set. I caught a glimpse of Grandma's traditional Russian piroggi cooling on racks in the tiny kitchen to the left of the entryway. The aromas of roasting meat and freshly baked bread filled the air. With the understated excitement, smells, and cadence of the familiar Russian language, the apartment held the essence of family.

Tink led me to the archway that announced the living room, tapping her toes on my shoulder. She whispered that they couldn't see me, that this was a scene from long ago. My Uncle Bob had a small glass in his hand, and he wasn't wearing that thing in his eye — the jeweler's telescope I remembered from visits to his jewelry shop in Manhattan.

My mother's Russian family — the dancing crew from the Bronx in my childhood.

My mom, 1944 N.Y.C.

My mother's side of the family came to America through Ellis Island, leaving Russia to escape persecution in the early 1900s. Grandma Fanya made the journey pregnant with my mother and carrying an infant, my not-quite-two-year-old Aunt Ruth. Women traveling alone were unheard of, but my grandfather was delayed by authorities and insisted that she get out while she could. He joined the family just over a year later. Despite their affluence in Russia, they, like most immigrants, had started their new lives with grit, determination, and hope. They had done well.

Aunt Genia gently lifted the arm of the Victrola and set the needle carefully on the groove where Uncle Bob's favorite song began. The men shed their suit jackets, loosened their ties, and rolled up the sleeves of their shirts. As the song began, my grandfather and two uncles lined up side by side in the center of the spacious living room. The song began slowly and then built up to the powerful, steady beat of a familiar traditional Russian folk song. Left legs moved forward while right ones held the weight of their bodies, and they miraculously did that squat-and-kick move of the traditional Ukrainian Hopak, commonly known as the Cossack dance. Their physical strength and stamina were astounding, and combined with an intense masculine grace, the dance was a beautifully choreographed marvel. Women clapped their hands, and we children sat respectfully on the high-backed chairs, watching our heritage of dignity, vitality, pride, and joy.

• • •

Uncle Bob was an old soul with a warm, endearing spirit. He held my hand, looked into my eyes, and in his thick accent, said the words for which he was to be remembered: "Everything'll gonna be all right." We walked hand in hand down the hallway toward the kitchen where a new door appeared. He opened the door, hugged me, and whispered in my ear. I was to move through this door and be a big girl, he said. When I looked back, he sat on a stool at his workbench with the monocle in his eye, setting a black pearl in my mother's ring.

I walked through the door, certain that Uncle Bob had rearranged the universe for my benefit because Uncle Bob could do stuff like that. Once through, I wasn't surprised to find an older version of myself on a plane with Mary touching down in Tel Aviv. Tink perched herself on my shoulder in a parrot-like position as we landed. She whispered that I'd been paralyzed not long ago but had fought my way back. I was nineteen, the year was 1972, and I was on a victory journey.

"Watch," she said.

• • •

A uniformed woman touched the older me's elbow and led her out of the customs line into a small room.

"Welcome to Tel Aviv. I am going to search now."

The orange backpack was methodically emptied, its contents carefully examined. Then the woman looked over and said, "Take your clothes off."

What? We watched me race through the childhood Hebrew vocabulary words. *That can't be right.* My questioning eyebrow raise elicited a "yes indeed" nod.

• • •

Me holding a strange-looking orange at the kibbutz, 1972.

The bus stopped on the side of a dirt road, and the driver pointed toward a stand of trees.

"Gal Raim," he said.

If the hippies in the States in the early seventies thought they knew what a commune was, they had a lot to learn. Kibbutzniks invented the ultimate alternative lifestyle. Everyone had a job to do and did it with great care and pride. At the end of the workday, dinner was ready in the dining hall. Prayer, dance, and song were part of daily life.

Young travelers hailed from all over the world and, once cleared through an application process, were welcomed to live and work. Kibbutz Gal Raim had dormitory-type housing for visitors, and most were assigned to pick oranges or work in the small factory where fans were made. Many spoke passable Hebrew; most knew broken English. Through combinations of Hebrew, English, German, Swedish, Spanish, Chinese, Dutch, and the rest of the world, communication happened. We lived for many months and another lifetime feeling honored and honorable, swelling with the pride that is born of honest hard work.

Why could these Sabras, people born and raised in Israel, with their fierce pride and pure, unwavering faith, not be left in peace on their tiny plots of land to live as they saw fit? Instead, child-soldiers patrolled kibbutz parameters with machine guns. Never have I known a people so pure and strong. With their sweat and against all odds, Israelis turned barren desert into lush, productive land that supports a people as they support the land itself. God's presence is palpable in the midst of pure, proud devotion and dedication to the earth.

Once I had absorbed the lessons of diligence and devotion, I left Gal Raim, walking with my fading orange backpack down a dirt road toward the next lesson.

• • •

Dr. Sharret shook my hand and assured me that we would meet soon and ease the pain. A week later in Seattle, the good doctor and his team completed the trial procedure, leaving me with wires poking through my skin and a remote control to adjust the level of sensation emitted from the battery to the wires attached to my lower spine. Once the butt was stitched back together, I stood up, and for the first time in many months, found that I could stand without the excruciating pain of flames coursing through my body.

This guy was smart.

I could walk. A month later came the surgery to implant the permanent version. When the anesthesiologist came in for the usual chat, I learned that he too was Israeli. As I was wheeled into the operating room and we spoke in my barely findable Hebrew, I heard him telling Soldier Doctor about his kibbutznik father and that I'd lived near Eilat as his kindly face and gray hair faded softly into the drugs that took me floating away.

I moved forward figuratively and literally.

I understand that my body will rebel against the battery from time to time. When it does, the good doctor must perform another surgery to make repairs. A damaged battery cable must be replaced; a delicate wire can migrate from a nerve root thinking it doesn't like the cul-de-sac and wants to live down the road. Surgery is never desirable or easy, but we do what we have to do and move on.

Round Two

For a second time, I was blessed to have one of the country's top researchers and neurologists. Dr. Mannis (aka Dr. Angel) specialized in neuropathy, and his ultimate goal was not to manage the pain but to make it go away. Why, he wanted to know, had I developed neuropathy in the first place when I fit into none of the neuropathy boxes? In his research lab, he had studied, experimented, test tubed, waved wands, filled flasks, stirred cauldrons. Okay, maybe not the cauldrons. But he had developed a viable theory that made a case for a relationship between hepatitis C and neuropathy. Testing the theory would involve finding just the right human being in the right circumstance with the right outlook.

I raised my hand in the air like an eager second grader who knows the answer to the question on the blackboard. *Oooh, ooh, pick me! Me! Ask me! Let me answer the question. Ooh! Ooh! Ooh!*

Chosen I was, chosen I was meant to be.

It wasn't like there was anyone else with their hand up.

Off we went. When Dr. Mannis spoke in his soft, humble tone, the hospital grounds trembled, the waters of Puget Sound parted, and his subjects raced to do his bidding. Scalpels pierced my body as carefully and deliberately as an archaeologist moves earth atop an ancient burial ground.

I was pleased that my body potentially had something to teach.

"No guarantees," he explained. "But even though we can't see it, Hilary, I am convinced that there is a connection between hepatitis C and peripheral neuropathy. If we eradicate the hep C virus, the neuropathy should theoretically reverse."

Okay.

Incivik, the first new hep C medication to be developed in twenty years, was awaiting FDA approval in 2010. My second journey to hell would begin as soon as the drug was available. Since I would not be working full time during treatment, this time around would be a breeze.

I know that hep C treatment is *not* a breeze.

I know that I am spared a great deal of suffering through my connections to the — oh, let's just call it the Great Beyond.

I picked up the white Styrofoam cooler that had been left on the front porch that sunny June morning and set it on the floor in the entryway. When I slit the tape and lifted the lid, bags of syringes and boxes of medicine resting quietly in ice packs reminded me that it was nearly time to begin. I suddenly felt a 1,000-pound elephant tap my chest, crushing the butterflies. *Oh shit. Here it is — this is real.* Knowing that Interferon needed to be refrigerated, I took the small box into the kitchen and placed it carefully under a bunch of spinach in the vegetable bin. If I didn't look at it, it wasn't there. If it wasn't there, I didn't have to think about it for a few more days.

When the cooler was empty and in the garage, a band of helpers began to gather. Tink darted over to the paddle by the garage door, perched on its tip, and lit up from inside like a blinking holiday ornament. Mary appeared beside me as my delightful Alfie Smile bounced energetically about, throwing sticks in the air and chasing invisible monsters. When the phone rang and I saw "Leia" on the caller ID, my soul smiled.

"Interesting timing," I said. "My evil medicine just got here."

"It doesn't have to be evil. It can and needs to be your ally, your partner in healing."

What a load of crap, I thought. *She has no idea*. When I told her it was under the spinach, she laughed that loving laugh of hers.

"Take it out, Hilary, and let it be your friend."

"Okay. Right."

What a load of crap, I thought again. But Leia had planted the seed. It was to grow.

"Check this out," my head whispered to itself.

I joined Tink on the paddle and did just that. There I was, about to begin a year of drug-induced hell. I chopped the white Styrofoam with an X-Acto knife and stuffed it in a trash can, leaving little white pieces of that impossible white stuff all over the ground.

Mary's calm presence is comforting as always. Alfie is the smile, the bounding, joyful being connected to me like no other. He speaks truth through those old-soul eyes and would be my reason to get up, get outside, and keep moving. I pondered first the Leia call, and then the call yesterday morning informing me that I was the first patient whose health insurance has approved the new medication, that the hepatologist working with Dr. Angel had already ordered blood work.

I see beyond this gathering of disguised blessings. I close my eyes for a moment, say a wordless silent prayer, and move my hand to grasp the paddle.

"Let's go, Alf."

Ten minutes later, Smile and I are in our lifejackets at the edge of the lake getting into Old Yeller. Alfie perches himself on the front hatch, sitting straight and tall like a figurehead on a viking ship, and off we go.

The next morning, I free the Interferon from its spinach prison and move it to the butter compartment where we can see one another. Two days later, I sit at the dining room table with the medicine. I easily swallow the pills and clean a spot on my stomach with an alcohol pad. I take out a new-and-improved-pre-filled syringe of Interferon, shoot it into my body, and head off to the familiar wild blue yonder.

The first blood test showed a lowered viral load but not the expected zero. It also showed anemia that required the addition of a weekly injection of Procrit to keep my red cell count up. I would need two injections a week throughout the remainder of treatment. The second month results didn't make the zero mark either, and by the third month I was weak, foggy, and frustrated.

The thing is, I've never felt that there's any option other than to move forward. Regardless of what happens to my physical body, I am, in my way, detached from it. Giving up on healing is never an option as I blindly muddle my way through each obstacle. An invisible support system has kept me going through the darkest days. Call them what you will — angels, friends, hallucinations, leprechauns, or faeries. Labels make no difference.

• • •

During my first round of hep C treatment, my mind wandered to a profound state of depression that was unquestionably foreign to my being. It was nevertheless a reality that I visited for a short period during which I saw an indistinct version of myself sitting on my couch in Idaho with a .44 Magnum moving toward my head as a "make my day" a la Clint Eastwood chant played over and over in my mind. Dr. Johnny "happened" to call in that moment. Shortly after that, Mary shut my computer down from across the room as I was studying exactly how many of which kind of pills in my possession were certain to cause death rather than just make me sick.

Oh yes, I've been there.

Yes, I am ultimately safe, surrounded by guardians.

By the third month of round two, thoughts were wrapped in little cloth drawstring bags inside my head and couldn't get out. They couldn't visit with each other or join forces to produce anything approaching coherency. Speech was as difficult as eating or moving, nausea constant, energy sapped, confusion the norm.

The neuropathic pain initially increased to the point where I wondered whether foot amputation could be an elective surgery. The neurostimulator company people were unable to program their elaborate system in a way that provided relief. There was a bout of begging, whining, changing settings, and working my way up to a conversation with the corporate president. In his ever so kind and tactful way, he explained that since Interferon had me in "uncharted territory," they really didn't know how to properly program their product. From the depths of my fog, I saw myself place the external controller carefully in a drawer, knowing that relief would not come through my bionic-ness.

I clung tightly to the white horse on the merry-go-round.

My weight dropped forty pounds over the next few months. Walking across a room was exhausting. When I looked from my couch at the loaf of bread on the kitchen counter, I knew that making myself a piece of toast required more energy than I had. Every dust ball in every corner taunted me with that teasing child melody, singing, "You ca-an't clean me, nee-ner-nee-ner ha-ha." I needed a nap after a five-minute phone conversation.

• • •

One morning in the mirror, bones were particularly prominent on the emaciated frame of a body. I saw an older version of the very young, thin woman who left Mount Sinai in New York so many years ago. That me had found strength. That me had also traveled through death and paralysis without self-pity or delay. Searching the mirror for a glimmer of recognition, I found Tink sitting on my left ear waving cheerfully. At my side, Mary touched my hand, locked eyes with me in the mirror, and took me back forty years. She brought me to the trailhead of my life after leaving Mount Sinai, when I brushed myself off and kept moving.

There are moments in life when we choose one path over another, like those stories that are written with different endings.

Tink took my hand as she and Mary led me through the mirror.

• • •

A medical marvel accompanied by an invisible entourage boarded a plane from New York to Rome in 1972. The willowy teen held her head high as she hefted the orange backpack and stepped confidently into her future. Tink, mischievous and lighthearted, was always in her field of vision. In the background, Mary quietly orchestrated the balance it took to move through the world.

She traveled because she could.

She traveled not as a tourist but as a seeker.

Tourists see nothing of the reality that surrounds them. They blindly follow the all-important, planned-to-the-minute, stay-safe-inside-the-tour-bus itinerary.

Travelers step into whatever the universe places before them, open their eyes and hearts, and experience realities that gently alter their own.

A small bus sped and weaved from the airport into the city, honking through the chaotic maze of streets and traffic. The scenario was somehow familiar when the bus door opened to let the girl out at a random stop. She wandered to an outdoor café and sat down to get her bearings. She toasted her victories in silence and slowly sipped a glass of wine.

Paolo appeared with a knowing, charming smile, as though he had been waiting down the street for her. He was well dressed in jeans and a beige, lightweight sport coat. His ivory-colored shirt was unbuttoned to reveal his deeply tanned chest and silver chain. Green eyes danced and grinned when he removed a fedora and waved it before his body in a dramatically exaggerated theatrical bow of introduction. She laughed aloud and caught a glimpse of Tink playfully cheering, pompoms and all. Paolo and his antics joined her at the table.

He was a local, at once a gentleman and a rogue. He spoke to her in Italian;

she replied in Spanish. They had a picnic on the top step of the Coliseum with fresh bread, cheese, and fine wine. He showed her tourist spots and hidden streets, history, art, sculpture, old men passionately playing checkers in the small plaza near his home. They delighted in faux romance and the glory of Rome. It was a time of undisguised, absolute abandon.

That time had been a perfect beginning to the Second Life of Hilary.

• • •

I drifted into a thick fog of medications, this one far thicker than the first. The all-new, ready-for-primetime Incivik was hellacious. Despite the stubborn viral load, I was again certain that I would beat hep C. The universe would support me. I would never, ever fall down and not get back up.

"Look at each challenge, Hilary, and walk through it."

OKAAAYYYYYY. Dr. Angel had done years of research working amid cloudy visions of people rising from scooters and wheelchairs to run on the beach, to hike Boulder Mountain, to be well again.

I watched myself in the lab amid a group of wheelchair-bound patients. We slumped miserably during the first part of the show, writhing in silent pain, unable to find relief. I sat perfectly still, looking around the room before suddenly standing up in total bewilderment. I was told that my eagerness to be the guinea pig could help others in the future. I looked around, stood on one foot, then the other, raised my arms in the air, and locked eyes with Dr. Angel as we timelessly connected souls.

• • •

One painless step, and I am wiggling my toes in the sand as I stand next to the pier of First Street and Ocean Drive. South Beach, 1969. It is as it has always been — peaceful and perfectly calm. I look to the south and see the jetty in the distance, far past the dog track parking lot, beyond the surfboards resting on the beach. I begin to walk, slowly at first, kicking up a bit more ocean with each step before breaking into a gleeful run. Halfway to the jetty, Mary sits in the sand, waves washing up over her feet as she playfully lifts Tink in the air. Sitting beside them, we remain silent for a time, enjoying the past/present/future until we burst into laughter — the joy and absurdity of it all!

• • •

Earthquakes shift the earth causing fissures in the ground, visible cracks large enough fall into and maybe never get out of. Consciousness shifts are that dramatic without being visible.

Elements of Healing

Rest and medical care.

Love.

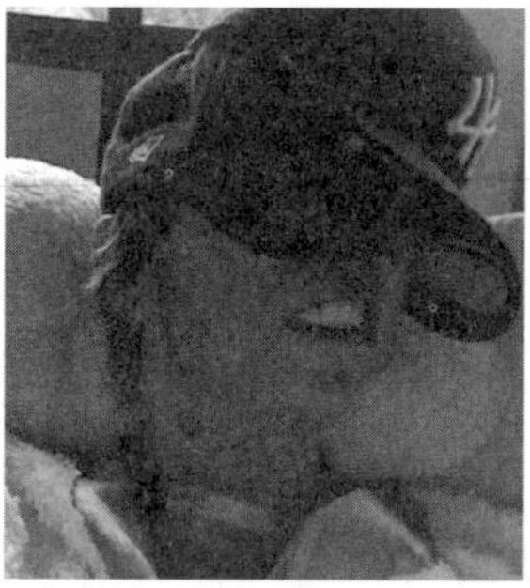

Humor.

Prayer.

Faith. There is always a way to move forward.

Fog

Undetectable hep C viral load. *YES!*

Eleven foggy months later, my emergence from treatment was akin to a butterfly going backward and coming out a caterpillar. I come out with increased cognitive confusion. I notice that my memory is worse than ever, and I'm constantly losing things. I ban all questions that begin with "where is …" or "have you seen …." I embrace a shiny new clarity about "what is" and ponder whether focusing on the world of things and stuff had been taking up space that was needed for intuition and knowing. I talk less and communicate more.

I see and access my other life more clearly: the familiar parallel life where I live in the upstairs of an adobe building. My balcony overlooks the ocean. The breeze is warm, tropical, and soothing. It's a white building with blue trim. It's always been mine. I've seen it for as long as I can remember. It's small, the inside, and very comfy. Private but not isolated. I spend time on the balcony reading, writing, drinking coffee, talking with my dog. I can't tell how well I'm ambulating, but I've found a way to get around this environment that works for me, and I am at peace. "Stuff" is a non-issue because I've gotten rid of most of it. If I don't have it, I don't lose it. Simplicity suits me.

My consciousness continues to shift as the poisons leave my body.

Another parallel life emerges. Adobe again, this one is a home in the desert surrounded by glorious wildflowers. The house is Santa Fe pink though it's nowhere near Santa Fe. There are open breezeways and a small courtyard. In the center is a statue of a little girl with water trickling gently down her body making an endless, flowing fountain. I stand comfortably on stone slabs looking out at a vast expanse of desert — cactus, tumbleweeds, and wildflowers as far as the eye can see. A brilliantly colored kite floats easily with the desert breeze.

I notice that this altered mindset embraces random acts of kindness, actions without words. I again ponder what is truly important in any of our lives, what is real and what is not. Mary and Tink are real, perhaps existing for the sole purpose of helping me evolve. They live, teach, dance, and play in their reality while encouraging me to follow suit on this earthly level, and I love them.

• • •

The pain in my feet and ankles has become quite tolerable, a testament to Dr. Angel and his hypothesis. The doctors discover that in my unrelenting determination to remain active, Battery Butt had adopted a crooked walk that with every step should have given me excruciating pain. Pain, the body's way of getting attention, was masked by sophisticated technology, tolerated, and ignored, leading to structural changes in foot bones.

"I've never seen this before" has become a pronouncement that fills me with dread and pride at the same time. My experience with the all-too-familiar phrase has been that while no one knows what to do, they will nevertheless embark on another quest that may help others in the future. Meanwhile, my feet are damaged, painful, and currently living in corrective braces in hopes that the bones will go back to where they used to live.

• • •

I am not an emotionally mature person. I scream, holler, whine, and throw tantrums on a regular basis. Where self-pity might be, there is only perseverance, frustration, and anger. While there is no fear of death, there is profound disgruntlement with suffering. I believe there is a lesson in tolerating the level of pain I live with. I ponder this as I ponder most things: in a circular fashion that inevitably leads to whispers of answers and more questions:

Remember when I started telling you not to kayak so much, not to fight choppy water and wailing winds? Remember when you began to feel twinges of pain in your wrist, elbow, and hand? Do you remember that you consciously decided to continue doing what you were doing despite the increasing discomfort? Well, how about two more surgeries? How about a fancy De Quervain's tendonitis in your wrist and a pinched ulnar nerve in your elbow? Oh, and let's make your hands and fingers ache and turn blue.

Here you go. Learn moderation.

How's that "nothing in moderation" mantra working out for you?

Pay attention, Hilary.

Desert

Tink was getting dizzy.

"Do you not see why?" she asked. "I have followed you around these carnival grounds forever. Your exemplary combination of the Indio Date Festival and Coney Island has become completely familiar. Bumper cars, go-carts. Roller coasters and Ferris wheels. I've watched you get off one ride only to look around and eagerly move on to the next. In that transitional moment, you make a choice that takes you to the next step of this journey, our journey, your life. You've fended for yourself as best you could since you were a baby, and even when the roller coaster takes you upside down, inside out, and the bumper car crashes into the house of mirrors, you brush yourself off and move forward. Sometimes the only comfort you have is holding on with all your might to the merry-go-round horse that moves in time to the merry-go-round music.

"Sometimes you stagger but not for long. Oh, no. Staggering is not your style.

"You must have a lifetime unlimited ticket — the kind that, for a price, allows you unlimited rides and cotton candy and games with barkers urging you to shoot the bouncing duckies, throw the ring onto the peg, and win the giant stuffed monkey bear. Coney Island's Cyclone terrified the little girl whose knuckles turned blue. Never did you let on, though. Oh no, no time for that — the next challenge was waiting right around the corner.

"When exhaustion sets in, you find solace on the merry-go-round, where you flow with the gentle movement of round and round and up and down, listening to the delightful music that defines your life, that never-ending, always-changing circle of music and life.

"I've watched, listened, and always done my best to help you. I am the child you didn't have a chance to be until you grew up, and together we capture moments and silly antics and fireflies. Rather than put them in a jar in traditional childhood fashion, we prefer to watch them glitter and dart and dance through nighttime skies.

"Alfie likes to run round and round and round chasing his tail. The puzzling part is what to do when he catches it. He doesn't understand his connection to that tantalizing furry extremity any more than most of us understand the connectivity of the moments in time that define our lives.

"There are no coincidences. It's all connected. I am connected to you as you are connected to Mary, as every moment, every ride, every choice is connected to the universal plan."

When Mary holds out her hand, Tink lands on her index finger, and they hold me in their hearts. No magic. I am blessed with the highest caliber of teachers. Everything is connected.

• • •

Mary and Tink urged me to listen to the depth of my soul, to my soul's calling. So listen I did. I felt compelled to return to my beloved desert where I learned so many lessons, where my daughter was born, where I met and fell in love with my Michael.

I've never been certain what it is that calls us back in time to somewhere we have been. Perhaps we are called back to complete part of our journey, a fragment of a lesson. Perhaps the memory is so strong in our heart that we have no choice but to physically revisit this place one more time. But is it ever the same?

Pay attention, I tell my brain. *Compensate, accommodate, harmonize. You are returning to your desert home, the California destination that followed the time of the Orange Backpack.*

The time of the Orange Backpack, my traveling period after rehab, was a chapter of my life that was as vital as the Ice Age or the Stone Age in the history of the world. It was the period during which I learned how the part of me that came back from death would harmonize with the world. The Hilary who disembarked the flight from Zurich to JFK after a year and a half was a confident, comfortable new version of me.

I could easily have been lying in rehab somewhere.

I could easily have become bitter and angry, resentful of my misfortunes.

I could easily have been defeated, a paraplegic for the rest of my life.

Had I listened to the white coats' prediction that I would never walk again, I would have fulfilled that prophecy. There are moments when we must focus on that place inside us where we have unlimited access to strength, will, and power. I'd made the choice to replace the white coats' picture with my own, I'd chosen mine, and I acted on pure will.

We always have the power to dictate our own lives, our ideal future, because we are the ones who create it. We must never lose sight of that.

• • •

When I realized that New York no longer suited me, it was time to head West. It was a time when the highways from east to west accommodated a steady trickle of Volkswagen vans carrying Deadheads, seekers, that loner from high school, everyone who believed in "Hair," and all manner of blossoming hippies, everybody heading to California, the Promised Land.

I chose my future, found an alternative college, applied, and was accepted with an academic scholarship.

Redlands turned out not to be the powerful, awe-inspiring place where massive ancient trees ruled but a bland little town off a freeway in Southern California. Redlands and redwoods were not equally stunning, despite sharing the same prefix.

Oops.

I desperately drove a hundred miles in every direction, my new mind whirling with strange and unusual escape plans. Since Johnston College at the University of Redlands was "alternative" in its policies, I was determined to create a graduation plan that would somehow alter the unfortunate geography.

Beyond that, I discovered that the new me was not going to function in any traditional manner whatsoever. My brain was instantly overwhelmed with social pressures, memory issues, classrooms, and expectations. I recall the first college classroom I attended with my new brain. I was appalled to find a room full of students with a woman in front whose framed paper and title indicated that she had something to teach us. If we learned whatever it was that she and her colleagues had to teach, we would eventually earn our own frame-worthy pieces of paper redeemable for admission tickets into the carnival of the American Dream.

The sign on the bulletin board at Johnston Center read, "ACTION! University Year for Action, a part of the Peace Corps' domestic unit — VISTA. Do good work, give your heart and soul and time and energy to a cause, work tirelessly around the clock. If you think THAT sounds good, wait until you hear the rest! We will PAY you for this honor, the sum of $210 per month on which to live WHILE you dedicate yourself to the cause, take your full load of classes, and share a dwelling with a group of like-minded world savers. So, you get college credits, work ungodly hours, barely sleep, live with strangers, and get to struggle with poverty to boot!"

Well, who could possibly pass up a chance like that? Certainly not someone with an alternative brain and a new skin who had moved across the country to attend an alternative college.

Idealism ran deep back then. Not a speckle of cynicism — just pure good intention combined with boundless energy. Fifteen or so of us were chosen. We would create a center for juveniles taken into custody by law enforcement, and we would devote ourselves to setting them on a path to their own dreams.

We would live in a crowded apartment, work, eat, study, and sleep together, united in our cause. We, the ultimate believers, would do our part to change the world.

• • •

Indio, California, is a drive down highway 10 from Redlands. I distinctly remember the air suddenly changing. It didn't change color — no cloud shifting, no vortex. The air simply feels different in the desert, the sky more vivid, more beautiful, as though God has a stronger presence, as though God perhaps hangs out in what, to some, is a barren wasteland. In the desert, the sky is more alive, more intense, as though created from colors crafted by apprentices of the old masters, oils made from pigments of the earth extracted from magical trees and secret berries growing on fairyland bushes picked by winged angels, mixed by the queen of the gnomes. Brilliant pinks, oranges, and blues are so pure that they take your breath away. The moon rises and spotlights each and every cactus and tumbleweed from above.

My connection was instantaneous and deepened so slowly and subtly that I barely noticed. I became part of the landscape, one with the spirits and history of the sacred grounds.

It is forty years now since I first beheld the desert, yet it still holds my soul and soothes my restless spirit. I return now, knowing that the desert air will provide sustenance. The old friends who remain there are family now, having familiar, shared history. Some have moved on or passed on to their next existence, but they return to greet their wayward sister.

This I know in the instant I get off the airplane and feel the warm breeze like a familiar old lover's caress. I breathe deeply and know that I have come home. My traveling companions witness the years rewinding and watch as I move backward in time. In the present, every step I take is fraught with pain. In the present, I travel with my thirty-year-old daughter, my disabled-people scooter, and my service dog, Alfie.

My homecoming stops me in my tracks and propels me forward.

I have arranged the circular expedition to begin where memories are most vivid, at the place where I learned some of the most important and enduring lessons of my life: a not-famous, not-fancy, not-public retreat that used to be known as the Desert Lakeshore Ranch.

Thirty miles and a planet away from the Palm Springs airport are several hundred acres of pristine desert where I spent a tremendous amount of time in my youth. Now in a land trust, Ruth and Allen's Desert Lakeshore Ranch will remain forever as it is today.

• • •

Thirty-five years have passed. He stands next to the rented car looking at me through his father's eyes — thinning gray hair on a broad face, wire-rim spectacles, and the knowing hint of a smile that turns up just a hair on the left corner of his mouth. His hands are in the pockets of his khaki pants that flow casually on the body that has precisely the amount of weight to be stocky without crossing over to heavy. A broad-brimmed straw hat jauntily sits atop the not-quite-bald spot. His ruggedly functional, stylish shoes can walk from Eisenhower Medical Center, where he works, to the scrub-brush mountains of his desert canyon roots. We spend a moment letting memories swirl through the space between us before he opens the car door and I step easily into the warmth of his arms — Tony, son of Allen. Years melt away and

Desert Living

Part of Ruth and Allen's Desert Lakeshore Ranch.

Ruth and Allen's yard.

The Desert Conservation Land Trust and the living Desert Reserve are part of Ruth and Allen's legacy.

become yesterday. We hold each other, comfortable, familiar, my daughter the only evidence that time has passed between our yesterday and this moment.

"You look exactly like your dad," I whisper into his shoulder. "Exactly."

"Thank you, Hilary. Thank you."

When the moment is over, Misty Dawn introduces herself, providing proof that we are no longer in our twenties. She is greeted as family into the first square of the beloved quilt left behind when I wandered off to Idaho with her father.

There is no statute of limitations on the seventies. We are as we were, only more so.

Lunch is at Teresa's, a favorite Mexican restaurant that had survived the decades by being passed down through generations. The delectable food is prepared and brought to the table by Teresa's son, Alberto, who has maintained the traditional recipes and cozy dining area through the years.

Misty and I are hungry after a late night and early morning flight from the present to my past. My life before Michael is about to unfold, the life about which she is curious, interested in who her mother used to be.

After lunch, I drive with Tony. Misty follows in the rental car when we head out to the ranch that represents, to me, the essence of my desert years. Ruth and Allen's ranch was always filled with memories and spirits, knowledge, books, grace, power. When Ruth passed a few years ago, the ranch became part of a Desert Mountain Land Trust, hundreds of acres protected by gates with locks and codes and secret special paths for secret special vehicles.

A caretaker is off taking care of something, so Tony invites me to look in the windows of the well-maintained old house. Ruth's chair remains in the very spot where it was forty years ago, looking south out of her living room window at a never-ending landscape, a world filled to the brim with desert, cactus, palm trees, and the incomparable desert sky, forever fueling the imagination.

Though walking is difficult for me these days, walk I must. I shall gladly pay the price later, when nerves and bones in my feet will undoubtedly punish me for the extravagance. Every step is familiar. I follow my own footprints, and I see them clearly.

We approach the house, Ruth and Allen's, where centuries were spent in the living room talking about books and ideas and the universe. Ruth, granddaughter of former *Los Angeles Times* Publisher Harry Chandler, always said she had an "embarrassingly abundant amount of money" and that she and Allen strived to do a good job at being rich. They did.

The house is simple, compact, and efficient, like Ruth. We walk around the side where Ruth's flower garden thrived, where desert roses delighted the senses with a kaleidoscope of colors and aromas. I see them in all their glory. Though most are gone now, my memory brings them back with ease. The roses surround this house, this oasis of my world. Beyond the house and gardens is endless desert.

Long ago, the land was sacred ground of the Cahuilla Indians. We had visited when Misty was a toddler, and Allen had taken her little hand, walked with her, carried her to his favorite spots, and whispered secrets of the canyons. Seashells can be found in the hills, ancient Native American land first stolen, then purchased and loved, now preserved forever in the grand circle of life. The man-made lake is dried up now and the waterfall is gone.

I jolt back in time, landing barefoot in the sand at the edge of the water. Swimming, soaking, hippies are scattered about, lying on homemade bridges, sitting in small gazebos, reading, always reading, playing, loving this land like no other. We walk past Ruth's garden to the small back patio where the metal table remains, where the same chairs are arranged to look out at the desert, to look toward the mountain. I stand where I stood so long ago, grateful beyond words that the view remains the same. Nothing shall ever spoil this place.

Lost in time and space, Tony stands in front of me, facing me though he does not approach. We look at one another through timeless eyes, and he hands me a perfect orange rose.

"One of Ruth's," he says. "For you." I hold perfection in my hand. It fills in decades as it releases the powerful fragrance it has saved for me through these many years.

"Thank you, Tony."

We meander to the other side now, where metal sculptures 20 feet tall reach toward the sky. These stunning geometric shapes were built, Tony explains, to teach geometry to the students of Ruth's small private school, a school that brought her ideas of education to fruition, where Tony's children studied beside campesinos and Native American kids in the classroom of Everland.

Dear Lord, I see *the* living room of my youth, a modest room. Bookshelves cover two walls from floor to ceiling, and they are still full. Ruth's chair has not moved — a faded red armchair, low-backed, well used, at the end of the coffee table. Ruth sits with her hand on a small, moist glass of gin and bitters set on the coaster next to a small stack of books. To her left, several twenty-somethings share the couch talking passionately, gesturing with conviction — more books, more coasters, a drink or two. Allen stands behind us scanning the shelves for the book from which he wishes to make a point. Ruth stands up and walks in her brisk, efficient way toward the kitchen. She is a small woman brimming with energy. A simple woman, despite her very entitled birthright. Sensible, brilliant, generous. I see her never slowing down, body and mind busy doing, thinking, giving, teaching, learning. She whips together plates of hors d'oeuvre, bustles hither and yon, and now the coffee table is filled with sustenance for the hungry minds. It is the time of Seth. Animated conversations are mixed with bonds that span lifetimes.

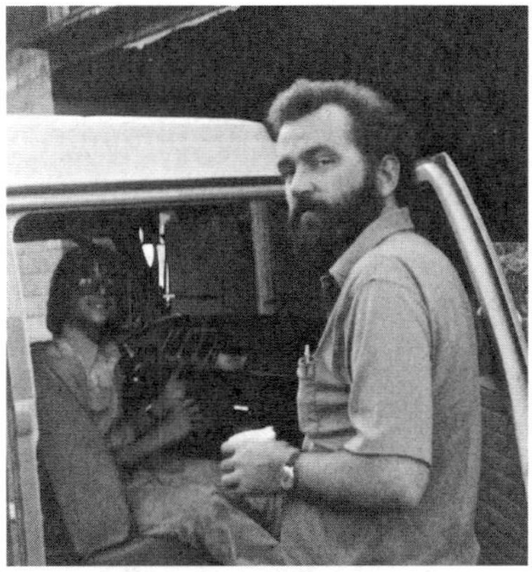

Barry, *top,* with his son, Jay.

Dodo, *bottom*, the matriarch of Barry's family.

• • •

I put my hands to the side of my face to shield the glare of the sun.

"Those were some of the best days of your life, weren't they?" Mary, beside me, speaks quietly. She too is taking in the past.

"Yes. Indeed they were."

I was filled with the passion of giving, devoted to the causes and bursting with energy. *Look, there's Barry meandering through the front door*. He catches my eye, and his lips part ever so slightly when he smiles the sweet Barry smile. He winks and moves a chair over to join the conversation. *Barry*.

The ranch hosted more than college students. Everyone was welcome, ideas the only cost of admission. There was the San Francisco clan, Barry, Newall, Lawrence, Carol, outcast idealist intellectuals a decade older with jobs or lives that intersected ours. Barry worked with probation. Gerry ran a halfway house for paroled heroin addicts.

The living room was a magnet for diversity and learning. On this day, it was *Seth Speaks*, the first volume in a series of five books about the eternal validity of the soul, the unlimited awareness, intuition, and knowledge to which we all have access.

Gordon smushes himself next to me on the couch with a "Hi Hil," just like I heard the other day when we spoke on the phone. Gordon, my brother, fellow moccasin maker, enduring friend. Gordon holds memories of my past and understands the depth of my gratitude when he discloses pieces of my history that elude me.

Barry, who fancied himself several hundred notches smarter than the rest of the world, begins speaking in his best "clear my throat/smarter than thou/I have the best insights" voice to which we have all grown accustomed. He famously insisted that he drank "to make people more interesting," and he drank like I did: in a classically functional alcoholic manner.

An intellectual snob and another heir to another fortune, he had charm, looks, class, and money. Barry and I were to become lovers. I would, for a time, be stepmother to his children, Jordan and Jay, and I would become an integral part of his family forever.

I have remained connected to Barry's extended family throughout the decades. They are exceptional and diverse, connections strong and unconventional. Dodo, the matriarch of the clan and mother of Barry's first wife, lived in San Francisco and passed away a few years ago. For ninety-five years, Dodo lived in the moment, vivacious and brimming with love, life, red wine, Marlboros, wit, whimsy, knowledge, and awareness.

In Barry's family, every ex is family. Every child and every parent of every ex and exes of exes and steps and in-laws and friends and lovers are all family. Bound together as we are spread throughout the world, everyone is engaged in his or her own definition of life. This alternative definition of family is based on a logical premise that is beautifully different. Once you have loved someone, a part of you always has a speckle of love left for that person. Since that person has lots of people they love, you are automatically connected to those people through your love for the original person. The children of these connections are included and embraced. Their friends and lovers join in the circle, as do others over time. It's so simple it can appear complicated at first glance.

This is the way the rest of the world has forgotten to be. This is the way the universe intended humans to behave — with love. Pure love. Perhaps it sounds like a bunch of mind-altered hippies having a love fest, and perhaps that's precisely what it has been these past forty years. If so, then good for us! We had the right idea then, and we have never let it go. We have never lost sight of the joy that comes with gracious, loving acceptance, defining family in a way that could work for all of humankind.

• • •

Between worlds with Mary and the desert rose of my youth.

Mary puts her arm gently around my shoulder — barely a touch, a whisper of an invitation to return. I look at her with tears in my eyes, complicated tears of joy and gratitude, grief and knowing. Tears that are essential to this arc of the circle, tears that had to be shed here at Ruth and Allen's, looking into the living room while holding the desert rose of my youth.

Absolutely Cherished Memories.

With Mary at my side, I turn slowly back to the present. Memories have flowed powerfully like floodwaters, washing across the sand into the dry lakebed, filling it now as the waterfall begins with a trickle. I remain still while the circle of life shifts the sands of my desert to bring forth the perfect picture of my memory, to bring back the water, to move the circle around a bit more, filling in parts that have not yet connected. There is a visible line being drawn.

The circle of my life is visible as a circle, oddly enough, and just for fun, it creates a center with a face so that the face can wink at me. Space remains. The line around the edge is not yet connected to itself, but the wink makes me smile and assures me that I am on the right path.

Tony stands near the arrow sculpture smiling his father's gentle smile, watching me return from the past. Misty is off a ways watching her mother's healing journey through time.

Thank you, I pray. *Thank you, Ruth and Allen. We have met again and will do so unto eternity.*

I am between times smelling the desert air, remembering this incomparable oasis that can never be touched. They can build and ravage and create a

Life in Joshua Tree

Our house in Joshua Tree.

Joshua Tree Garden.

Michael, Misty, and friend.

horror show of gated, walled communities, but they cannot change Ruth and Allen's Desert Lakeshore Ranch or the glorious sky. Not ever.

• • •

Tony and Misty have moved toward the mountain. She will hike and camp for a few days. Tony provides guidance: "Seven miles to the nearest water source. Watch for snakes. You will have to climb at mile two." He knows these canyons. They were his backyard growing up and his children's backyard. Stories of the land passed down through centuries and generations are now being handed down again to my daughter. She looks over at me and tells me with a glance that she understands now. It is sacred. It is home.

• • •

I don't drive much any more. Can't feel my feet on the pedals.

Misty drives to Joshua Tree in the high desert, where she lived the first years of her life. Things have changed. Though plenty of space remains and Joshua trees still outnumber people, poverty cries out from trailers and ramshackle homes. It feels as if time has forgotten to care for its majesty and instead the land appears ravaged, even a bit raped and pillaged. I am saddened by the trash strewn along the highway. Cactus, decorated with plastic bags as if they are Christmas trees, cry out their lack of love. There could be a main street now. Someone has made a feeble effort to arrange a town of sorts. The crooked row of funky stores reminds me of the façade town in *Blazing Saddles*, and I expect to see Gene Wilder appear to tip it over with a flick of his finger. Yet the few people walking through the sand appear content, as we once were, with the sparse surroundings.

How have I unknowingly gotten so far away from the person who was one of the sand wanderers, when the windows of our rented shack were covered with cardboard? The swamp cooler did little to ease the 125-degree days, and our water lines were so close to the surface that cool water could be drawn from the taps only between three and four in the morning. That was the hour I would awaken to fill Misty's plastic pool for the next day, and that was when we bathed. The rest of the time, tap water was too hot.

As we drive, I am certain that water pipes are still barely covered with sand, that cardboard and plastic remain on windows and door panes. I wonder whether it was love that made such living conditions not only tolerable but somehow noble. Yes, we were tough. Life was rugged. My garden didn't mind the heat of the days or the temperature of the water. It thrived and produced an abundance of food. Little Misty and I sat in the coolness of the tomato plants eating our fill of cherry tomatoes, lettuce, and peas. We lived outdoors, for the most part, and were one with the desert.

Misty drives silently, trying, I think, to see beyond the surface here as she does in the jungles of Central America where she has spent the past several years. She is a child of the desert, and it is not foreign to her soul.

"The desert is older than the jungle," Misty says quietly. "It is silent and does not give up its secrets easily."

Mary stands beside the entrance to the Joshua Tree National Park with her head down, acknowledging the sadness of the housekeeper, erasing the surface to reveal the beauty that remains untouched and unchanged. Tink darts about, collecting plastic as it flies through the air with the breeze that has just kicked up. Mary is on the side of the highway as we drive, reminding me to see beyond today, beyond the surface. We are certain that a few miles back, someone has arranged a living room out of used furniture, and people sit and visit and drink and are neighbors in this communal outdoor living room as they are nowhere else.

Stump

Where we going, Mom?"

"To Stump, sweetie."

"We get to ski across the lake to get there today, huh, Mom?"

"We do!"

"You always have a way for us to get to Stump, don't you, Mom?"

"There's always a way to get anywhere we really want to go, Misty."

"Yeah. We've swam, canoed, taken a rowboat, skied, snow-shoed — we get there all kinds of ways."

"You bet. There's always a way, and don't ever let anyone tell you different."

"Okay, Mom. Why do you stand on Stump, Mom?"

Mom kneels down, fastens clips and zippers, and gazes into her child's ageless, sea-smoke eyes.

"Stump is a special place to me, Misty. I meet with God there and talk and listen and stuff. Lots of people go to churches or temples; your strange old mom goes to Stump. Gods are everywhere, and it feels really, really good to keep in touch with the universe."

Tying the little gloves to the jacket sleeves, Mom looks up quizzically at her child.

"Do you have a special place, Misty?"

The little girl's old-soul eyes travel beyond Mom to another galaxy. They return with the familiar jolt that has forever sparked these two powerful spirits.

"There's a giant log that's really a chair in the woods behind our house where I like to go. It's like a hidey spot."

"We all need a place like that, sweetheart. Does you heart feel special when you're in your hidey spot?"

"My heart feels safe."

The wisdom of a five-year-old easily defining a basic need of humanity.

• • •

Across the vast frozen expanse of lake are two skiers and three dogs. The cats turn back after the first half-mile. We see no on else out today. Most days, really. We live in Donnelly, Idaho, on Cascade Lake. It's two miles wide and fifteen miles long, busy in the summer with boaters and weekenders escaping the cities. It's winter now. Three feet of ice cover the lake, and the few inches of fresh snow that fell last night create a pristine, unsoiled paradise. Later in the day, a few of the old-timers may be out for a bit of ice fishing. Misty and I join them sometimes — have become familiar neighbors with our flaggy stick poles that old Ray made us. Everyone keeps watch on the red ribbons just above the fishing holes waiting eagerly for the movement signaling a fish bite. The sun shines brightly through familiar ice crystals that fill the wonderland air, and trees create their own decorations of frozen pine needles interspersed with the occasional cone. Owls call from one of the distant shores.

Here there is no hurry. Here life is as it was meant to be. Here, in nature, in paradise. Twenty feet off the shore of Cascade Lake, Stump rises several feet above the surface. Roughly four feet in diameter, he reaches toward the sky, surrounded by water, snow, ice, or a combination thereof. His top is a level surface. Someone took a chainsaw to Stump many years ago, but Stump didn't seem to mind. Stump is one of the specks on this planet from which I can reach out, touch the universe, and be revitalized. It's something like recharging a battery.

• • •

After brutal winters, every summer day in Donnelly is cherished. Stump and I met many years ago while I was swimming in the lake. Neighborhood

Misty with Stump.

kids played safely in the sand, water wings permanently attached to tiny arms. That day, my neighbor Brian was there with his daughter, so he watched the little ones while I swam around the point.

There was Stump. I felt rather than saw it. I paused for a moment, continued out a ways, then felt drawn to turn around and head back. I returned to Stump and swam circles around him, looking, feeling. I knew what I needed to do, and spotting a foothold, I easily climbed out of the water and onto Stump. There was an overpowering need, then, to stand up, to firmly plant my feet and connect. When I did, it began. Physical sensations coursed through my body, my being.

Stump and I are alone now. I face West Mountain, thickly forested and rugged. To the south, water is clean, clear, and teeming with fish. Our house is the only one visible to the east, the turret that is Misty's room sparkling like a beacon in storybook land. The beach is to the north, but since I rounded the point of the peninsula, no one is visible. Lines of vision blur all at once and then fade as a tremendous burst of power rises from the earth and courses through Stump into my feet, up my legs. I am not feeling power; I am becoming power. Up, up, I raise my arms to the sky as I am completely encompassed by a familiar foreign entity. No thoughts, no movement — nothing but power. Surprised, accepting, appreciating the experience, I stay with it until I am not only filled to the brim but have long since overflowed, a battery charge strong enough to light the world, to love without measure.

What was it I told my five-year-old?

"There's always a way to get to where we need to go."

Palm Springs

I return to the hotel, to Palm Springs and the privilege and the pool and the statue of Marilyn Monroe. I am comfortable here now. Another arc in the circle, these resorts are essentially no different from the hotels of the Catskill Mountains in New York. Here too the Rat Pack partied and performed and charmed the world. From the resorts of my youth, I have traveled far and wide through opulence, poverty, motherhood, being a mountain woman with a fulfilling and successful career, and ill health. Here and now, a lounge chair of my South Beach youth beckons me to the deck of the hotel room, and I am charmed.

My battered body is grateful for the reprieve from the cold and wet. As the pain eases in the warmth and sun, I can move and breathe more easily. I am alive again, and grateful, knowing that my soul has taken root once again in the shifting sands of this desert home.

I close my eyes and drink in the splendor, the warmth and stillness of my body, the reprieve from pain. I feel as though I am alone drifting on a cloud with no thoughts beyond the pleasure of the exquisite surroundings that engulf me.

In the silence, memories of Michael fill my head — and my heart.

• • •

Michael and me, 1980.

An unlikely pair, we met in Palm Springs when Michael arranged to buy a pair of my custom-made moccasins. I had recently parked my bright-yellow VW pop-top van following a long bout of wanderlust. After working my way to a supervisory capacity in the State Social Services system within two years of finishing college, the persona felt, to me, like a pair of stiff new Levis. The blue jeans and me wanted to be liberated, wanted to be soft, ragged cutoffs. At twenty-five, I had a prestigious, well-paying, secure position, interesting work, great benefits, and a retirement plan.

I got to work one morning and went directly to the manager's office. Helen Edams was an efficient, hard-working woman who had fought through a man's world to rise in the ranks of public service. She stood up and came around the desk to greet her young protégé whom she'd met at a dinner party at "the ranch" years earlier. Bright, fair-minded, and ambitious, Helen's soft-spoken manner belied a firm hand and watchful eye. A delicate woman in her early sixties, she dressed impeccably and wore her blond hair in a short, stylish cut. When I put an arm around her shoulder that morning, the boss looked at me and smiled. In that moment, I saw Mary's eyes and felt the unmistakable familiarity of her touch. Over in a flash.

"Good morning."

My Michael

Michael and me.

"Old Friends' Last Crossing": Divorce painting by Michael O'Loughlin.

My Michael's new mocassins.

We moved to the door of her office and stood looking out at the large room filled with desks and workers and telephones and buzzing bureaucratic busyness.

"See those people, Helen?"

"Yes, Hilary. I see."

"See how they don't care anymore, Helen?"

"Some do; some don't. They do their best."

"I have to leave, Helen. It's time. I care too much."

"I know. I understand."

And she did.

There was a time of grueling physical labor landscaping for a Palm Springs company before I morphed into a textbook hippie and headed north on highway 1. A portable smoked salmon stand put the VW to good use and lent a vague sense of purpose to camping on the beautiful beaches along the coast. In Monterey, I found several of the desert book club crew from Ruth and Allen's ranch, and other desert family welcomed me in San Francisco. In an apartment in the Haight one evening, all of my senses were unexpectedly overwhelmed when a woman walked in wearing a very unusual pair of leather moccasins.

I asked a few questions and the next day found a tannery, bought a collection of exquisite elk and buffalo hides, and presented myself at the doorstep of Hank, the King of Moccasins. His home and studio were in the foothills of the Sierra Nevada Mountains, and Hank laughed at my precocious audacity before agreeing to take me on as an apprentice. The moccasin makers of the seventies were an elite and creative group, custom designing and fitting each and every pair right down to the handmade buttons. Grace Slick ordered a pair from Hank during this time, which made me an instant celebrity by association.

Donning the new hat, our chameleon moved on. The VW now smelled like South Beach and was equipped with an industrial sewing machine, hides, and tools of a new trade.

• • •

"Something about the air and your soul," Allen had somberly explained. "You will always return."

When I did, I rented a room from friends in a modest mansion in a

West Coast Living

Me with my yellow Volkswagen, *above*, and smoked salmon stand.

La Quinta, 1977. My forever brother, Gordon, with load of hides.

Fitting moccasins.

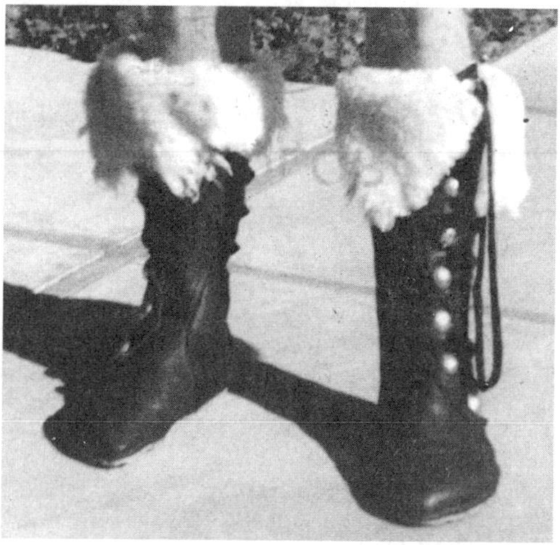

The finished product.

star-studded neighborhood and began to sell moccasins in downtown Palm Springs. It was a time of excess. Alcohol, money, parties by the pool, night clubs, and leather spun me around as I experienced this other end of the desert, this stereotypical lifestyle that, along with golfing presidents and celebrities, flashes through many minds with the mention of *the* Palm Springs.

In the shop, my roommate's friend Jeff scheduled my appointments to fit moccasins and take orders, which I did several times a week. Michael was sitting quietly in a chair by my display examining a pair of chocolate-brown buffalo knee-highs. He was a sight to behold in downtown Palm Springs. Long black hair cascaded from beneath a well-worn, sweat-stained cowboy hat. The long fringe on his gray leather pants hung evenly and had been cut with care, I noted, from top to bottom. The soft leather of his shirt hugged his lean frame and was carefully beaded at the neckline. His dark, round sunglasses were reminiscent of John Lennon, whom he vaguely resembled. He was barefoot. Jeff shrugged his shoulders, shook his head, and walked off to show a customer one of the intricate sculptures he sold.

When I walked toward Mr. Leather, he turned to me and stood up instantly. He actually tipped his hat as he said, "I'm Michael."

I introduced myself as Hilary the Moccasin Maker.

"How do you do, ma'am?" He nodded politely. He had a thick black beard and mustache that, combined with the dark glasses, made me wonder whether he was hiding from the world. Michael was tall and striking, his manner subdued and self-possessed. "I ain't never seen shoes like this." He was cradling the buffalo moc gently in his hands. "I'd like to buy me a pair."

Everyone wanted a pair. Depending on the leather, trim, and buttons, a pair of knee-highs ranged from $300 to $400. The sign in the shop window was clear.

"Sure. Here's how it works: Since each pair is custom fitted, the first thing I do is put you in a pair of socks and cover the sock with duct tape. I draw my pattern on the tape, then cut it off to size the moccasin. I'll need half the money down before I start, the rest when I'm finished."

"I don't carry money on me. Sanette, my manager, has my money."

Sure. "Well, I'll need a down payment. Then we can decide on color, trim, buttons, and talk about exactly how you want your moccasins. That's how it works."

When he lowered his sunglasses, I beheld the deepest, most beautiful brown eyes I'd ever seen. He looked through me, smiled, and nodded. He took my breath away.

"No problem. I'll just have to get it from Sanette. I'm a painter. My work is in Sculptures Three Gallery over there, and I'm pretty sure she's around. Can you wait here a few minutes?"

Sculptures Three was a high-end art gallery in the same plaza.

"I'll be here for a half-hour or so."

"Be right back."

He tipped his cowboy hat again. *Who is this guy?* Jeff and I watched him walk across the courtyard in silence.

"Not *my* type, but definitely interesting," Jeff said. "Think he'll come back with the money?"

"I have absolutely no idea," I admitted. "Where the hell did he come from?"

We watched as Michael headed toward the gallery. He moved like a panther, lithe, mysterious. *Who looks and dresses like that in downtown Palm Springs, and why would someone else take care of his money?* This one was definitely an outcast. Maybe even an oddball.

He was back with the down payment in ten minutes. I admired the tastefulness of the design he wanted and wrapped his feet for my pattern. He asked whether I could have them done within the week — said he had some kind of a show coming up.

"What's so important?" I asked.

"It's an unveiling of one of my paintings. The gallery is putting on some big, fancy invitation thing at a place called Rockefeller's Center. I don't even want to go, but they're kind of making me."

"So, an artist. Where you from? Certainly not around here."

"No, ma'am. I'm from the mountains of Idaho. A friend of mine flew me here 'cause this gallery wanted to handle my work. Do you want to see it, maybe, when we're done here? I mean, if you have time."

This guy was a strange one; I always did like the strange ones. "Sure. Why not?"

Jeff was with a customer when I did the "I'll be back" wave. He nodded, grinned, and went on selling. Michael and I crossed the plaza and went in the rear door of Sculptures Three Gallery. A well-dressed, heavyset man whom Michael introduced as Les, the owner, greeted him warmly. Les was reclining with his feet on the desk, talking with Sanette, an attractive blond who said she was Michael's manager.

Michael lightly touched my elbow and guided me to a spacious room that opened to Tahquitz Canyon Road. This was the street entrance, and in the center of the room was a gigantic canvas set on an easel that was more like a pedestal. Other canvases hung on the walls. Remingtons and other fine sculptures dotted exotic tables and rose up from the marble floor. When he stopped in front of a painting in a handsome wooden frame, I looked up and felt both chills and joy course through me.

The longhaired hippie guy looked a lot like Michael. He wore a different hat and had an easy smile, his right arm around a young woman wearing faded blue jeans and cowboy boots. Both tall and willowy, his hair loose under the hat, hers light brown past her waist with an orange scarf for a headband and an orange tank top. Her jeans hung casually on her hips, and she wore a stunning beaded vest. The couple looked at each other, both smiling, eyes sparkling. When I moved closer to the painting I saw that this artist had actually painted magical sparkles in the lovers' eyes. Walking toward the right side of the canvas, they were riding off into the sunset of happily ever after. Every crease in the clothing, every hair, every inch of the painting was absolutely, perfectly real. Their emotion was palpable. I was transfixed.

"You did that?"

"Yes ma'am."

"It's incredible."

He led me around the room, his room, while I marveled at each painting in turn. Not only were they well done, but each piece held a story, evoked emotion, had power. A red linen cloth covered the canvas that dominated the room. It was tastefully veiled and surrounded by thick red-velvet cord attached to gold stands that formed a protective barrier. He moved toward his creation.

"That's 'Dying Cry of Blue,'" Michael said quietly. "They say it's a big deal. Anyway, it's what the show is about. Custer's Last Stand, 4 x 8 feet and over 700 figures. Took me years. Hell, the frame cost them thousands of dollars."

He carefully lifted the linen to reveal the canvas. I nearly fell over. The battlefield was alive; each figure was as detailed as the couple walking off the canvas. Every blade of grass, horse's hair, weapon, wound, facial expression — all there as real as a photograph. Starting at the bottom corner, it would take weeks to look at it properly.

As I looked over at Michael, Les and Sanette wandered over.

"You must be the moccasin maker."

"I am."

A delightful, beautiful woman in her late thirties, Sanette was a Palm Springs fashion statement: shoulder-length blond hair perfectly layered and styled, pale-green lightweight pants suit, yellow cotton shirt with matching shoes and accessories. She wore jewelry that sparkled like the eyes of the young lovers in the painting.

"Good, isn't he? I've known this guy since he was a kid. Hell of a painter. My husband, Anson, and I flew him out here a few months ago. Had to get Michael to a place where his work can be seen and he can make some money. Idaho just isn't the place for high-end art." She looked at him affectionately and chuckled. "Wasn't easy to get him into our plane. He'd never flown before, *and* it was his first time out of Idaho. But it's working out well for him."

The mystery man hid behind his dark spectacles.

"He's *so* shy. Wouldn't think it to look at him, would you?" Sanette laughed as she walked over to give him a hug. "He's not exactly at home in Palm Springs."

Shy, talented, sexy, mysterious, and rich worked for me.

"Palm Springs is its own little world, for sure. But things change pretty quickly once you get out of town. My roommates own a great little café up the canyon about half an hour. It's another world."

"I'd love to get out of here," Michael said. "Any chance you would let me buy you dinner?"

"A burger and drinks at Sugar Loaf sounds great."

It turned out that Michael actually drank as much as I did. Perfect.

• • •

Palm Springs Life Magazine did a photo shoot and wrote a raving article. The newspapers gobbled him up, this mountain-man master painter in the desert. The flow of money easily kept pace with the flow of liquor.

Rockefeller's was a red-carpet, black-tie event. Chuck Mangione's "Children of Sanchez" filled the intimate auditorium as the curtains parted to reveal Michael's masterpiece to the gasps of Palm Springs' elite art connoisseurs. Clad entirely in leather and wearing his brand-new moccasins, Michael hid behind his trademark sunglasses throughout the show and reception as he held on to my arm for dear life.

Two weeks later, he asked me if I would marry him and move to Idaho.

"Where's Idaho?" I asked. "Isn't that one of those 'I' states like Iowa, Illinois, Ohio? I need a map."

Idaho was precisely where it was supposed to be.

• • •

She didn't know what it meant to be poor until the checks stopped flowing in from the gallery in Palm Springs. Michael had been paid in installments for several paintings, and they had grown accustomed to having income.

Mary and I watched over her. We knew that they needed to move on. She had forgotten her purpose somehow, was lost in an alcoholic haze and needed help. With a battering ram and cosmic connection, we managed to break through the cloud just enough to remind her to move forward. Their friend Buck sold them a beat-up Ford pickup for a dollar. A few tanks full of gas later, they were back in the desert. With commissions, advances, and promises of paintings to be done, Michael had cash in his pocket within a few hours.

Whispers of desert breezes guided the wayward couple away from town and up into the high desert. They pulled over near Joshua Tree Monument and decided to stay. Desolate and forbidding, wild, untamed, uninhabited. Tiny, run-down shacks and trailers randomly dotted the vast expanse of nothingness. Human beings were as sparse as the landscape.

• • •

Our lifestyle in the high desert was every bit as rugged as the harsh, extreme environment. In our shack, boards covered broken windows and duct tape kept the swamp cooler in. We were surrounded by tumbleweeds, wildflowers, cactus, Joshua trees, and gods. Wildlife, though abundant, blended into the environment like the chameleon humans who lived there, showing themselves only when disturbed or hungry. Scorpions, jackrabbits, coyotes, and lizards coexisted with a variety of rattlesnakes, each with its own brand of deadly venom. The "desert rats," a breed of their own, inhabited trailers and shacks, few and far between. Roads were nonexistent, but we knew which path in the sand got us to where we wanted to go.

Outcasts old and young escaped to the Wild West of the high desert where the law of the land was survival, where sandstorms, flooding, and unrelenting heat were taken in stride.

Mary had a friend in her circle of angels who was the guardian of a weathered old desert rat named Skeeter. As our black pickup cruised the hinterlands, Skeet wandered out of his shack to sit in his favorite chair, smoke a cigarette, and pet his dog. He walked a bit bent over these days, a few wisps of long gray hair still sprouted from under the straw hat. The teeth were gone — his own first, and then the set his grandson had bought him. He could still gum his food and spit, though, and he did both with gusto. Skeet was getting on, and though he tried not to let the aches and pains bother him much, there were days when fetching water was becoming more than he could manage.

Timing is everything. Old Skeeter waved when he saw the truck; there hadn't been a car or person around for a couple of days. The Ford stopped at his house, and the die was cast. Skeeter liked his wine, his dog, his "dead chicken" cooking pot, and his desert. Skeet became family.

Jingly Joni lived in a trailer someone had abandoned. She'd fixed it up and had been there fifteen years, mostly alone. Dale, a young Vietnam veteran, carried his .45 in a holster on his hip and felt it was his job to protect his neighbors from snakes and other dangers, real or imagined.

Michael and me, 1984. Trails West Gallery, Laguna Beach, CA.

The one-room shack we rented was on the periphery of the 29 Palms Marine Corps Base, on the edge of thousands of acres used for training and war games. Tanks rolled around the dunes, and gunfire, bomb blasts, and fireworks were everyday fare. Water was delivered in a truck and stored in a large tank outside. When we moved in, Skeet was our friend, neighbor, grandfather, and wise teacher of desert ways. When Skeet got too old to care for himself, we moved his trailer next to our place and helped him — desert rats stuck together then.

Ken's house was the only "real" house for miles around. The 200-acre fortress was a world of its own, set on a sand dune with high chain-link fences and telescopes that provided incomparable 360-degree views. He and his family had a thriving business breeding and training German shepherds. The kennels, immaculate and well appointed, housed thirty or so dogs ranging from pups to adults in training. The dogs were trained for whatever the customer needed — be it drugs, explosives, or protection. Ken's clientele included the LAPD, USMC, the Hell's Angels, and numerous celebrities and professional athletes. The dogs, bred from elite champion lines, had American Kennel Club papers that boasted backgrounds of royalty. His protection dogs were legally registered weapons. Michael and Ken shared a fascination with firearms and explosives; both men had plenty.

Our part of the desert was, at the time, a fascinating remnant of the Old West. There were often rumors of dead bodies found in the wilderness around us, and though we tended to ignore the details, we knew that most of what we heard was true. Bodies were found in shallow graves, having been shot execution style. Ken expended tremendous time and resources converting his home into a fort with heavy gun power, explosives, and machine guns ready to go. Michael joined in the cause with enthusiasm.

Around Christmastime that year, Ken asked Michael to go to Bakersfield with him into deliver some pups. He was to meet the buyer at Denny's restaurant to review pedigrees and papers, collect his money, and come home. Ken was playing both sides of the fence with his business. Although he'd commented about potential dangers of selling to drug dealers and law enforcement, he was making an outrageous amount of money. A bulletproof vest subsequently became part of his wardrobe. Though Michael planned to drive with Ken that day, he bowed out at the last minute to finish a painting. Ken left our house alone with the pups. He uncharacteristically removed his vest when he got to Denny's, locked his car, and joined the customer at a table. They talked a bit, signed paperwork, and went outside to get the dogs.

As he exited Denny's, a man dressed in a Santa suit came toward Ken carrying a long, festively wrapped rectangular box. Three shots in rapid succession from the gift box killed Ken instantly. Merry fucking Christmas.

It was time to go back to Idaho. We loaded a trailer to pull behind the pickup and left Joshua Tree swarming with good guys and villains. They would work it all out on their own. Or not.

• • •

I know that beyond the trash-ridden exterior there is a new Skeeter, a new generation of cast-off misfits inhabiting the wild spaces. Misty does not see the mysteries here as she does in the jungles of Central America. Yet the desert is in her, and she too will return. It is foreign to her eyes but not to her soul.

Misty Dawn

When I stopped drinking that morning of the pink desert sunrise, I was already eight weeks pregnant. Prior to that day, I'd been drinking a fifth of Jack Daniels a day for years. The sunrise knew what I did not.

My daughter comes from a long line of Tender Hearts. Her gentle-souled father destroyed his body and mind with alcohol in an unsuccessful effort to make sense of a nonsensical reality. When I could no longer reach him, my heart broke in two. I love him far too much to have continued watching his tenderness vanish into a cultural and spiritual vortex.

Our daughter struggles mightily to survive with the fragile essence of a Tender Heart. While some cultures honor those who are special, ours does not. Our society clearly ostracizes all who do not fit in a box.

In addition to being a Tender Heart, Misty Dawn also has a very significant family history of mental illness on both sides of the family. I am blessed to be able to comfortably blend professional training with spiritual knowing.

My paternal grandmother was a unique woman. My grandfather had her placed in a mental institution due to "bizarre behavior." In America in the late 1920s, it was not uncommon for abandoned immigrants to be labeled and locked away for being different. Having very recently emigrated from Russia, my grandma spoke little English. Unable to communicate with her wardens,

Grandma Sarah was diagnosed with paranoid schizophrenia. She remained institutionalized until she died in 1976, over forty years later. Her existence was kept secret until I found a faded old hospital record in an uncle's attic years later.

My father stole a mule after serving in Anzio and walked off into the mountains. The army stamped a Section 8 "you are crazy" label on his forehead when they found him in a small Italian village taking photographs of locals in exchange for food, using a camera without film.

My dad's brother Harry has ranted angrily and loudly for as long as I can remember. When I was seven, he stopped his car on a road in upstate New York and made me get out. My thick New York accent, he said, was intolerable, and I should go learn how to speak properly.

Uncle Patrick, ever the favorite uncle on Dad's side, shot himself in the head when he was thirty-four years old. A lovely, sensitive soul — handsome, wealthy, tortured.

Cousin Roger lives in a trailer in the woods in Northern California with two doctorate degrees and an allergy to life that prevents him from communicating with the world or leaving his secluded acre of land.

Et cetera, et cetera — such is a history of ancestors who could not or would not conform. In my professional world, the genetics of mental illness are not questioned. In my personal world, Tender Hearts beget Tender Hearts.

• • •

It has been said that we choose our parents. I recall the moment my daughter decided that I would be her mother. A surge of energy coursed through me, reaching my heart with unexpected surprise. Prior to that moment, the notion of being a parent had occurred to me only as a position that would be heartily inconvenient.

When I bought the pregnancy kit, Misty had been with me for about eight weeks. Michael was doing more drinking than painting, and I worked in the commissary on the marine base for three dollars an hour. I drove 5 miles of unmarked dirt roads to work each morning, rarely seeing anyone else until I got to the back gate of the base.

It was hot.

On my way out the door that morning, a 4-foot Mojave green rattlesnake greeted me with a hiss as my feet hit the concrete slab of a porch. Mojave greens are known for having the most lethal venom of any snake in North

America — venom ten times more toxic than any other rattler. I grabbed a shovel and, with one slick move, chopped its head off. Nothing personal, but there was no other exit, and I didn't have time to mess with a deadly reptile in a foul mood. I had to get to work.

I climbed into the pickup and headed off on one of the paths that we called roads.

I drove a few miles as the sun rose that morning, in awe of the beauty surrounding me — I mean we. We stopped, Baby and me. I explained the basics of survival to Baby, a lesson in the context of "ye who hesitates can be dead in an instant, and we must do what it takes, no matter what — even if we don't necessarily want to." He was in the wrong place at the wrong time. *Sorry, Green Guy.*

The pink sunrise was tinged with impossibly beautiful purple- and orange-layered paint strokes and magic. Sounds of glorious silence. The desert in all its majesty.

Nice job, God. Incredible, actually. I have something to talk to you about. Your power is without limits — that we know. Please, please, I know that what Michael and I have done to our bodies would have gotten all of LA stoned. I know I'm screwed up, but I'm still going to ask. Please, can my baby be healthy? Can my baby be okay and have fingers and toes and not be a victim of my many mistakes in life? I speak to you from the center of all that is beautiful, pure, and good as your creations surround me — the powerful silence of your sunrise, your mountains, the understated elegance of your deserts. Let this baby be born with the essence of your wisdom in its soul. I don't ask forgiveness. I ask that my child be healthy. That's nearly more than I should/could hope for or deserve, but if you can create all this, you can make the arrangement. Thanks, God. Doesn't hurt to ask.

God always answers us.

• • •

Remembering in forward motion, circumstances forced me to sell my 1992 Saab. It was the one and only material possession I have ever loved. Odd, I know.

Absurdly sad and needing a vehicle, I went to a dealership and drove off in a brand-new, leather-seated, sunroof-sporting, flashy, shiny, black Subaru Legacy Sedan.

On the way home, I stopped at the courthouse to tend to some business before heading up Little Donner Pass. I clicked the CD control to replay my favorite song of the day and cranked up the volume. David Gray sang of debauchery. I reached to the back seat for the other half of my biscotti. As I rounded the curve coming out of the pass, I noticed that I was floating through the air in slow motion. I continued listening to my song, feeling little more than a background befuddlement.

"An afternoon's ..."

The music stopped. *Darn, I like that song. I hope the CD is okay.*

I pondered the upside-down angle of the fields outside my new car and pondered David Gray until the wail of sirens interrupted my rambling thoughts. When Bob Gorman's face appeared at the window and asked if I was okay, I took fresh stock of the situation.

Oh, I've spun off the road and landed upside down in a ditch.

Ah, I've been in a wreck.

I nodded to Bob that yes, I was okay. More sirens and more people quickly surrounded the car, and I was instructed not to move. They would get me out. I was lifted out of the driver's side window on a stretcher. They were taking me to Cascade Hospital.

Okay. "How about tipping me up so I can see the car?"

"Hilary, you do *not* want to see your car."

Okay.

Though the car was completely totaled, I wasn't injured, nor had I experienced even a fleeting moment of fear. I'd been in Mary's hands gliding through the air with a comfortable unconscious memory of death.

Of course I was safe. I always have been. I always am.

• • •

Oh yes, back to the desert and my prayer for the baby.

The sky turned brighter pink as I felt a tap on my shoulder, a whisper in my soul. Mary spoke to me from the brightest part of the sunrise, her eyes holding mine. She told me it was time to quit drinking and get my act together.

Okay, I can do that.

And in that instant, I did.

I closed my eyes and stood tall and proud as the first ray of sunlight landed on the Joshua tree beside me. Slowly, I raised my arms to the sky. Without warning, a rush of sensational energy began at the tips of my fingers and flowed

Pregnant in Joshua Tree.

through my body until it connected me firmly to the sand beneath my feet. The flood of emotion surprised me.

I turned four times, giving thanks to the north, south, east, and west. "Amen" took the form of a moment of extra gratitude to earth and sky.

Then I hopped in the old black truck and went to work.

• • •

The baby was due on Thanksgiving Day, 1982. Our friend Ernie and his wife, Tammy, graciously offered us their finest goose for the holiday. Along with the generous gift came Tammy's plan to come over and teach me how to get it ready for the oven.

Oh dear.

I'd seen how she grabbed the birds by their little legs and chopped their heads off. Our dinner was squawking in a cage in the bed of Ernie's pickup when they drove up to the house. Bursting with pride, Tammy set the crate in front of me as she handed me a rather large knife. It would have been inhospitable and rude not to appreciate their gift.

A huge metal pot sat on the sturdy grate over the wood fire as Michael wandered in and out of the shack, he and Ernie stoking the fire and drinking. Food was hardly abundant in our house, though there had never been a shortage of beer. Though I hadn't had a drink since that sunrise in the sand, Michael hadn't missed a sip.

The knife made short work of the goose's head, and then it was straight into the pot of boiling water. Tammy thoughtfully set a stool next to the pot so I could lean on it during my plucking lesson. *So that's how they get the feathers off, eh?* It felt suspiciously like work getting the bird ready for cooking. The men kept the water boiling, Tammy gave me tips, dogs barked, children played, and Baby and I plucked.

Wearing a gigantic red-and-white-checkered shirt that billowed over my denim maternity pants with a scarf for a headband, I felt like a *Little House on the Prairie* woman that night. Though the whole goose-plucking thing was not a scenario I would ever have imagined for myself, I recall thinking about how natural it felt to do whatever needed to be done for the benefit of my child. I closed my eyes for a moment, pledged my love to Baby, and promised that I would forever and always be the very best mother I could be.

That was the night I went into labor.

• • •

Most of us have read about near-death experiences — stories of white lights and being greeted by relatives in another realm. Much has been written about the concept of continuity of self, the notion that the soul progresses through past lives to an intermediate phase, to Earth life, and on to life after death.

It is less common but no less fascinating to hear about people who recall consciousness before their birth into this world — the "pre-birth experience" that seems to occur on a plane similar to near-death experiences.

Misty remembers the day before she was born. She wrote about it, unsolicited, when she was about ten years old.

She didn't know who she was. She didn't know who she became. A thousand lives had filled this one, yet none of them fit. Or perhaps all of them fit. Her identity was ever changing.

Her path started before she landed on this planet to walk it. Her memories started before she was born — the day before she was born, to be exact.

I remember my mother plucking geese. It is my first memory. She sat outside in the desert sun in a cheap folding chair outside the shack that was our home. A pot of water boiled on a fire and the dog milled around hoping that something cooked would come his way.

Me and Misty when she was a toddler.

The only pot big enough to accommodate the geese was the one he drank his water from and he kept an eye on it from a respectful distance. Mom wore a red-and-white checked shirt and a red bandana around her head kept some of the sweat from her eyes. My father was inside drinking beer and painting. A traditional, talented but starving artist. But not this night. Tonight there was goose meat.

My first memory is vague yet clear. The only thing that confuses me is my perspective in the memory. I seem to be sitting on the ground on the other side of the fire from my mother. But, I also remember seeing her from behind. The entire time I was silently watching her. When I told my mother about it, it was at random when I was about ten years old, I think. It came up that I recalled her plucking geese. She looked at me with some measure of surprise.

"I have only plucked geese one time," she said, "and that, is the night I went into labor with you. Are you sure someone didn't tell you about that and you just think you remember it?"

I thought hard. I didn't recall having heard the story, but even if I did, the memory seems exactly like all my other ones. I have always felt that my memories could be memories or dreams, or memories of dreams. They never quite show up in order when I try to call on them specifically. I see the pictures in my mind as unruly as old films that refuse to play from a rusty reel. They are often grainy and seem unfinished somehow. The beginnings and ends are always fuzzy or faded. My first memory is the same. Only, it happened before I was born into this world. Checking in on my mother before I was to be encased within this body that I carry along with me this time around. Whatever meaning there is, I have only this: I have been here before and will likely come back here again. My lessons certainly are not finished and there is so much yet to do.

— Misty Dawn, 1992

When I realized that Misty was cognizant before she was born, I was not as surprised as I could have been. This life, for her, is a special assignment, an act of love for humankind beyond anything you or I can fathom. She chose to come here to help bring our world back to the place of light it's meant be. Given the purity of her motives and soul, however, such a goal causes excruciating inner turmoil.

Michael and I knew that she struggled from the time she was born, yet we had no idea how to help. One night after watching a *20/20* segment on television about maternal alcohol use, Michael held my face in his hands and looked in my eyes.

"That's Misty," he said.

He was right. My alcohol use during those earliest months of pregnancy had caused part of her difficulties. Within a month, she was diagnosed with Fetal Alcohol Spectrum Disorder (FASD) and enrolled in research being conducted by an angelic professor named Dr. Ann through the University of Washington in Seattle. Her department's expertise validated our concerns and gave us practical, useful support to help ease a part of Misty's suffering. With her deep spirituality, high intellectual functioning, and the comorbidity of psychiatric diagnoses, however, Misty has always been an enigma to the world of Western medicine.

Like her father, Misty feels things far too deeply to function in our society.

Michael drinks.

Misty cuts.

When I ended our marriage of over twenty years, I assured Michael that our souls will meet again. He knows. Misty wanted to save him, to rescue him from himself, and she tried. Those were tumultuous, heartbreaking times. I had to let her learn that her father does not want to be saved from himself. The lesson allows her to recognize a part of own struggle.

It is too difficult for souls as sensitive as those of Misty and Michael to exist here. Though they are always looking for the exit sign that will provide a way out, they must endure this existence in order to fulfill their purpose.

Michael lives an isolated life in the mountains of Idaho. I will always love him.

Misty is occasionally still restrained for her own safety in various ways, and I am never surprised to be contacted by police, hospitals, friends, or an embassy here and there. I love and support her unconditionally and strive to understand her journey and her purpose here on Earth. That's the very best I can do.

• • •

I realized on day one that taking my job with the outpatient mental health clinic meant actually *being* the person to manage the clinic. That meant being the one person in a county roughly the size of Connecticut to be called whenever there was a mental health crisis. In those days before cell phones, I was given a pager that connected me to law enforcement, physicians, hospitals, and other key agencies — 24/7, 365 days a year. When the beeper beeped, I would find a phone and call the number appearing on the read-out.

Misty quickly learned that when the beeper beeped my attention would be shifting from her to somewhere else. She alternately encouraged me to turn it off, leave it at home, or smash it with a hammer. So began a ferocious rivalry between a pager and a tender little girl.

• • •

In the summers, Misty and I grabbed our fishing poles, found worms and marshmallows, and moseyed down the washboard dirt roads to cast our fate to the wind. Though the lake teemed with trout, the "beaches" (I had trouble calling them beaches) were usually empty except for a few hardcore fisherpeople intent on catching their limit. Though Misty and I were far from hardcore, we did add new dimensions to the local fishing scene with our ultra-casual approach. I found forked sticks, buried them in the sand, and then rested the poles in the crooks of the sticks so no one had to actually hold them. After that, it was simply a matter of watching the bobber. The other favorite option was to lie in the sand with the fishing line between my toes and read until I felt a toe wiggle. Old-timers scoffed at the newbies' lazy ways and lack of attentiveness. They believed that the harder you stared at the water, the more likely the fish were to take your bait.

Nevertheless, there were days when we jumped and cheered on the sand, catching one trout after another while the old-timers looked on. Sometimes they packed up and walked off, grumbling and shaking their heads while secretly smiling at Misty's glee and our lighthearted ways. Summers were glorious in the high mountains. We fished from shore until late fall. Soon after that, the snows came, the lake froze, and ice fishing season began.

One summer Saturday, Misty and I walked to the lake early in the morning with poles over our shoulders and a cooler packed with worms, sandwiches, and cold drinks to get us through the day. We chose a spot toward the end of the peninsula where the water was deep and the fish were plentiful. Since it was Stump's neighborhood, he sat watching us, his bark beaming at mother and daughter's shared pleasure. Our neighbor Ray fished nearby, and we saw Jill the Mayor/liquor store owner in her chair way down by the Willards'

Misty Dawn

Misty Dawn, 2007.

In Central American jungle, 2011.

My mom and Misty Dawn, Donnelly, Idaho, 1986.

summer house. I was reading aloud to Misty as she worked on a sand sculpture and we kept one eye on the bobbers.

When the beeper beeped, my little girl instantly burst into tears.

"Mom, don't go. Please don't go. *Please*, not today, Mommy."

As her distress escalated, I recognized that in her mind the pager was a rival for my love. I took her in my arms and held her until the sobbing subsided. Then I picked up the beeper and turned the damn thing off. I felt a lump in my throat as her eye color turned from hazel to gray to a blue that rivaled the bright summer sky. With a trace of a whimper, she asked if I was really going to stay with her as I smiled and tucked her nemesis into the tackle box.

I continued reading *The Great Big Book of Why* until Misty's bobber summoned our attention to her pole. I sat behind her as she struggled with the reel, and soon a good-sized trout was flopping on the sand. When she held the fish up, she could barely lift it off the ground.

"You caught dinner! Wow!"

"I did? Really? Daddo is gonna be proud of me, huh?"

"You bet he is. That's some fish you've got there, and all by yourself!"

Old Ray moseyed over to congratulate her. He'd been fishing since dawn without a nibble. Misty beamed as we put her trout on the stringer and tossed it into a bucket. Ray smiled and baited her hook for her before helping her cast it back out. When her pole was safely back in the crook of the tree limb, she resumed her sculpture and I continued reading about why the grass is green.

Another day in paradise.

An hour later, we heard footsteps coming from the woodsy area behind the beach. When I turned around, the sheriff appeared through a stand of trees with a wave and a smile. Michael and I were friends with Sheriff Greg and his family, but this was not a social visit. He cast me a meaningful glance before meandering over to visit with Misty and admire her sand sculptures.

"Got your dad's knack for art, don't you, Misty? That's really something! Nice work."

"It's gonna be a horse ranch. I'm finishing this house now. Then I'm gonna build stables. Look, Greg, I even brought my horses, and they're gonna fit in there."

"Wow, they are! Even the one with the pink mane. Very cool. I'm going to talk to your mom for a minute while you do that, Misty."

"Okay, Greg."

He parked himself in the sand next to me and put his arm around my shoulder.

"I figured you might be here, Hilary. And catching fish, I see."

"Yes sir, having a nice day with my daughter. Didn't you get the hint when I blew off the page?"

"I know. I'm sorry."

"No."

"Yes."

"NO."

"Sorry. It's a doozy, and we need you. Otherwise I wouldn't have come all the way out here. We've got a guy who sped through town at 70 miles an hour running from one of my deputies. When we caught up with him, he told us that he was being chased by a biker gang from California. Says they're after him because he knows where their hidden treasure is. Something about his grandmother leaving him a map when she died and this gang finding out. Anyway, he says a bobcat told some biker he was camping by the river in Riggins. I didn't catch how he knew that, but apparently when they find him, he'll be tortured until he gives up the map. Then they're going to drag him, off to a cave, I think. Stuff you would understand way better than we do. He raced through Adams County too. They contacted us when he left their jurisdiction. The guy has put a lot of people at risk, so we have him in a cell."

I sat with the *Why* book opened to "Why is the Sky Blue?" and wondered Why Minds Become Tortured.

"Why today, damn it."

"I don't know. The guy is screaming in a jail cell, and I'd sure rather see him go to the hospital."

Misty knelt in the sand with her toy horses. When she walked over, I sat her on my lap while Greg wandered off to give us privacy. Her eyes filled with tears as they held my heart.

"Why?" she asked.

"Sweetheart, this is a big, giant world we live in, even bigger than us and Stump. There's our piece of the world, and then there are a bunch of other big, humongous pieces that stretch way, way far all over the place. Inside of us there's a special string that connects us to stuff outside our part of the world — all the gazillions of people and things that are out there."

"Really? Do I have a string part like that?"

"You sure do. It's the part that belongs to the universe, Misty. It's the part that exists to help others by sharing some of what we have inside. That part cares deeply and wants to help people. It's sort of a big, giant chunk of love."

"I have a chunk like that!" Tears stopped flowing as the wise little soul connected lifetimes of dots.

"Oh, you certainly do! You have a *huge* chunk of love inside of you. That's why you're so kind to people and why you always rescue sick animals. Remember last week when you helped the wounded bird?"

"Yeah, the one that bonked his head when he flew into the window and then Sylvester got him in his mouth. I yelled at that bad kitty, then he dropped her."

"You did indeed. Sylvester was just being a kitty. He didn't know he was hurting her until you told him. But that bird needed your help to get better, didn't she? And we took care of her until she could fly away home to her family, right?"

"Oh yes, Mom. I fed her with a dropper and did a really good job taking care of her. Then she could fly away again!"

"She could and she did, didn't she? Did it make you feel good that she got better?"

"Yeah. She flew right off."

"Why did you take care of that birdy, Misty?"

"Because it needed help, and I could be the one to help her." Misty was silent as her eyes filled with compassion and wisdom before capturing mine with our familiar jolt. Her moment of knowing created a current that flowed through the wise little body into the big mom body, then back to eternity. "You help the people you work with, like that nice Sophie lady I met who moves funny, huh Mom?"

"Exactly. I have to go with Greg, Misty, to help somebody. That's part of why we're here on Earth, my love. To help others whenever we can. And we help from our hearts because that's just the way we are. It's a very, very good way to be. Even when there are other things we feel like doing, Snookerdoodle, helping to ease pain comes first."

As the little body got up from the sand, toes wiggled and bare feet rose above the earth for an instant. Then a spot of light left the beach to sit lightly on Stump for a moment before returning to shore, entering the body, and sitting gently on the ground.

"I get it, Mom. You have to go help someone. But you'll be back soon, and we can play here some more, right?"

Another jolt, two old souls connecting with the wisdom and love of the ages.

"That's exactly right, Misty. So how about we take your giant trout and our stuff and make Greg put it in his police car so it gets all stinky?" We laugh with the delight of our mischievous plan while Greg starts walking toward us.

"Hey, I'll gather up the gear and bring Misty to the house while you get changed, okay?"

"Okay. It'll just take me two minutes to walk home. See you there."

The little girl does her adorable crooked wink and gives her mom a hug while sweet knowing courses through them.

• • •

Hiking was my favorite pastime for many years. I loved the silence and solitude of the vast wilderness and the feel of my body moving through space. For the most part, I preferred to hike with my dog Molly for companionship rather than a talking, walking person who would interfere with my Very Important Thoughts.

I hiked in remote areas with little likelihood of seeing other people because Molly and I preferred to be alone. I loved the movement, the solitude of the forests, and the dozens of high mountain lakes that rewarded those long treks with an invigorating swim.

Idaho has more undeveloped public land than any state other than Alaska, including the largest area of unbroken wilderness in the lower forty-eight states. Nearly 10 percent of the state's 83,000 square miles is available to explore, respect, and love. The Frank Church River of No Return Wilderness alone covers nearly 2.5 million acres.

God's Country. Unspoiled.

When Misty started wanting to hike, she was about four years old, and I simply carried her when her little legs got tired.

There was a particularly notable hike, a rare one with a planned destination that included a small group of friends. We would meet Barb and her two teenage boys for a hike to Loon Lake to celebrate Sam's thirteenth birthday. A magnificent river hike, the trail begins by going 4 miles downstream on the Secesh River through granite outcroppings, meadows, and lodgepole pine forest. The river is clear with occasional white sand pocket beaches that made perfect resting spots along the way. Across the bridge, we headed up a slope and through a stand of aspen trees that opened to a meadow on top. The 6,000-foot high lake is surrounded by fir forests and is steeped with history. The area is home to an abundance of wildlife including moose, elk, deer, and bears. The silence is deafening, the landscape stunning.

Misty and Angel.

We met early in the morning and took our time going up and in. Misty and the boys had grown up together, and the older boys treated her like a little sister. Molly and her herding instincts would keep tabs on everybody as she tried in vain to keep us all together. Ultimately, she stayed with me when cooperation was lacking. We spent the morning leisurely making our way to the lake, where the hungry children were delighted to see a feast of a lunch appear from our daypacks. In midsummer, the high mountain lakes are delightfully cool and brisk, so swimming and exploring lasted for hours.

In January 1943, a B-23 bomber crash-landed on the frozen lake and came to rest about 150 feet from shore during a snowstorm. After almost three weeks of surviving in the Idaho wilderness, all eight crew members were rescued. The World War II bomber has been sitting in the trees near the shore for seventy years. The crash site made a perfect playground from which all manner of journeys and stories could be imagined and played out. We swam in the pure, icy water, lazed on the grassy shores, and were vividly alive. Watching the children, we recognized how blessed they were to be familiar and at ease in such a dramatic mountain environment. This was what they knew, and their memories would begin in harmony with nature. The boys tried to catch fish with their hands in the crystal clear lake while Misty studied the shallow tadpole section on the west side. She came back with her canteen and announced that she had captured some tadpoles and would take them home to watch them evolve. Molly kept a vigilant eye while endlessly fetching sticks.

She was prepared for the appearance of a monster and would leap into action in a heartbeat when danger struck. We could count on her.

It was midafternoon when we packed up to head back. We would easily make the trailhead with plenty of daylight. Barb and the boys went ahead while Misty, Molly, the tadpoles, and I followed closely behind. Misty opened the canteen lid every few minutes to check on them. Despite having walked all day, the little trooper was determined to make the entire hike on her own. We were nearly back when I told Misty to wait as I stopped at a bush to relieve myself while Molly ran off in chase of a rabbit. Within two minutes I was heading down again with everyone ahead of me on the clearly marked trail. It wasn't long before the trailhead was in sight. We would drive back to town and have dinner at our favorite Mexican restaurant. I saw Molly begging jerky from Sam before we realized in horror that Misty was nowhere to be seen.

Horrified, we immediately turned around and ran back up the trail. The boys disappeared into the thick forest along the riverbank, Barb took the higher road, and Molly and I retraced our steps. Misty had continued walking when I'd stopped but had somehow gone off the trail within the last half-mile. It was dusk, the sun had gone behind the mountain, and darkness would come quickly.

This was the stuff of nightmares and bad movies, not the kind of terror that belonged in our lives. I remember my heart stopping as my little girl's name echoed through the endless forest. She was all alone out there. How could this have happened to such seasoned, savvy hikers? Where could she possibly have wandered off to?

What must have been less than five minutes felt like weeks as I pictured all manner of dangers and wild animals. She sat leaning on a tree by the side of the trail, tiny, vulnerable, and sobbing. I whisked her into my arms and held her so tightly she had to wiggle her way out of my arms to breathe. Relief permeated the forest as we all came together. Molly was thoroughly embarrassed that she'd followed Sam and the beef jerky rather than doing her designated herding job.

Misty had decided to let the tadpoles go in the river. It wasn't nice to take them home when they were creatures of the forest. She had changed her mind and wanted them to stay out here where they belonged. She'd ventured off the trail for only a moment to set them free just as I'd come out from my bush and passed her by on the trail. Night was falling now as I carried Misty to the car with her arms wrapped tightly around my neck.

"Mommy, I was scared."

"I know, baby. So was I."

"I didn't know what to do when I couldn't see anybody."

"You did exactly the right thing. You sat down."

"I sat down 'cause I was so tired, and then I heard a voice tell me not to keep going."

"Your voice inside you gave you guidance, told you what to do. Inside you have a big self that helps you when you're afraid, helps you always survive. You maybe didn't hear it out loud because it's not usually very loud. It's a survival instinct, and you must have been listening very, very carefully to your own wisdom, sweetheart."

"I was?" The sobbing had subsided now as a lesson emerged from within the panic.

"You were. You are. Always, always, listen for the voice inside you, Misty. It will never lead you astray and will keep you safe. You have a big grown-up bunch of stuff that comes out when you need it, and you've always been wise enough to pay attention. When you're afraid, always be very, very quiet, and you'll hear it like you did just now."

"Mom? I love you."

I squeezed her more tightly again, my own tears welling up in my heart. "And I love you. And Molly ran right to you. She is a good finding dog."

"Yeah, I'll always sit still so she can find me. I promise. But can you just carry me the rest of now, Mom?"

"You bet. I'm gonna hold on to you really tightly."

"Me too, Mommy. You and me and Molly, right?

"Right. And the wisdom inside."

Breast Cancer

"Your mammogram shows an abnormality, Hilary. You need to get it checked."

Okay.

With the blessing of continued access to the finest medical care, I called the Seattle Cancer Care Alliance and scheduled an appointment. I felt no fear or trepidation about having a mass in each breast. Instead, I was rather annoyed with the prospect of another medical hassle.

When I scheduled the appointment, it hadn't occurred to me that buildings of brick and mortar had personalities, yet walking through the front doors of the SCCA was like being enveloped in the arms of a lover — comfortable and safe. The air was filled with competence and compassion, and the blinking neon aura assured all comers that "we do *not* screw around here."

The first appointment lasted six hours and included a team of five collaborating doctors.

"Hilary, you have breast cancer, but if you have to have breast cancer, this is the good kind."

Okay. Lucky me.

"The biopsy of your right breast confirms that the mass is cancer. The one in your left breast appears to be benign, but we'd like to remove it so we can be 100 percent certain.

Okay.

The surgeon, Dr. Lucas, was a beautiful young woman with a heart that filled the room and the reputation of a goddess. Her sharp blue eyes missed nothing. Her hands glowed subtly and emanated palpable skill. I trusted her instantly and implicitly.

"We'll do surgery, and then you'll need radiation but hopefully no chemo."

A date was set to operate on both breasts. I explained that if she saw any indication that a mastectomy was advisable, I was perfectly fine with having both of my breasts removed. She appeared to understand that I did not have a significant emotional attachment to my body and nodded in agreement.

I came out of anesthesia with two breasts and Dr. Lucas's assurance that she had removed all the cancer and left clear margins. I believed her.

The cutting-edge option in terms of radiation at that time was called brachytherapy. It involved the insertion of tubes, or catheters, through the breast directly around the surgery site. They were to be left in place for two weeks, during which time radiation was to be administered through the tubes twice a day, like a firing squad with rifles sited in and aimed at their target. Only the offensive spot would receive radiation, increasing the intensity and shortening the time frame for post-surgical treatment. I would stay at one of the SCCA's partner hotels for two weeks and get this done. No muss or fuss.

"Okay. Let's get on with it." Always in a bit of a rush, I am forever impatient, needing to move through, over, or around every obstacle in order to make my way forward. When I went in for the catheter insertion, I was confident and prepared.

"I'll be fine," I'd told my husband. "Two short weeks, and it's all over. No need for you to come to Seattle."

A miniature platoon was assembled in the small procedure room when I was brought in and instructed to lie face down with my breast hanging through a hole so it could be accessed from below.

Cool Boob Table.

The breast would be numbed, and the catheters placed. Radiation would begin the next day. Little did I know that was to be the day I would learn the true meaning of a ten on what I used to think of as "that silly pain scale."

The lead radiation oncologist, Dr. Cheng, calmly explained the procedure. It sounded very straightforward. Selena, the nurse positioned by my head, was the designated hand holder, and of course, behind her, Mary's face faded in and out.

So it began. I have only a few still snapshots in my head with which to account for the rest of the day. The catheter placement procedure was done in the SCCA building on the campus of the University of Washington Medical Center. Local anesthetics were administered, and catheter insertion began. It was immediately apparent that the anesthetic was completely ineffective as I found myself lying on my stomach gripping the table with white knuckles and tears streaming down my face.

General anesthesia, they apologized, was not available in this facility, and it was too late to move me to the main hospital. I begged the hand holder to "please conk me on the head with a hammer." I screamed. I cried. I yelled. I held my breath and pleaded to be knocked out — *Please, Lord, make this stop, for Christ's sake, and stop putting those idiotic Q-tips in my mouth and telling me they're pain medicine.* "Hammer," I begged. Tears soaked the table, and Hand Holder looked into my eyes with helpless compassion.

I thought of the Indian sun dancers, and it occurred to me that perhaps I too had a spiritual purpose in withstanding such a level of physical agony. Had I known ahead of time, perhaps I could have been in a different space. But I hadn't, and I wasn't. As Mary made every effort to hold my heart with her own, eighteen catheters were inserted through my breast that morning, each one slowly, methodically, and precisely.

I exhibited zero stoicism, tolerance, graciousness, understanding, or guts. I was reduced to a melted, blubbering puddle of whinery and had to be pried off the boob table with the jaws of life.

When I was wheeled out, Ron, who had taken the day off and come down despite my bravado protests, did not immediately recognize the battered woman in the wheelchair as his wife. When he did, he crossed the room to hold me, to do his best to soak up part of the suffering.

We heard the familiar, if not well-loved, mantra: "We've never seen this happen before."

But it was done. Radiation could begin. I was transported to the hotel room where Ron made sure I was settled in and knew that everything would be all right before he headed home.

I know. But DAAAAMMMMMNNNN, that hurt.

The protocol was changed that day.

That procedure was never done again.

I have the dubious honor of being the catalyst for an instantaneous procedural change in a facility that does not screw around with patient care. I also learned that the true meaning of a pain-scale ten is having eighteen tubes jammed through your breast without anesthesia.

It was three years before I learned that the local anesthetic injections had missed their mark. Human error.

The following morning, radiation began. Kate, the nurse in charge of administering the secret potion through the evil tubes, surprised me with the gift of music. I was as comfy as one can be on a cold metal table with a pillow, blankie, and kind faces above my head. Kate held out a set of headphones and several CDs. Out of all the zillions of CDs in the world, there it was in her hand: *Joshua Tree*. I smiled and asked her to please play Molly's song, "Running to Stand Still."

I knew that Kate knew that I knew that she was only as real as the invisible cure being run through the catheters. Twice a day for two weeks, my organic brain sang silently Loudly and Out of Tune. Then the cancer was gone.

"Take the poison from the poison stream."

Yes, Molly. Again.

When I went back to thank Kate during one of my follow-up visits, she was not to be found. I didn't pursue it. In fact, I wasn't the least bit surprised.

I've heard that five years of being cancer-free is a good omen.

I'm at four years and six months.

Last month, I felt a new lump in the same breast. I saw the same winged surgeon woman, who held my hand as a butterfly lit on her shoulder. She looked into my soul as she said, "Let's look at it again next month, Hilary."

"Okay."

• • •

She had tried, done her best, to be a Walton, to keep the family together and make it all work. She'd worked tirelessly for years, saved, bought a spectacular ranch with a studio for Michael, a barn and land for Misty's horse, and plenty of space for everyone's projects. Despite the divorce, she still loved him and thought it could all come together. If she only tried harder, the "Good night, John Boys" and wide-open spaces would define their lives. The idyllic spot was supposed to make everything better.

It didn't.

Michael had been "removed" from the shop/studio by Hilary's friend Jack when he refused to leave. This drinking binge had been the scariest ever; each one was predictably worse than the last. The guns got bigger, the finger itchier, the threat of death more real. The sheriff was too afraid to come over since the time he had responded to a call and been greeted by the barrel of a Browning automatic rifle machine gun.

She knew he was capable of killing, and she knew she would be the first one to be shot. Her knees, body, and voice quivering, she had told her then-husband that this time *she* was not the one leaving. She was genuinely surprised to be alive at the end of the sentence. When the bullet hit the ground beside her, she knew it was not his aim. It was his special way of saying that he was not going to leave. She had been living in fear and very real danger, yet this time, she had held her ground.

Only Jack and Dog could have gotten Michael out. Nothing else intimidated him. Her friend Jack knew no fear. A big man — 6'4", broad shoulders, powerfully built. He tied his blond hair in a ponytail that reached past his waist, and his eyes — Jack's piercing blue eyes — were full of tricks. Jack stared without blinking at Michael's arsenal of weapons, straight through his fierce façade and mysterious persona. Jack looked into Michael and smiled his special bone-chilling smile. His *Shining* smile. Both Jack and his dog, Dog, had the same smile — and a reputation that went with it.

A living legend in the rural Idaho community and dubbed Crazy Jack by locals because he liked to play with explosives, he lived in a secluded house 15 miles from town. He stayed out of trouble for the most part and occasionally indulged himself by blowing up a vehicle or building that nobody was using. And his eyes — he had an uncanny ability to look at people and prevent them from looking back. He was unpredictable, wild, solitary.

When she and Jack were first introduced, they had shaken hands, looked at one another, and burst into laughter. There was intensity in the unspoken irony of their instant connection. Years later, she understood that Jack was an angel in the unlikely guise of an ex-Hell's Angel. Jack had appeared when she was in trouble, taken care of her, and asked nothing in return. Jack was her protector.

The loaded .44 Magnum stayed under her pillow for two months after Jack moved Michael out. She knew that in his grief and sickness, he would kill her, and she'd been completely prepared to shoot first. She didn't know that Jack had been staying in his camper down the hill, where he could watch the road and her driveway. Her angel had moved on only after Michael stopped stalking her, once Jack was certain that she and her daughter were safe.

• • •

There was a sigh of relief now that I could get on with my life, that Misty and I could live in peace without Michael's drama. But it was not to be.

• • •

A cry of anguish pierces the world and rises swiftly through the suddenly meaningless walls of her house, shooting past hawks circling above, up, up, until it lands at that place in the sky where pain lives. The heartache is physical and heavy with so much weight that her body slides from the couch to lie face down on the floor.

Molly knows. The dog is beside her in an instant, nuzzling the body, loving her, telling her she isn't alone. She reaches out and hugs the aging Blue Heeler and together, always together, they cry until there is nothing left.

Spent, they get up and walk outside. They are alone. Their surroundings, when they can focus, are majestic. Snow-covered mountains, the Gold Fork River visible through the strong, old stands of pine trees. A dirt road down the hill hugs the river and goes on forever, back through boundless wilderness where isolated cowboys and enormous cattle ranches have sustained themselves for generations. Past the fence in the front yard, where pastureland seems endless, the cows live their trouble-free cow lives, unaware of potentially scheming teenage cow tippers.

She turns, looks at the barn and shop. Empty but for the bales of hay now. Misty's beloved horse, Angel, is in one of the back fields, perhaps visiting with a neighbor horse near a fence, always waiting for those moments when Misty grabs her mane and gracefully, effortlessly, flies through the air to light on the back of the giant Appaloosa, waiting for those times when they move as one and gallop to that land of total freedom. Angel will be sad.

She looks at the road and beyond, knowing that this is where she belongs; her home is the ultimate refuge. A few stray Loomis sheep are grazing out back on the hill. The heeler ponders going into livestock alert mode but decides to focus on her human instead. Above West Mountain, the sun is beginning its leisurely late afternoon ritual, moseying to the place where it will settle in for the night.

The child had decided to live with her father now, to save him from himself. Misty haphazardly packed some bags and tossed them in the back of the little crinkled copper truck — after hitting that deer last month, the headlights, stuffed back in their damaged sockets, point in random directions. No matter, it left a cloud of dust as Misty sped down the long dirt driveway. This was *not* going to be okay. She was *not* safe. Fourteen-year-old Misty had become increasingly obstinate, confused, and angry. She was moody, sullen, and rude, refusing counseling, boundaries, curfews, conversation.

The truck was long gone now, up in the next town raising dirt on the road where Michael had a trailer to stay in.

Dear Lord.

She felt her heart break, leaving her soul open and vulnerable.

In that instant, that stabbing excruciating moment when the piercing, inhuman sound left her, it did not travel alone.

• • •

Switching from my reality to the present illusion, I catch my breath long enough to realize that I'm again in a hospital, this time in Seattle.

The hospital's ninth floor is for the sickest of the sick. It has been five days since Ron was admitted through the ER with extremely labored breathing and a rapid, irregular heartbeat. He'd been sick for nearly two weeks before he'd finally agreed to go in. Despite stabilization and sophisticated testing, a diagnosis beyond "severe lung injury" remained elusive.

I was physically, mentally, and emotionally exhausted when I got on the elevator. I had to find a new hotel room because Kenny Chesney's concert the following night had every room in town reserved, including mine.

Forcing one flaming foot in front of the other, I was lost in my head when I stepped into the empty elevator car. After a while, I noticed that not only were the doors still shut, but the elevator hadn't moved. It was another minute or two before I realized that the elevator was stuck. When I pressed the alarm intercom, it was promptly answered.

"Yes, hello," she said.

"Hi there. I'm stuck in the elevator."

"Oh, the elevator is stuck?"

"Yes. And I'm in it."

When the voice assured me that she would call security, I thanked her, and she politely clicked away.

I leaned against the elevator wall and let my body slide down to a sitting position, grateful for the rest. As I closed my eyes, my brain wandered to a less complicated reality. When I checked my watch, thirty minutes had passed without a sound. Nothing. I scooted on my butt to the buttons and pressed the alarm again.

"Yes, hello."

"Hi, elevator voice. I'm still stuck in the elevator."

"Oh. They're working on it."

"Okay, thanks. Bye now."

At my security wall, I snuggled into the luxurious cloud of the other reality. I awakened as the tip of a shiny sword slid between the closed doors.

Camelot, I thought.

"Well, hello!" The sword and I are old friends.

Silence. Sword never was much of a talker. Soon the doors opened to reveal Richard Harris in a suit of armor looking at me through layers of truth. When I held out my hand, King Arthur gallantly helped me to my feet before leaning over for the hand kiss. I thanked him with a smile and stepped out of the elevator as he faded away. Dizzy and too exhausted to take another step, I spotted an empty gurney parked against a nearby wall. Without a second thought, I lay down and continued my travels.

The hospital's reality was very far away, little more than a distant background shuffle. I vaguely heard someone asking whether I was okay and heard myself answer that I was very okay, just resting and a bit lightheaded. I wanted to lie there for a moment or two. *Thanks for asking, now go away*. I'm pretty sure I didn't say the go away part out loud.

As I rested comfortably, I watched a nurse quietly raise the rails of the gurney just as "code 4 by the ninth floor elevators" was announced over the hospital's loudspeaker. As I heard the code, I saw myself lying contentedly on the gurney. Next thing I knew, I opened my eyes and the gurney was surrounded by a small army of medical people.

I'm not a Code, silly people, I thought. *I've just reached my limit. I can't walk, I can't think, I can't fix Ron, and I don't have the energy to be evicted from my hotel. Misty took my Alfie home, and my feet feel like they're standing on hot coals. I've simply reached a limit and decided to check out for a while. I'm fine. Be back shortly. Just resting my soul.*

The gurney was moving. From another time and place, a whispered memory moved on a gurney. When I opened my eyes, a handsome young man with hazel eyes leaned over me.

"I'm David," he said.

"David," I whispered. My dad was a David. "Roll me to Nordstrom Rack?" I heard myself ask.

"I don't think so." Good-natured laughter from dear David and several assistant gurney drivers. I watched a short film clip of the body being pleasantly wheeled around the new downtown Seattle Rack accompanied by stylish shopping helper nurses. *Perfect.*

"We're going to take you to the emergency room so they can make sure you're all right. What's your name and date of birth?"

I was sure I blinked and answered that question, but I told them again. I saw myself lift my head every few minutes to see how I was doing. The body was not willing to move. A banner floated by reminding me that as long as I was agreeable, they wouldn't make me get up.

Okay.

ER staff took over checking vitals and bustling about. When a warm blanket appeared, I gratefully snuggled in. The nurse assigned to watch over me, Nanette, was in her early forties with a broad, almost cherubic face and gently probing pale-blue eyes. She leaned over and quietly asked me what was really going on, as old, familiar tears slipped from my eyes, even as they remained closed.

"What?" she asked kindly.

"I'm just resting," I heard myself say. "My husband is very ill, my feet are on fire, the hotel next door is kicking me out, and I'm dizzy."

She arranged the blanket and touched my shoulder ever so sweetly. "Relax. I'll be back."

Tink drifted out of the room, taking a piece of my consciousness with her. A mini-huddle arrived at a consensus that no one knew what happened to me, but I was medically stable. Nanette was talking on the telephone in a firm, authoritative manner as Tink darted in closer to listen. She was reminding the hotel manager that patients' families come first and demanding that I be moved to a different wing and be given a better rate. "The hospital owns the damn hotel," she muttered. "How dare they!"

Juice and a graham cracker appeared along with a lovely presence at my side. "You okay, Hilary? You aren't being evicted. They've found a wonderful room for you. Just stop at the front desk and ask for Caroline. She's going to move you across the street and get you set up."

"Wow. Thank you so much. I didn't know what I was going to do. Thank you." Feeling better now, I opened my eyes and looked at her. Her essence morphed slowly through time as her eyes wandered back through the ages and became many angels rolled into one. Mary's eyes appeared just long enough for us to make contact. When I recognized her, I was not surprised. I breathed deeply. "You're awfully special." *Understatement of the millennium.*

"Thanks. So are you. If you have any problems, just give me a call. I've written my number on your discharge papers."

The doctor came in to run through another mental status exam. I passed with flying colors since I knew my name, birthdate, and where I was.

"Did you lose consciousness?"

"Not completely," I answered, smiling to myself as clear pictures of JFK and knights in shining armor meandered about my consciousness. Hovering above a landing pad in a familiar foreign reality, I considered what an incredibly complicated question that was.

"Are you feeling well enough to leave?"

"Yes, I'm good. I was just tired and dizzy. I'm better now."

"All right, then. Your discharge papers are ready, and you can leave any time."

I slowly stood up and put myself back together, then parted the curtains to my ER room.

"Thanks again," I told Nanette.

"Be seeing you. Take good care of yourself."

I had no doubt whatsoever that we shall meet again.

I hobbled to the hotel desk and was ever so graciously moved to a room in their building across the street. Still partly in another realm, I had to keep shaking my head to gather myself into the present moment.

Ron was doing a bit better on oxygen, though his condition continued to baffle the doctors. We didn't talk, but I held his hand and he rested comfortably.

• • •

I was a bit surprised when I heard myself book a seat on the 7:30 train to Bellingham the next morning. The Amtrak ride was soothing, and when I got home, Alfie and I agreed that a trip to Stickyville and a dip in the lake were the perfect way to celebrate the end of our very first separation. Within a few hours, a higher authority told me to pack my bag and go back to Seattle.

Despite my exhaustion, I knew better than to question myself, and we made it to the station just in time to catch the 2:30 back to King Street Station.

The doctors had come and gone by the time I reached Ron's hospital room, but he was breathing better and resting more comfortably. Relieved and exhausted, I said good night and headed to the new hotel room. When Alf and I greeted the bearded old man smoking cigarettes on the corner, the inevitable dog conversation ensued. He was from Alaska, down to be with his son during surgery. He talked of his dogs and the splendor of the wilderness where he lives.

I followed him to the grandeur with my heart, remembering the bewitching splendor of the Idaho mountains.

"Idaho is like a small Alaska," I explained. "Absolutely as beautiful in the right places but on a smaller scale. I love it there."

He itched his beard, smiled, and nodded his head.

A tiny voice chimed in. "I'm from Idaho!" Olivia had appeared from nowhere. A delicate, tiny young woman with round green eyes, long, light-brown hair, and a tentative air, it seemed to have taken great effort for her to join the conversation. In her early twenties, she was frightened, fragile, and vulnerable. We were immediately familiar.

From Caldwell, Idaho, she was in Seattle to be treated for complicated pancreatitis. Her condition is rare, she explained, and requires a sophisticated level of treatment available only in a few select hospitals in the Northwest. I understood completely, absolutely. Virginia Mason was paying all of her expenses; she was having a procedure done in the morning. Little Olivia was clearly frightened and clearly very ill. She kneeled down to pet my Smile before looking up with her own as our hearts connected. I felt her goodness, saw her courage, and knew her soul. When she saw that I had difficulty walking, she offered to take Alfie up the quiet street to a grassy spot at the top of the hill. Because I had known her essence, I easily handed her Smile's leash and watched her face light up like a three-year-old on Christmas morning. Alf looked at me, and when I nodded, he totally got it.

Olivia didn't want to be alone with her fear. Having changed rooms during this time of straddling realities, she and I were now next-door neighbors. When we got to my room, Olivia told me about her illness and pain, her medical procedure, her life, and the dim future she saw for herself given the nature of the disease. She spoke matter-of-factly, not with a hint of self-pity but rather with incredible courage. She did not expect to see thirty.

"Why don't you get a new one?" I asked.

"New what?"

"New pancreas."

"A new pancreas?" She smiled sadly. "I wouldn't know where to begin, and no doctor has ever mentioned it. But I've secretly had that dream ever since I was a little girl."

I opened my MacBook and pulled up the University of Washington website. The first paragraph talked of breakthroughs in pancreas transplants. The article went on to places filled with hope and promise for my new old friend.

Olivia looked into my heart as tears welled up in her eyes.

"I feel like we met for a reason."

"We absolutely met for a reason, Olivia. We were put on that street corner at the same moment in time because I am here now to help you in any way I can."

"I wouldn't have been brave enough to talk to you if I hadn't seen how sweet your Alfie is. Those eyes of his kind of called to me, Hilary, in a very different way."

That would account for the train trip.

When she returned to her own room at midnight, we both knew that our newfound friendship was as old as time itself. During visits to her hospital room over the next few days, I learned that she was on five different narcotics without getting significant relief from the unrelenting pain. She explained that the only thing that really helps is marijuana. Medical marijuana is legal in the state of Washington. Any marijuana is an evil crime in good-old-boy Idaho.

The following morning, I hijacked a wheelchair and realized that getting around was a breeze without walking on fire-feet. As a legally certified service dog, Alfie was on my lap, and together we spread heartfelt smiles among people who desperately needed them. When we wheeled into Ollie's room, she absolutely lit up. Knowing that she'd just undergone a major procedure, the furry empath moved gently to her feet and rested his head on her knee as the tears welled up in her eyes. Word of Alfie's talents spread quickly, and requests for visits piled up. After Ron and Olivia had their time, Alf was honored to share his spirit with a few other eager patients.

On the day of Ron's release, Olivia told me that she and her mom had been wanting to relocate. They talked about Bellingham and would be planning a trip back very soon.

Alfie at Virginia Mason Hospital with "Olivia," 2013.

"You'll stay with us. We have plenty of room."

"We really want to move to Washington, Hilary."

"Yes."

When we hugged, I clearly felt the prominence of her delicate bones. Olivia and her mother would be visiting very soon.

When I pressed the elevator button to return to the ninth floor, I felt another jolt and watched the body rise from the parked gurney to rejoin itself in another reality. There are no coincidences. I fell into bed that night knowing that the universe had been hard at work. The arrangement to meet Olivia began days ago when I stepped onto the elevator that let me out in another reality.

No coincidences, only divine power.

Ron 2

The connection between Ron and me had deepened over time. Having fallen deeply in love, we were married the spring after I moved to Seattle.

Ron was a man's man — quiet, self-assured, and powerful, with the class and sophistication it took to bring me to an elusive arc in the circumference of my life, the piece leading back to my oddly privileged youth. Though I had happily wandered far from materialism, it was easy to fall into the comfort of his lifestyle.

His love and devotion to me was pure and sweet.

After all the other experiences I'd had with men, I wondered what I had done to deserve him. He was so different from Michael and the others. It took Ronny time to truly believe that I loved him for the good man inside, not what he had or could give me materially.

He bought me expensive, glittery gifts. I created things for him, things I made from my heart, things money could not buy. I taught him to be more in his heart. He taught me to accept being loved and taken care of in a way that was different from anything I had experienced in my life.

Ron was a great provider. He helped me release the need to always be in charge, the need to make all the decisions for myself and others. I felt relieved of the responsibility and gratefully accepted him taking care of me, especially as

My Husband, Ron

Ron and Me.

Misty and Ron.

my health issues escalated. Ron took loving care of me through fifteen surgeries and eleven months of painful debilitating hep C treatment, through the attack on my nervous system that rendered me unable to walk. I wore leg braces and suffered constant, extraordinary pain. He bought me a disabled-people scooter and a golf cart. Ron was always there for me with a positive outlook, a smile, and a way to make my life better. He would watch tenderly as I journeyed off in my kayak, Alfie riding proudly on the bow, and he would wave as the two of us happy mariners set sail for our favorite island. Ron helped me feel free.

Ron Pellegrino, my husband.

"You'll get through this, baby. I'm with you."

• • •

Through my union with Ron, I lovingly learned that family is what matters most. Misty was given a glimpse into what that world really means. We were welcomed and embraced with love and warmth into the folds of Ron's amazing Italian family. These people give meaning to the word "family." They represent and exemplify a feeling I am uncertain I have ever known before. I didn't know this kind of love and togetherness from my own family. My heart overflowed with joy as I watched three generations of Italian women making pizza together in my kitchen — talking, laughing, loving. Dinner was exquisite.

Ronny was the only man my father would have ever accepted and approved of. They would have hit it off splendidly had my father been alive when Ron and I were together. My father's energy came back to embrace me during that time.

• • •

Ron learned about spiritual laws and truths by watching the way I handled my life. He was able to take God out of the box of his childhood and embrace the universe in a way that both surprised and delighted him.

I loved Ron. I still do. He helped me through some of my most difficult moments. In return, I taught him that he did not have to buy love. He deserved to receive it unconditionally.

We both had obstacles to overcome. Misty and her challenges were always a part of our lives. Despite the fact that her brand of suffering was completely foreign to him, he quickly learned to love and support her while we worked to help her in every way possible. Ron had issues with his son. I helped them come together again toward the end of Ron's life. I believe he learned to be present in the moment with our children and with all those we love. Remember, this moment is all there is until we move into the next phase.

Ron lived through my pain and my challenges. I lived through his. He kept moving forward despite setbacks, heartbreaks, and career devastations. He began a new career at age sixty and was extremely successful financially. Ron had that charisma, that confidence that said, "I will always do well. I will always make it happen." And he did.

• • •

I had a very difficult time watching this once strong, quick-witted, never-give-up kind of guy wither and die. But Ron's illness took charge. It finally claimed his life. Ron held on to life, to the memories — the times that were good and abundant, times that were filled with love and sharing. Then this great man's body shut down and he merged into the light. Holding his hand, in that moment, I was heartbroken but relieved that the suffering was over for him. I know where he went.

Alfa Romeo Pellegrino and I walked out of the Catholic church after the memorial service with the dignity I knew Ron was proud to see.

We carried his ashes to New York, back to his family. Home.

Looking Back

I can feel the circular motion of existence over and over, from student to teacher, from being helped to giving help, around and around it moves. I am here to evolve to another place and time and to help others do the same as best I can.

It remains true that there is always a way to get where we need to go. It is true in every aspect of life. Motivation is the desire to get from where you are to where you want to be. Everything is possible so long as there is forward movement. The impetus for such movement comes from within and may not be allowed to falter, hesitate, or lose momentum. Obstacles must be taken in stride, roadblocks obliterated with the force of pure will.

Existence here is not intended to be easy. Each of us has the ability to put one foot in front of the other and keep going in the face of adversity. While we may slow down and take note during times of hardship, we must remain vigilant lest we linger too long and lose sight of the need to resume our forward motion.

We also have within us the capacity for unconditional love, the ability to forgive, the strength to embrace life wholeheartedly.

We need not wonder what is real or what may be an illusion, for it is all real when we are one with the universe. We are never victims in our lives when we choose to view experiences as opportunities to learn and refuse to allow negativity and resentment to impede us.

Certainly life happens, certainly we are challenged, surely we can become overwhelmed.

The important thing is that we view obstacles, no matter how big, as speed bumps rather than brick walls. Easy to say, not so easy to accomplish such a mindset in the midst of daily existence. No, a speed-bump mindset requires a particular arrangement with the universe. For me, that mindset must be as flexible as the definition of reality. That definition must maintain with conviction the reality of Coma World and other realities that can be easily misplaced, doubted, denied. The issue of what is real and what is an illusion is simple once we realize that everything is real. Coma World is as real as the Dream World I visited last night, which is as real as this moment in which I write.

In the physical world, definitions are a requirement, conversation, sights, and sounds, and comings and goings that allow for everything to be placed in its proper box. The physical world, for the most part, precludes the inclusion of "illusions." Yet illusions are just as real as the ground on which we walk. Mary and Tink are as real as you or me.

It is in nature that this version of reality is most clear. It is in nature that the soul most effortlessly becomes one with the universe, where lines of separation vanish and the knowledge that reality is everywhere is clear.

I have frequent out-of-body experiences that validate all of my realities. They remind me that one of the lessons from Death and Coma is that we are unquestionably one with the universe. When I was gone in the Land of All is One, there was no need to define or label. There was a pervasive, peaceful knowing in that world without walls or lines that every point of view, each perspective, all dreams, fantasies, illusions, cultures, planets, and imaginings are true and real. All doubt, separation, and judgment is created by the mind and based in fear or religion or other limits created by our earthly selves.

The noise of the physical world is extremely annoying because, for the most part, sound is a barrier to knowing. Most conversation is nothing but interference that, combined with ticking clocks and other constant sounds, becomes (to me) like fingernails scraping on blackboards, an irritating jumble of frustrating annoyance from which I must escape. I need only slip the headphones on my head and flick the on switch to block out the world and attain the profound power of silence.

While geographically getting away from it all has become significantly more challenging given my multitude of physical limitations, motivation, by definition, allows me to find a path to wherever I want to go. Unable now to hike to a "magical" spot, I learn that the most crucial step is the one that crosses the threshold beyond any place with four walls.

Once outdoors, I do the best I can do to seek out a reasonably private spot, and from there, I can create solitude with my own inner power. I close my eyes and give my soul the freedom to be alone in nature, to travel unencumbered to that place where it is forever embraced by heaven.

• • •

There are no limitations where Hilary and heaven meet. In those places, lessons are clarified and reinforced by the power of the universe. The higher power of which she speaks must speak for itself now, for that is the way to gain insight and clarity into the purpose of this writing.

What is it that she wishes to share with others?

What qualifies her as a spiritual teacher?

Why does she think she has something important to say?

All good questions.

The answers are found in the story of this life, a life that has been fraught with challenges and obstacles that would defeat most people. Yet time after time, I see her move forward without hesitation, and I marvel at her resilience.

How does a human being find places to meet heaven?

What magic are we talking about? Who are her teachers?

Her soul connects with heaven in nature, in places where she feels peace and hears silence. The further away from people, distractions, and noise, she is, the stronger the connection. She knows full well that these moments are, for her, a primal need, as crucial as food, water, and air.

At the age of twelve, she became fascinated with hurricanes. People spoke of boarding windows, stacking sandbags, and the importance of protecting themselves and their property from the onslaught of the deluge. It was at the beginning of her first hurricane season that she decided to harness the power of the storm. She didn't know exactly what that meant; what she did know was that instead of joining the fight *against* the storm, she was going to somehow embrace it. As the winds kicked up, she slipped away to the beach and stood alone atop the stone sea wall. She wore a long blue cape with luxurious red lining. As the winds increased and the ocean warned of its power, she closed her eyes and stood facing the water. Then she turned and ran barefoot along the sea wall, increasing her speed as she opened the cape wide and leapt into the wind.

Did she fly? Why yes, of course she did.

She believed in everything, even then.

She knew that nature was her ally — that for her, joining with its power would always make her stronger. Together, she and nature made magic. She innately understood her ability to reach out, reach up, and be reborn in this body, this life, this time on Earth.

Afterword

This book is dedicated to the spirit of my husband, Ron Pellegrino.

There seems no rhyme or reason when it comes to life or death, yet somewhere within the universal circle, there are always reasons.

My husband Ron began to neglect his body in our later years together. That, for me, was extremely troublesome, given my lifelong struggle with physicality. Still, we helped keep each other going. I felt my husband would be around much longer than he was. Misty and I used to chuckle picturing him at ninety, standing on a New York sidewalk next to a table with a red-checkered tablecloth, eating a sausage sandwich.

But he taught me to expect the unexpected, to wade through the darkness of emotional, grief, pain, and loss and embrace the light. I had already been there. He had not. My job was to help him peacefully slip into the other reality absent of fear. Ron left his body and this physical plane shortly before the completion of this writing. He never failed to encourage me through the years. His gentle soul will remain with me throughout time. He is the best man I have ever met, and he had his reasons for moving on.

I believe that as a loved one passes, we go through our own memory banks to reflect on life experiences together. We see the good, bad, and ugly with a strong focus on what was good in the relationship. Ron and I had our differences, yet somehow we found balance together, understanding, and compassion. I long for him now — his gentle, caring, and loving presence — yet I feel him in my own way all around me. Ron is no longer Ron but part of all that exists — the wind, the rain, the trees.

• • •

I reflect on Rock, my gentle place of embracing all the universe. I look up to the stars in my mind, hands held high, reaching, connecting.

With Alfie at my side, I have begun my personal journey now of grieving. It is not the same process as others might experience. I need to be quiet and cry and fly with the angels. I listen now to the whispers of the breezes. I feel a sense of peace and knowing in every drop of rain throughout the long Northwestern winter. The natural forces driving my life are now gathering at this juncture, providing direction to me intuitively amid all the chaos in my life. Such is my world, the world in which I feel at home. This is the world I relate to. Each day I awaken to the moment and breathe in the next. In this part of my journey, I am at peace.

• • •

I am now involved with another world, a world that I can only describe as one where I need to sing Loudly and Out of Tune. It is a world filled with everything my mind cannot deal with — attorneys, paperwork, probate. It is not my world, but it's certainly one that has done everything in its power to crush any remaining bit of energy that I have.

But this second world is our society's result of my husband's illness, suffering the indignities of our health care system and the outrageous economics of an unexpected death. Somehow, Misty and the greater me held it all together this past year. Together always in spirit, we will continue to do so.

• • •

Since leaving Idaho for Seattle, going through the second round of hep C treatment, neurological problems, and innumerable surgeries, I have not had any specific "patients" to work with. My purpose in life, my dedication to the outcasts, has not changed. My work is simply subtler now. I can be seen on the streets of downtown Seattle or in the local mission floating between worlds of reality and illusion.

My familiarity with the "system" allows me to help others navigate through life so that their basic needs are met. Housing, health care, food, and companionship seem so commonplace to most of us. However, to the outcasts of society, these needs are the basis of life. Survival needs.

The work is the same. Everything else seems different. It isn't.

If anything, my work has taken on a new dimension with projects that require as much energy as ever. I am a spokesperson and advocate working with administrators of several hospitals. My purpose is to alter the protocol used in intensive care units as it relates to end-of-life care.

If a patient is ready to make his or her transition, that patient should absolutely be granted the dignity of choice without delay. No one should be forced to suffer in order to satisfy egos of doctors who say they have the knowledge and equipment to keep the patient alive.

I have seen the expense.

Not only does the patient suffer abominable pain, humiliation, and more, but so do the family members, who in many cases are left to feel powerless at the mercy of the medical team, even when there is no hope for the patient to recover. Palliative care must never be ignored, minimized, or tossed to the bottom of a stack of papers. I now deal with projects that could make death easier for the next patient and his or her family.

• • •

I don't know where I will go from here — Bellingham, Washington, that is. Misty has traveled on to her beloved Belize to work with a shaman in the jungle who is one of her teachers. Alfie and I sit alone in this huge house looking at the golf course and the lake. It is lovely, but it was Ron's dream and a reality that I can afford neither economically nor spiritually. This place is familiar in the moment, but my possessions are packed, and I will soon move on. I remind myself in this alone space that I am never alone, that Mary and Tink are always here. Alfie too is an angel. I know I'm watched over, protected, and loved.

• • •

There is a purpose in writing this book. Leia and I saw the potential for it to be a teaching tool to others. It is not just about death and a return to life in the same lifetime; it is so much more.

I will enumerate some of the lessons. Some you will glean on your own.

- **I am not my body.** Where I have been and where I have returned from make that very real.
- As I learn to focus not only on myself when making decisions but on the good of the whole, I **have complete faith** that the universe will take care of my personal needs. And it does.
- **We are not here to quit.** Certainly, if any one of you lives with substantial pain, you realize the difficulty of embracing that one more day. But as we find the soul's purpose, as we discover why we are here — to serve God, to make a difference — the pain subsides. We can get up with a smile, and do it another day.
- **Fear is only an illusion.** Fear is a learned emotion. It is used to control people, to keep us from moving forward. Fear is one of our earthly teachers, and as we pass the test of seeing through this illusion, we are free to find divine love.
- Learning to **understand detachment** in all its complexity is an important part of moving forward. In learning to be true humanitarians, we must detach our egos and adjust our consciousnesses to that of the masses, thinking not only of ourselves but of humanity. Any of us who strives to teach must do so with the utmost love and respect for humankind. At the same time, it is essential to retain a strong enough sense of ego to prod ourselves to achieve what we set out to accomplish.

  When we are able to detach, it becomes easier to allow people and things to flow through our lives, thereby allowing for more and more lessons.

  At times, it may serve us well to detach from our own expectations. It is important to learn to give love without attachment to whether or not it makes the other person love us more. This can be a difficult lesson. By giving love freely because we feel love for the other person, we can act without self-interest. There is pure joy in giving love without the expectation of attachment or adoration.

  The idea is to be able to let go of attachment, proceed to the next level, and love for the sake of loving. That is the road that leads to experiencing the joy of being loved for who we really are.
- **Never look back** — except to understand the lesson. If you spend too much time back there, you can be enmeshed in a box marked "my past." This is

where you've been, not where you are now. You can't change the past, but you can learn from it. Never repeat what you already know.

- **We are all equal.** When we judge one another, this spiritual truth does not seem real. Labels and judgments are part of belief systems passed on to us from family, friends, societies, and cultures. The only way to help change our worlds is to love and accept each other as equals. Each of us may be learning similar lessons, each in our own way. We must find the courage to stand in our power and speak out against old beliefs, to integrate spiritual truths and realities — not from anger, but from a clear voice within, a voice of higher consciousness, a voice of divine love, compassion, and understanding,
- **Loyalty and integrity matter**. Being loyal to a person does not mean being loyal to his or her path. I have, at times, become confused and found myself being loyal to someone else's path and repeating lessons I have already finished. Only when we learn to recognize such diversions can we pursue our journey, fulfill our purpose, and accomplish what we are here to do.
- **Lessons do not have to be serious.** We are all children in life's eyes, and it is my joy and duty to lighten up and teach by example. This is part of my purpose, and to fulfill it, I must consistently be mindful of remaining centered and not allow those around me to knock me off balance or change my way of looking at life. By remaining buoyant, I have, both in my career and personal life, been able to help people learn to love themselves.

    We must always maintain that playful energy that allows us to set aside our worries and travel to places like Stickyville with ease and Smiles. Laughter, playfulness, loyalty, and love help to light up the universe. We must let the child shine through!

• • •

Ron has not yet settled into the arms of the universal All That Is. Part of his spirit is spending time at my side in the delightful company of Tink. I hear them playing squeaky toy with Alfie in the night. They awaken me with a song to speak silently with unmistakable clarity.

My work will continue for as long as human beings struggle to find inspiration and strength, for as long as we strive to find meaning in life, for as long as love and hope ignite our hearts to move forward.

Me and Trikey.

Because he understood my struggles and because he loved me, Ron consistently sought ways to give me what I need most of all: to be free and active in the natural world, to feel the earth beneath me, and to revel in nature as I recharge the essence of my soul. I remain, for all intents and purposes, without balance and unable to walk any distance without enduring immense pain.

Shortly before he left for the Other Side, Ron gave me a Greenspeed Magnum Recumbent Tricycle — Trikey — an exquisite machine that requires none of the physical skills I don't have while allowing me to utilize all the ones I do have in perfect synchronicity.

My ticket to freedom.

My wings.

As I feel the ground beneath me and my body hard at work, my spirit soars and my soul

is in ecstasy.

Ron left me with a secret: the hidey hole of Trikey. I am no longer scooter- or wheelchair-bound. With the freedom of movement afforded me, I pedal with all my heart, the music plays, and Alfie runs beside me, offering the other end of his sticky. "RIIIDDDDE," he says, "RIDE LIKE THE WIIINNDDDD, RIDE FOR YOUR LIIIFFFEEEE!"

And I do.

Thank you, Ron. I love you too.

About that road trip we had planned? I intend to do that road trip down the California coast on my Greenspeed Trikey. I look forward to you joining me in God's glorious church of the Sequoia National Forest, in Mendocino, at Asilomar Beach.

Soon you will rest, and we will meet in the not-too-distant future. We will relax in recliners and talk about life, love, and soul lessons.

Thank you for being.

I love you.

About the Author

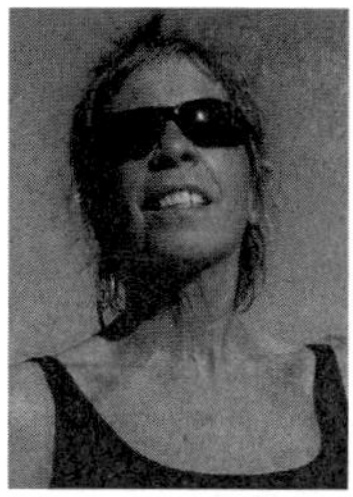

Hilary died from a drug overdose at the age of eighteen and journeyed to the Other Side. Defying all odds, a grim prognosis, and a lengthy coma, she managed not only to survive but also to maintain conscious contact with both her higher self and her guardian angel.

Despite having sustained a permanent brain injury, she went on to earn a master's degree in community social psychology and establish a successful career in the mental health field, working in substance abuse, dual diagnosis, and, for the past twenty years, primarily with schizophrenics.

Her writing has been published in both national and international educational and professional publications available through the University of Washington, the Federal Substance Abuse and Mental Health Services Administration (SAMHSA), and the Public Health Agency of Canada.

The impact of treatment for her hepatitis C exacerbated Hilary's brain damage and ultimately forced her to give up her career. Her health issues progressed and now limit her physical mobility as well as cognitive functioning, yet she teaches by example that we must *never give up*. She maintains the belief that she is not her body but a higher consciousness moving through life lessons one day at a time.

Hilary currently resides in Bellingham, Washington, with her helper and trusted advisor, Alfie. An avid recumbent tricyclist, she plans to continue her journey forward on three wheels and a prayer.

Light Technology PUBLISHING Presents

Tina Louise Spalding

Great Minds Speak to You

"Many in spirit look on these times of difficulty, abundance, trouble, and innovation and wish to share with you their experiences and ideas. Some famous names and faces will come to mind as you read this book, and you will glean some fine information about their own learning, their own suffering, and indeed their own experience in the life after this life, for they all wish to tell you that there is no death as you perceive it to be. They are all there in their astral forms, enjoying their continued growth, their continued expansion, and their continued joy in living."

— Ananda

Chapters Include:

- Albert Einstein
- Jerry Garcia
- Marilyn Monroe
- John Huston
- Amy Winehouse
- Princess Diana
- Elizabeth Taylor
- John and Robert Kennedy
- Michael Jackson
- Cecil B. DeMille
- Pablo Picasso
- Queen Mother Elizabeth
- George Bernard Shaw
- John Lennon
- Jesus Christ

$19.95 Softcover, 192 PP.
ISBN 978-1-62233-010-2

CD of Live Channelings Included!

Making Love to GOD
The Path to Divine Sex

"We are here to teach the way to divine bliss, and we know you are scared — scared to lie naked caressing your lover with rapt attention and honor. Give love all day, and you will be guaranteed to receive love all night. The divine sexual experience connects you, God, and your lover — if you have one — together in a dance of divine bliss."

— Ananda

Topics Include:

- How We Came to Misunderstand Sexual Energy
- Using Divine Sex Energy
- Specific Steps and Sensations
- Blocks to Transformation
- A Transformed View of Sex and Sexual Energy
- Following the Path to Transformation
- Reaping the Harvest

$19.95 Softcover, 416 PP.
ISBN 978-1-62233-009-6

Print Books: Visit Our Online Bookstore www.LightTechnology.com
eBooks Available on Amazon, Apple iTunes, Google Play, and Barnes & Noble

Light Technology PUBLISHING Presents

PLANT SOULS SPEAK
A NEW WAY OF INTERACTING WITH PLANTS
THROUGH ROBERT SHAPIRO

"What we intend to speak about — if I may speak in general for all plants — is how you can interact with plants in a more benevolent way for you as the human species. For a long time, you have been clear on medicinal uses of leaves and stems and seeds and flower petals and so on, but you are only getting about one-tenth of the energy available to you that way. It is always better to interact with the plant and its energies in its live form, but you need to know how.

"The intention of this book is to reveal that formula so that you can stop searching, as a human race, for the magical cures to diseases by exhausting the supply of life forms around you, when a much simpler process is available. This book will not just comment on things you know about but show you what you are missing in your interaction with plants."

— Dandelion

$24.95

ISBN 978-1-891824-74-6
Softcover, 576 PP.

Chapters Include:

- Cherry Tree
- Pine Tree
- Crabgrass
- Bamboo
- Hibiscus
- Marijuana
- Maple Tree
- Redwood
- Oat Grass
- Corn
- Holly
- Orchid
- Palm Tree
- Walnut Tree
- Wetland Grass
- Daffodil
- Ivy
- Rose
- Peach Tree
- Brown Rice
- Angelica
- Dandelion
- Kelp
- Sage

Essences OF NATURE
BY MARY ANN ALTAMIRANO ANTENUCCI

Flower essences are living energies that can bring more vigor and vitality to our lives. They teach us how to evolve, how to utilize our elements, how to nourish and be nourished, how to be of beauty, and how to orient ourselves. They teach us internal integrity and structure. They teach us how to be.

Many of Mary Ann's interpretations of flower essences here are tailored to fit the needs of particular circumstances. Formatted with keywords for quick reference to whatever issues you would like to explore, this compilation of her columns from the past ten years serves as a friend, guide, and resource to help you grow and blossom.

Chapters Include:

- Apple Blossom
- Beech
- Chaparral
- Cherry Plum
- Echinacea
- Elm
- Garlic
- Golden Yarrow
- Honeysuckle
- Lavender
- Lemon
- Olive
- Pine
- Sage
- St. Johnswort
- Trillium
- White Chestnut
- Zinnia

$16.95

ISBN 978-1-62233-006-5
Softcover, 224 PP.
Over 300 full-color photos

Light Technology PUBLISHING Presents

Books by Tom T. Moore

THE GENTLE WAY

A SELF-HELP GUIDE FOR THOSE WHO BELIEVE IN ANGELS

"This book is for people of all faiths and beliefs with the only requirement being a basic belief in angels. It will put you back in touch with your guardian angel or strengthen and expand the connection that you may already have. How can I promise these benefits? Because I have been using these concepts for over ten years and I can report these successes from direct knowledge and experience. But this is a self-help guide, so that means it requires your active participation." — Tom T. Moore

$14.95 • 160 pp., Softcover • ISBN 978-1-891824-60-9

THE GENTLE WAY II

BENEVOLENT OUTCOMES: THE STORY CONTINUES

You'll be amazed at how easy it is to be in touch with guardian angels and how much assistance you can receive simply by asking. This inspirational self-help book, written for all faiths and beliefs, will explain how there is a more benevolent world that we can access, and how we can achieve this.

These very unique and incredibly simple techniques assist you in manifesting your goals easily and effortlessly for the first time. It works quickly, sometimes with immediate results, and no affirmations, written intentions, or changes in behavior are needed. You don't even have to believe in it for it to work!

$16.95 • 320 pp., Softcover • ISBN 978-1-891824-80-7

THE GENTLE WAY III

MASTER YOUR LIFE

"Almost three years have passed since *The Gentle Way II* was published. Yet as many success stories as that book contained, I have continued to receive truly unique stories from people all over the world requesting most benevolent outcomes and asking for benevolent prayers for their families, friends, other people, and other beings. It just proves that there are no limits to this modality, which is becoming a gentle movement as people discover how much better their lives are with these simple yet powerful requests." — Tom T. Moore

$16.95 • 352 pp., Softcover • ISBN 978-1-62233-005-8

Print Books: Visit Our Online Bookstore www.LightTechnology.com
eBooks Available on Amazon, Apple iTunes, Google Play, and Barnes & Noble

Light Technology PUBLISHING Presents

BY DRUNVALO MELCHIZEDEK

LIVING IN THE HEART

Includes a CD with Heart Meditation

"Long ago we humans used a form of communication and sensing that did not involve the brain in any way; rather, it came from a sacred place within our hearts. What good would it do to find this place again in a world where the greatest religion is science and the logic of the mind? Don't I know this world where emotions and feelings are second-class citizens? Yes, I do. But my teachers have asked me to remind you who you really are. You are more than a human being — much more. For within your heart is a place, a sacred place, where the world can literally be remade through conscious cocreation. If you give me permission, I will show you what has been shown to me."

— Drunvalo Melchizedek

Chapters Include:

- Beginning with the Mind
- Seeing in the Darkness
- Learning from Indigenous Tribes
- The Sacred Space of the Heart
- The Unity of Heaven and Earth
- Leaving the Mind and Entering the Heart
- The Sacred Space of the Heart Meditation
- The Mer-Ka-Ba and the Sacred Space of the Heart
- Conscious Cocreation from the Heart Connected to the Mind

$25.00 Softcover, 144 PP.

ISBN 978-1-891824-43-2

Drunvalo Melchizedek's life experience reads like an encyclopedia of breakthroughs in human endeavor. He studied physics and art at the University of California at Berkeley, but he feels that his most important education came after college. In the past twenty-five years, he has studied wizh over seventy teachers from all belief systems and religious understandings. For some time now, he has been bringing his vision to the world through the Flower of Life program and the Mer-Ka-Ba meditation. This teaching encompasses every area of human understanding, explores the development of humankind from ancient civilizations to the present time, and offers clarity regarding the world's state of consciousness and what is needed for a smooth and easy transition into the twenty-first century.

Light Technology PUBLISHING Presents

THE ANCIENT SECRET OF THE FLOWER OF LIFE, VOLUME 2

Topics Include:

- The Unfolding of the Third Informational System
- Whispers from Our Ancient Heritage
- Unveiling the Mer-Ka-Ba Meditation
- Using Your Mer-Ka-Ba
- Connecting to the Levels of Self
- Two Cosmic Experiments
- What We May Expect in the Forthcoming Dimensional Shift

$25[00] Softcover, 272 PP.
ISBN 978-1-891824-21-0

The sacred Flower of Life pattern, the primary geometric generator of all physical form, is explored in even more depth in this volume, the second half of the famed Flower of Life workshop. The proportions of the human body; the nuances of human consciousness; the sizes and distances of the stars, planets, and moons; and even the creations of humankind are all shown to reflect their origins in this beautiful and divine image. Through an intricate and detailed geometrical mapping, Drunvalo Melchizedek shows how the seemingly simple design of the Flower of Life contains the genesis of our entire third-dimensional existence.

From the pyramids and mysteries of Egypt to the new race of Indigo children, Drunvalo presents the sacred geometries of the reality and the subtle energies that shape our world. We are led through a divinely inspired labyrinth of science and stories, logic and coincidence, on a path of remembering where we come from and the wonder and magic of who we are.

Finally, for the first time in print, Drunvalo shares the instructions for the Mer-Ka-Ba meditation, step-by-step techniques for the re-creation of the energy field of the evolved human, which is the key to ascension and the next dimensional world. If done from love, this ancient process of breathing prana opens up for us a world of tantalizing possibility in this dimension, from protective powers to the healing of oneself, of others, and even of the planet.

Light Technology PUBLISHING Presents

$16.95 Plus Shipping

ISBN 978-1-62233-013-3
Softcover 340 PP.
6 X 9 Perfect Bound

DNA OF THE SPIRIT

VOLUME 1

channeled through Rae Chandran

WITH Robert Mason Pollock

The etheric strands of your DNA are the information library of your soul. They contain the complete history of you, lifetime after lifetime; a record of the attitudes, karma, and emotional predispositions you brought into this lifetime; and a blueprint, or lesson plan, for your self-improvement. Your DNA is also a record of your existence from the moment of your creation as a starbeing to your present incarnation. This information is written in every cell of your body.

CHAPTERS INCLUDE:

- Mudras for Activating the Twelve Layers of DNA
- The Awakening of Crystalline Consciousness
- Auspicious Times for Awakening Consciousness
- Angelic Support for DNA Activation
- The History of Human DNA
- Your Internal Compass: Nature's Body Intelligence

How God Did It, Not Why

by William Lowell Putnam

- *Creation is an ongoing process.*
- *God has not finished designing the Earth.*
- *Man is not the only creature in the process.*
- *This is the only world we know of.*
- *Time is a dimension.*
- *Fossils are our ancestors.*
- *We all have a right to our own heaven.*

$16.95 Plus Shipping

ISBN-13:978-1-62233-015-7
Softcover 160 PP.
6 X 9 • 4-color

CHAPTERS INCLUDE:

- Recent Geological History
- God's Mechanisms
- Before the Alpinists
- Peaks, Passes, and Glaciers
- Spots on the Sun
- Various Diaries
- The Astronomers
- Evolution?
- What's Next?

Light Technology PUBLISHING Presents

$16.95
Plus Shipping

ISBN 978-1-62233-016-4
Softcover 256 PP.
6 X 9 Perfect Bound

FIFTH-DIMENSIONAL SOUL PSYCHOLOGY

Vywamus through David K. Miller

This book is devoted to the techniques and information I have channeled from the spirit guide and soul psychologist Vywamus.

The first part of this book will be a more traditional explanation of some of the techniques and principles of soul psychology, which include a discussion of basic principles of soul psychology, such as past-life therapy; between-life therapy; different levels of self; how to do soul readings, soul lessons, and group healing methodologies; and finally, higher consciousness and the connection to your higher self.

The second part includes channeled lectures directly from Vywamus on his thoughts and ideas about soul psychology.

— David K. Miller

SOME TOPICS INCLUDE:

- Completion of Soul Evolution and Incarnational Cycles
- Thoughts and Sensitivity
- The Relationship between Soul Psychology and Illness
- The Nature of the Soul
- Dealing with Traumatic Memories
- Ascension

The Comprehension of the Holy Spirit within the Human Condition

Spirit of Space with Gabriel et al. through Arthur Fanning

TOPICS INCLUDE:

- The force of the Holy Spirit is coming: Are you ready?
- The forty-nine personalities in your chakras are unifying.
- Your soul force is expanding.
- Your birth name and birth date are vitally important.
- Your bones are becoming more fluid.
- The Moon rules the water in your body.
- Gratitude, appreciation, and prayer are essential now.
- Your thoughts: Are they yours or someone else's?
- All religions have the same god, the same idea, why fight?
- And much, much more.

$16.95
Plus Shipping

ISBN 13: 978-1-62233-017-1
Softcover 256 PP.
6 X 9 Perfect Bound

Phone: 928-526-1345 or 1-800-450-0985 • Fax: 928-714-1132

Light Technology PUBLISHING Presents

Gaia Speaks

Gaia through Pepper Lewis

SACRED EARTH WISDOM, VOLUME I

Many believe Earth to be sentient of feeling, but we are disconnected from her because we can't understand her vibrations and impressions. Gaia, the sentience of Earth, speaks through Pepper Lewis and teaches us how to listen and attune to Earth.

$19.95

Softcover, 432 PP.

ISBN 978-1-891824-48-7

WISDOM FOR AN AWAKENING HUMANITY, VOLUME II

Gaia is a living, learning, and teaching library of everything that is, was, or might be related to Earth. Because you are Gaian, you are also a part of the great living library that is Gaia. You are a library within Gaia, one whose contents are a collection of ever-unfolding experiences. You are a lifetimes-old master storyteller, unraveling each tantalizing chapter.

$19.95

Softcover, 448 PP.

ISBN 978-1-891824-51-7

Print Books: Visit Our Online Bookstore www.LightTechnology.com
eBooks Available on Amazon, Apple iTunes, Google Play, and Barnes & Noble

Light Technology PUBLISHING **Presents**

THE BOOK OF transformation

THROUGH ROBERT SHAPIRO

Topics Include:

• Heart Heat • Safety Exercises • Benevolent Magic
Living Prayer • Disentanglement • Deep Disentanglement
Disengagement & Engagement • Connections
and much more!

— Learn how to ask for clearing of old traumas and discomforts.
— Learn how to create a nourishing, benevolent life for yourself and others.

eBook ONLY $2.99

$25.00 Plus Shipping

ISBN 13: 978-1-891824-42-5
Softcover 448 PP.
6 X 9 Perfect Bound

with CD

Shifting Frequencies

Sounds for Vibratory Activation

by Jonathan Goldman

For the first time, Healing Sounds pioneer Jonathan Goldman tells us about shifting frequencies – how to use sound and other modalities to change vibrational patterns for both personal and planetary healing and transformation. Through his consciousness connection to Shamael, angel of sound, Jonathan shares his extraordinary scientific and spiritual knowledge and insights, providing information, instructions, and techniques on using sound, light, color, visualization, and sacred geometry to experience shifting frequencies. The material in this book is both timely and vital for health and spiritual evolution.

In this book, you will:

- explore the use of sound in ways you never imagined for healing and transformation
- discover harmonics as a key to opening to higher levels of consciousness
- learn about the angel chakra and what sounds may be used to activate this new energy center

Chapters Include:

- Sound Currents: Frequency and Intent
- Vibratory Resonance
- Vocalization, Visualization, and a Tonal Language
- The Harmonics of Sound

Print Books: Visit Our Online Bookstore www.LightTechnology.com
eBooks Available on Amazon, Apple iTunes, Google Play, and Barnes & Noble

Light Technology PUBLISHING Presents

Shamanic Secrets Mastery Series

Speaks of Many Truths, Zoosh, and Reveals the Mysteries through Robert Shapiro

This book explores the heart and soul connection between humans and Earth. Through that intimacy, miracles of healing and expanded awareness can flourish. To heal the planet and be healed as well, you can lovingly extend your energy self out to the mountains and rivers and intimately bond with Earth. Gestures and vision can activate your heart to return you to a healthy, caring relationship with the land you live on. The character of some of Earth's most powerful features is explored and understood with exercises given to connect you with those places. As you project your love and healing energy there, you help Earth to heal from human destruction of the planet and its atmosphere. Dozens of photographs, maps, and drawings assist the process in twenty-five chapters, which cover Earth's more critical locations.

ISBN 978-1-891824-12-8 • Softcover, 512 pp. • $19.95

Learn to understand the sacred nature of your own physical body and some of the magnificent gifts it offers you. When you work with your physical body in these new ways, you will discover not only its sacredness but its compatibility with Mother Earth, the animals, the plants, and even the nearby planets, all of which you now recognize as being sacred in nature. It is important to feel the value of oneself physically before you can have any lasting physical impact on the world. If a physical energy does not feel good about itself, it will usually be resolved; other physical or spiritual energies will dissolve it because they are unnatural. The better you feel about your physical self when you do the work in the first book, as well as this one and the one to follow, the greater and more lasting the benevolent effect will be on your life, on the lives of those around you, and ultimately on your planet and universe.

ISBN 978-1-891824-29-6 • Softcover, 576 pp. • $25.00

Spiritual mastery encompasses many different means to assimilate and be assimilated by the wisdom, feelings, flow, warmth, function, and application of all beings in your world who you will actually contact in some way. A lot of spiritual mastery has been covered in different bits and pieces throughout all the books we've done. My approach to spiritual mastery, though, will be as grounded as possible in things that people on Earth can use — but it won't include the broad spectrum of spiritual mastery, like levitation and invisibility. I'm trying to teach you things that you can actually use and benefit from. My life is basically going to represent your needs, and it gets out the secrets that have been held back in a story-like fashion so that it is more interesting."

— Speaks of Many Truths

ISBN 978-1-891824-58-6 • Softcover, 768 pp. • $29.95

Light Technology PUBLISHING Presents

Angels Explain Death and Prayer

by Cheryl Gaer Barlow

$16.95 Plus Shipping

ISBN 13: 978-1-62233-008-9
Softcover • 224 PP.
6 X 9 Perfect Bound

"We are the angels of the Mallbon. We are meant to tell those of Earth that the death of the body is never to be feared. We help in ways not understood by humanity. We can manifest anything we desire. We can live as humans on Earth. When we absorb the reality of Earth, we work God's wonders in ordinary ways.

"When the surroundings are not in focus or when you feel unable to cope with the people or circumstances around you, be still and ask God for help. God will respond to requests of help by mending emotions with aid from the angels. This is done by being aware of the angels. We surround you and bring you comfort.

"You must, as a human race, lift the quality of thought to the highest level. When the level of thought is low and miserable, it is generated through the entire world. When it is lifted to a level of joy, it lifts all minds. When you know the teachings of the angels, no ignorance will be left in the soul. You will no longer be afraid or in pain. Now is the time to stand with the angels of God and help humankind."

— The Mallbon Angels

Chapters Include:

- The Soul's Path
- The Death of Children
- Meeting God
- Dreams
- Birth on Earth
- Entering the Heavens
- The Joy That Awaits You
- Bonus: Prayer Guide!

$25.00 Plus Shipping

ISBN 13: 978-1-891824-42-5
Softcover 448 PP.
6 X 9 Perfect Bound

Homeopathy FOR Epidemics

by Eileen Nauman

Homeopathy in Times of Crises

Homeopathy's philosophy is like cures like. By potentizing a remedy through a series of dilution steps, only the energy signature of the original substance is eventually left in the alcohol carrier. Quantum physics will one day be able to explain why water has memory; similarly, homeopaths know that each remedy has its own unique frequency, whether there are molecules of the substance left or not.

The homeopathic community knows that in the past, homeopathic remedies have made the difference between life and death during global epidemics. It is my hope that you will pass the information in this book along to your relatives and friends. It might be the greatest gift you ever give them — information that can save their lives.

Light Technology PUBLISHING

OUT-OF-BODY EXPERIENCES

by Gene Schmitz

WITH CHANNELED EXPLANATIONS AND COMMENTARY THROUGH Robert Shapiro

This book not only tells the full story of Gene's life, but it also includes a detailed conversation with an angelic being who speaks through superchannel Robert Shapiro to reveal the meaning behind Gene's out-of-body experiences and his life's purpose. In the process of explaining the twists and turns of Gene's life, this angelic being also unveils some surprising truths about the connection between the body and the soul that apply to all of us.

$14.95 Plus Shipping

ISBN 978-1-891824-95-1
Softcover • 144 PP.
6 X 9 Perfect Bound

CHAPTERS INCLUDE:

- Soul Travel Begins
- Soul Travel Continues
- The White Light
- Floating Farther from Home
- My Soul Travels Resume
- Message from Grandpa
- Angels and Animals
- New Traveling Companions
- Soul Crossings

Hearing the Angels Sing:

A True Story of Angelic Assistance

by Peter Sterling

Hearing the Angel's Sing chronicles my extraordinary journeys into the higher dimensions of light where I met the angels who ultimately brought me to the realization that my mission was to be a channel for God's heavenly music. The book includes never-before-shared details of my journey of awakening. From the snowcapped peaks of the Rocky Mountains to the tropical jungles of the Mayan temple lands, the red rock towers of Sedona, and ultimately to the Incan highlands of Peru, this is a captivating story that will take you on an amazing journey of discovery!

— Peter Sterling

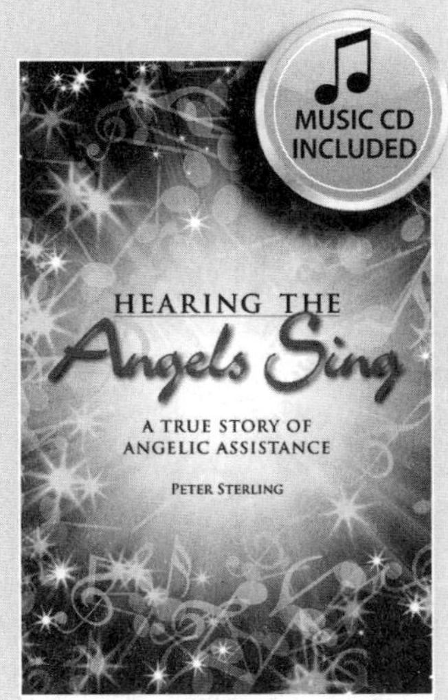

$16.95 Plus Shipping

ISBN 13: 978-1-891824-96-8
Softcover • 256 PP.
6 X 9 Perfect Bound

CHAPTERS INCLUDE:

- Descension and Birth
- Down the Rabbit Hole
- Windows to Heaven
- Rocky Mountain High
- Angels and Devils
- Harmonic Converging
- Red Rocks Calling
- To Hear the Angels Sing
- Fires of Purification

Phone: 928-526-1345 or 1-800-450-0985 • Fax: 928-714-1132

Light Technology PUBLISHING

12 Steps TO A Lightness OF Being

by Sarah Goddard Neves

This unique book has been designed as if you were taking a very special spiritual development course in the comfort of your own home. Through its wisdom and guided meditations – **included on the enclosed CDs to boost empowerment** – *12 Steps to a Lightness of Being* will gradually but surely lift your vibration and awaken you. Therefore, to get the most out of it, decide now not to rush it but to read it slowly. Take as long as you need on each step before moving on to the next. Commit to doing each meditation or visualization, giving yourself some quiet, undisturbed time to do this, and recall your meditation experiences and insights afterward. By doing so, you will get the most out of reading this book.

$19.95 Plus Shipping

ISBN 13: 978-1-891824-99-9
Softcover • 160 PP.
6 X 9 Perfect Bound

The Twelve Steps:

1. Meditation on the Light
2. Opening to Your Intuition
3. Master Connection
4. Being Happy
5. The Healing Power of Forgiveness
6. Evolving with Love and Light
7. Realizing Your Life's Purpose
8. Awakening to Love
9. You: a Creation and a Creator
10. Soul Reflection
11. Hope from the Stars
12. Becoming a Lightness of Being

$25.00 Plus Shipping

ISBN 13: 978-1-891824-72-2
60 min. CD • 31 min. DVD
192 PP. • Spiral Bound

Includes CD & DVD

HANDBOOK FOR HEALERS

by Frankie Z Avery & the OMA Group

Accompanied by an instructional DVD and a healing tones CD, the *Handbook for Healers* is intended for healers of all skill levels. OMA, channeled through Frankie Z Avery, offers advice on such issues as nutrition, lifestyle, and healing techniques. The companion DVD contains demonstrations of each of the meditations and exercises included. The *Healing Room Tones* CD is a creation of unique frequencies meant to enhance balance, harmony, and depth of perception in the healing room.

CHAPTERS INCLUDE:

- What Distinguishes Healers
- What Healers Do
- How Healing Works
- The Healer
- The Healer with a Patient
- Optimized Healing Environments
- Happiness
- The Importance of Eating Well

EXERCISES INCLUDE:

- Energize Your Day
- Check for Balance
- Expand Energy before Session
- Focus
- Balance with the Patient
- Stroke and Seal
- Cleanse between Patients
- Dust Off after Healing
- Restore: Catch Your Breath

Light Technology PUBLISHING Presents

THE EXPLORER RACE SERIES

ZOOSH AND HIS FRIENDS THROUGH ROBERT SHAPIRO

The series: Humans — creators in training — have a purpose and destiny so heartwarmingly, profoundly glorious that it is almost unbelievable from our present dimensional perspective. Humans are great light-beings from beyond this creation gaining experience in dense physicality. This truth about the great human genetic experiment of the Explorer Race and the mechanics of creation is being revealed for the first time by Zoosh and his friends through superchannel Robert Shapiro. These books read like adventure stories as we follow the clues from this creation that we live in out to the Council of Creators and beyond.

1 THE EXPLORER RACE

You are truly a result of the genetic experiment on Earth. You are beings who uphold the principles of the Explorer Race. The key to empowerment in these days is not to know everything about your past but to know what will help you now. You are constantly being given responsibilities by the Creator that would normally be things that Creator would do. The responsibility and the destiny of the Explorer Race is not only to explore but to create.

ISBN 978-0-929385-38-9 • Softcover • 608 PP. • $25.00

2 ETs and the EXPLORER RACE

In this book, Robert channels Joopah, a Zeta Reticulan now in the ninth dimension who continues the story of the great experiment — the Explorer Race — from the perspective of his civilization. The Zetas would have been humanity's future selves had humanity not re-created the past and changed the future.

ISBN 978-0-929385-79-2 • Softcover • 240 PP. • $14.95

3 EXPLORER RACE: ORIGINS and the NEXT 50 YEARS

This volume has so much information about who we are and where we came from — the source of male and female beings, the war of the sexes, the beginning of the linear mind, feelings, the origin of souls — it is a treasure trove. In addition, there is a section that relates to our near future — how the rise of global corporations and politics affects our future, how to use benevolent magic as a force of creation, and how we will go out to the stars and affect other civilizations. It is full of astounding information.

ISBN 978-0-929385-95-2 • Softcover • 384 PP. • $14.95

4 EXPLORER RACE: CREATORS and FRIENDS, the MECHANICS of CREATION

Now that you have a greater understanding of who you are in the larger sense, it is necessary to remind you of where you came from, the true magnificence of your being. You must understand that you are creators in training, and you were once a portion of Creator. This book will allow you to understand the vaster qualities and help you remember the nature of the desires that drive any creator, the responsibilities to which a creator must answer, the reaction a creator must have to consequences, and the ultimate reward for any creator. **ISBN 978-1-891824-01-2 • Softcover • 480 PP. • $19.95**

5 EXPLORER RACE: PARTICLE PERSONALITIES

All around you in every moment, you are surrounded by the most magical and mystical beings. They are too small for you to see individually, but in groups, you know them as the physical matter of your daily life. These particles might be considered either atoms or portions of atoms who consciously view the vast spectrum of reality yet also have a sense of personal memory like your own linear memory. Some of the particles we hear from are Gold, Mountain Lion, Liquid Light, Uranium, the Great Pyramid's Capstone, This Orb's Boundary, Ice, and Ninth-Dimensional Fire.

ISBN 978-0-929385-97-6 • Softcover • 256 PP. • $14.95

6 EXPLORER RACE and BEYOND

With a better idea of how creation works, we go back to the Creator's advisors and receive deeper and more profound explanations of the roots of the Explorer Race. The Liquid Domain and the Double Diamond Portal share lessons given to the roots on their way to meet the Creator of this universe, and the roots speak of their origins and their incomprehensibly long journey here.

ISBN 978-1-891824-06-7 • Softcover • 384 PP. • $14.95

Print Books: Visit Our Online Bookstore www.LightTechnology.com
eBooks Available on Amazon, Apple iTunes, Google Play, and Barnes & Noble

Light Technology PUBLISHING Presents

THE EXPLORER RACE SERIES

ZOOSH AND HIS FRIENDS THROUGH ROBERT SHAPIRO

7 EXPLORER RACE: COUNCIL of CREATORS

The thirteen core members of the Council of Creators discuss their adventures in coming to awareness of themselves and their journeys on the way to the council on this level. They discuss the advice and oversight they offer to all creators, including the Creator of this local universe. These beings are wise, witty, and joyous, and their stories of love's creation create an expansion of our concepts as we realize that we live in an expanded, multiple-level reality.

ISBN 978-1-891824-13-5 • Softcover • 288 PP. • $14.95

8 EXPLORER RACE and ISIS

This is an amazing book! It has priestess training, shamanic training, Isis's adventures with Explorer Race beings — before Earth and on Earth — and an incredibly expanded explanation of the dynamics of the Explorer Race. Isis is the prototypal loving, nurturing, guiding feminine being, the focus of feminine energy. She has the ability to expand limited thinking without making people with limited beliefs feel uncomfortable. She is a fantastic storyteller, and all of her stories are teaching stories. If you care about who you are, why you are here, where you are going, and what life is all about, pick up this book. You won't put it down until you are through, and then you will want more.

ISBN 978-1-891824-11-1 • Softcover • 352 PP. • $14.95

9 EXPLORER RACE and JESUS

The core personality of that being known on Earth as Jesus, along with his students and friends, describes with clarity and love his life and teaching 2,000 years ago. He states that his teaching is for all people of all races in all countries. Jesus announces here for the first time that he and two others, Buddha and Mohammed, will return to Earth from their place of being in the near future, and a fourth being, a child already born now on Earth, will become a teacher and prepare humanity for their return. This text is so heartwarming and interesting, you won't want to put it down.

ISBN 978-1-891824-14-2 • Softcover • 352 PP. • $16.95

10 EXPLORER RACE: EARTH HISTORY and LOST CIVILIZATIONS

Speaks of Many Truths and Zoosh, through Robert Shapiro, explain that planet Earth, the only water planet in this solar system, is on loan from Sirius as a home and school for humanity, the Explorer Race. Earth's recorded history goes back only a few thousand years, its archaeological history a few thousand more. This book opens up as if a light is on in the darkness, and we see the incredible panorama of brave souls coming from other planets to settle on different parts of Earth. We watch the origins of tribal groups and the rise and fall of civilizations, and we can begin to understand the source of the wondrous diversity of plants, animals, and humans that we enjoy here on beautiful Mother Earth.

ISBN 978-1-891824-20-3 • Softcover • 320 PP. • $14.95

11 EXPLORER RACE: ET VISITORS SPEAK

Even as you are searching the sky for extraterrestrials and their spaceships, ETs are here on planet Earth — they are stranded, visiting, exploring, studying the culture, healing Earth of trauma brought on by irresponsible mining, or researching the history of Christianity over the past 2,000 years. Some are in human guise, and some are in spirit form. Some look like what we call animals as they come from the species' home planet and interact with their fellow beings — those beings who we have labeled cats or cows or elephants. Some are brilliant cosmic mathematicians with a sense of humor who are presently living here as penguins. Some are fledgling diplomats training for future postings on Earth when we have ET embassies here. In this book, these fascinating beings share their thoughts, origins, and purposes for being here.

ISBN 978-1-891824-28-9 • Softcover • 352 PP. • $14.95

12 EXPLORER RACE: TECHNIQUES for GENERATING SAFETY

Wouldn't you like to generate safety so you could go wherever you need to go and do whatever you need to do in a benevolent, safe, and loving way for yourself? Learn safety as a radiated environment that will allow you to gently take the step into the new timeline, into a benevolent future, and away from a negative past.

ISBN 978-1-891824-26-5 • Softcover • 208 PP. • $9.95